ORTHO'S® All About

Carpentry Basics

Meredith® Books
Des Moines, Iowa

Ortho® Books
An imprint of Meredith® Books

Ortho's All About Carpentry Basics
Editor: Larry Erickson
Art Director: Tom Wegner
Copy Chief: Catherine Hamrick
Copy and Production Editor: Terri Fredrickson
Contributing Copy Editor: Carol Boker
Technical Reviewer: Ralph Selzer
Contributing Proofreaders: Steve Hallam, Margaret Smith, JoEllyn Witke
Contributing Illustrators: Jonathan Clark, Grant Jerding, Tom Mattix, Grant Maxson, Pamela Wattenmaker
Indexer: Nan Badgett
Electronic Production Coordinator: Paula Forest
Editorial and Design Assistants: Kathleen Stevens, Karen Schirm
Contributing Editorial Assistant: Colleen Johnson
Production Director: Douglas M. Johnston
Book Production Managers: Pam Kvitne, Marjorie J. Schenkelberg

Additional Editorial Contributions from Greenleaf Publishing
Publishing Director: Dave Toht
Associate Editor: Steve Cory
Assistant Editor: Rebecca JonMichaels
Editorial Art Director: Jean DeVaty
Design: Melanie Lawson Design
Additional Photography: Dan Stultz
Technical Consultant: Michael Clark

Photographers
(Photographers credited may retain copyright © to the listed photographs.)
John North Holtorf: Cover
Dan Stultz: 4, 5, 12, 13, 14, 16, 17, 18, 26, 27, 28, 29, 31, 32, 33, 34, 40, 41, 44, 49, 56, 57, 59, 62, 79

All of us at Ortho® Books are dedicated to providing you with the information and ideas you need to enhance your home and garden. We welcome your comments and suggestions about this book. Write to us at:

Meredith Corporation
Ortho Books
1716 Locust St.
Des Moines, IA 50309–3023

If you would like more information on other Ortho products, call 800-225-2883 or visit us at www.ortho.com

First Edition. Printing Number and Year:
5 4 3 2 1 04 03 02 01 00
Library of Congress Catalog Card Number: 99-75934
ISBN: 0-89721-436-6

Note to the Readers: Due to differing conditions, tools, and individual skills, Meredith Corporation assumes no responsibility for any damages, injuries suffered, or losses incurred as a result of following the information published in this book. Before beginning any project, review the instructions carefully, and if any doubts or questions remain, consult local experts or authorities. Because codes and regulations vary greatly, you always should check with authorities to ensure that your project complies with all applicable local codes and regulations. Always read and observe all of the safety precautions provided by manufacturers of any tools, equipment, or supplies, and follow all accepted safety procedures.

MATERIALS & TECHNIQUES 4

REPAIRS 44

CARPENTRY PROJECTS 62

MATERIALS & TECHNIQUES

Some people pursue carpentry because they love the toys—all those exotic tools, whether they are finely crafted traditional hand tools or the latest high-power gadget bristling with technology. If you take on a project merely to buy the gear, you can easily spend more on equipment than you would have paid a professional to do the work. On the other hand, a good set of tools makes the work go easier and faster and enables you to produce professional-looking results. So, assemble a modest collection of midpriced tools, and add more as the need arises. Here's a good start:

A ***speed square,*** *used to check or mark for 90- and 45-degree angles, also serves as a useful guide for a circular saw. A* ***T-bevel*** *allows you to duplicate an odd angle. A* ***framing square*** *helps you check projects for square and comes in handy as a straightedge. Many carpenters find a* ***drywall square*** *helpful for marking sheets of plywood or drywall.*

Your ***tape measure*** *will be a constant companion; a 25 footer with a 1-inch blade suits most jobs. Make long, straight lines with a* ***chalk line,*** *which doubles as a plumb bob to measure straight down from ceiling to floor. With a 2- or 4-foot* ***carpenter's level*** *and a little* ***torpedo level,*** *you will be able to check almost any object for plumb and level.*

A simple ***miter box with backsaw*** *lets you cut moldings with precision. You will need a* ***coping saw*** *to finish some molding cuts. And, a* ***handsaw*** *is useful when your circular saw will make too much of a mess. For other cutting and shaping chores, you'll use a* ***chisel, plane, rasping plane,*** *and* ***rasp.*** *A* ***utility knife*** *is a must; most people prefer one with a retractable blade.*

Your ***hammer*** *will see plenty of use, so buy one that is solidly built and feels comfortable; a 16-ounce hammer with curved claws is the most popular. With a* ***nail set,*** *you can easily finish driving nails without marring wood or set nail heads below the surface. Poke starter holes for drill bits and fasteners with an* ***awl.*** *A* ***flat pry bar*** *is indispensible for disassembling wood without marring it. To carry hand tools, buy a sturdy nylon or leather* ***nail belt;*** *you can even add a holster for a* ***cordless drill.***

A ***multiscrewdriver*** *takes the place of four normal screwdrivers. Use an* ***adjustable wrench*** *and* ***channel-lock pliers*** *to tighten and unfasten, and have a variety of* ***clamps*** *for holding wood together while you work on it or while the glue dries.*

A TOOL WISH LIST

In addition to the hand tools above, a basic set of tools will include a circular saw, a variable-speed reversible drill, and a saber saw. More specialized power tools include: a reciprocating saw for demolition work, a router for milling edges or making grooves, power sanders, a power miter saw, a table saw, and a radial arm saw. You'll find these tools described throughout pages 18–39.

IN THIS CHAPTER

These essential tools will equip you to handle most interior remodeling and repair projects. Add to your collection as projects require more specialized gear.

UNDERSTANDING YOUR HOUSE

This book focuses on projects for the interior of your home, from installing shelves to building a new wall. Despite the inside emphasis, you need to understand how your whole house goes together to complete these projects safely.

FRAMING

The frame of a house is like a skeleton. Wall frames are made of 2×4 or 2×6 **studs,** usually spaced 16 inches (sometimes 24 inches) apart. If you have an old house, don't assume the studs are evenly spaced. Horizontal top and bottom **plates** are made of the same material as the studs.

Often, a top plate will be doubled. There may be horizontal fire block about halfway up the wall. To span the distance above a door or a window, carpenters use a **header,** made of two pieces of 2-by sandwiched together.

Framing for floors and ceilings uses **joists,** usually 2×8 or larger. The longer they span, the larger they must be, or floors and ceilings could sag. Joists tie into **rim joists** running around the perimeter of the house. The bottom floor framing rests on a **sill plate,** made of rot-resistant lumber. It sits on a foundation or basement wall. In slab houses, a concrete slab takes the place of floor framing.

Roofs are framed with **rafters** or trusses, which use a rigid web of small-dimension lumber. Rafters join to a ridge board at the top, resting on the **top plate** of the wall framing near the bottom. **Balloon framing** runs two or more stories tall, without a top plate at each floor *(see inset)*.

SURFACES

Roof sheathing in older homes uses 1-by lumber; ½-inch plywood is common for newer homes. This is covered with roofing felt (tar paper) and asphalt shingles. (Wood shakes, roof tiles, and slate all require special underlayments.) An attic space must be able to breathe, so a series of vents is necessary.

Outside walls are covered with **sheathing,** made of plywood or fiberboard material in newer homes and 1-by lumber in older homes. This is covered with **roofing felt** or, in newer homes, **house wrap,** to keep moisture from entering and to protect against drafts.

Siding can be horizontal or vertical. **Horizontal siding** consists of beveled horizontal planks of wood, wood byproducts, vinyl, or aluminum. Vertical styles include board-and-batten siding and sheets of grooved plywood, often referred to as T-111. Other siding materials include cedar shingles, soft siding (which is like thick roofing shingles), asbestos shingles, stucco, and brick or stone veneer.

INSIDE

Inside the walls, between the studs, homes need to have **insulation** that stays fluffy over the years. Older rock-wool or cellulose insulation can become compressed over time. Some homes have asbestos insulation, which is dangerous if fibers escape into interior air. Fiberglass batts remain effective for many decades. Blown insulation, made of cellulose fibers, fills hard-to-reach places.

Floors often have two layers: a **subfloor** of plywood or 1-by lumber and a **finish flooring,** such as tongue-and-groove oak. Newer homes designed for wall-to-wall carpeting usually have two layers of plywood only.

Interior walls of older homes usually are made with hundreds of pieces of **lath**—rough strips of wood—nailed to the studs. Two or three layers of plaster cover them. Since the 1960s, most homes have sheets of **wallboard** nailed to the studs; joints and nail holes are covered with tape and joint compound.

Gaps between elements of the house—the floor and the wall, windows and the wall or the siding, doors, and so on—are covered with a variety of moldings, which are thin, decorative pieces of wood. On the outside of the house, most of these gaps are caulked to provide a weather-tight seal.

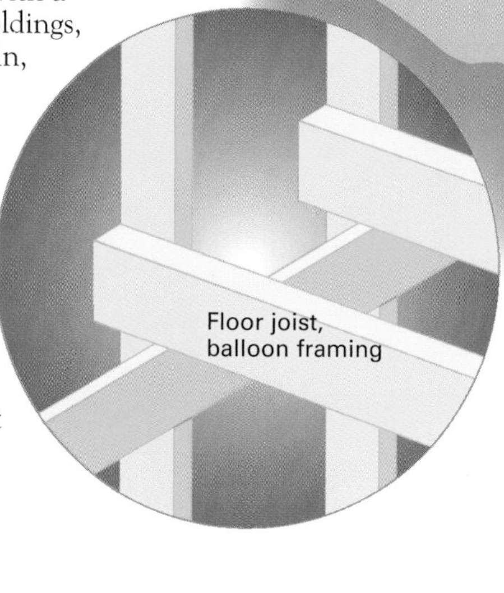

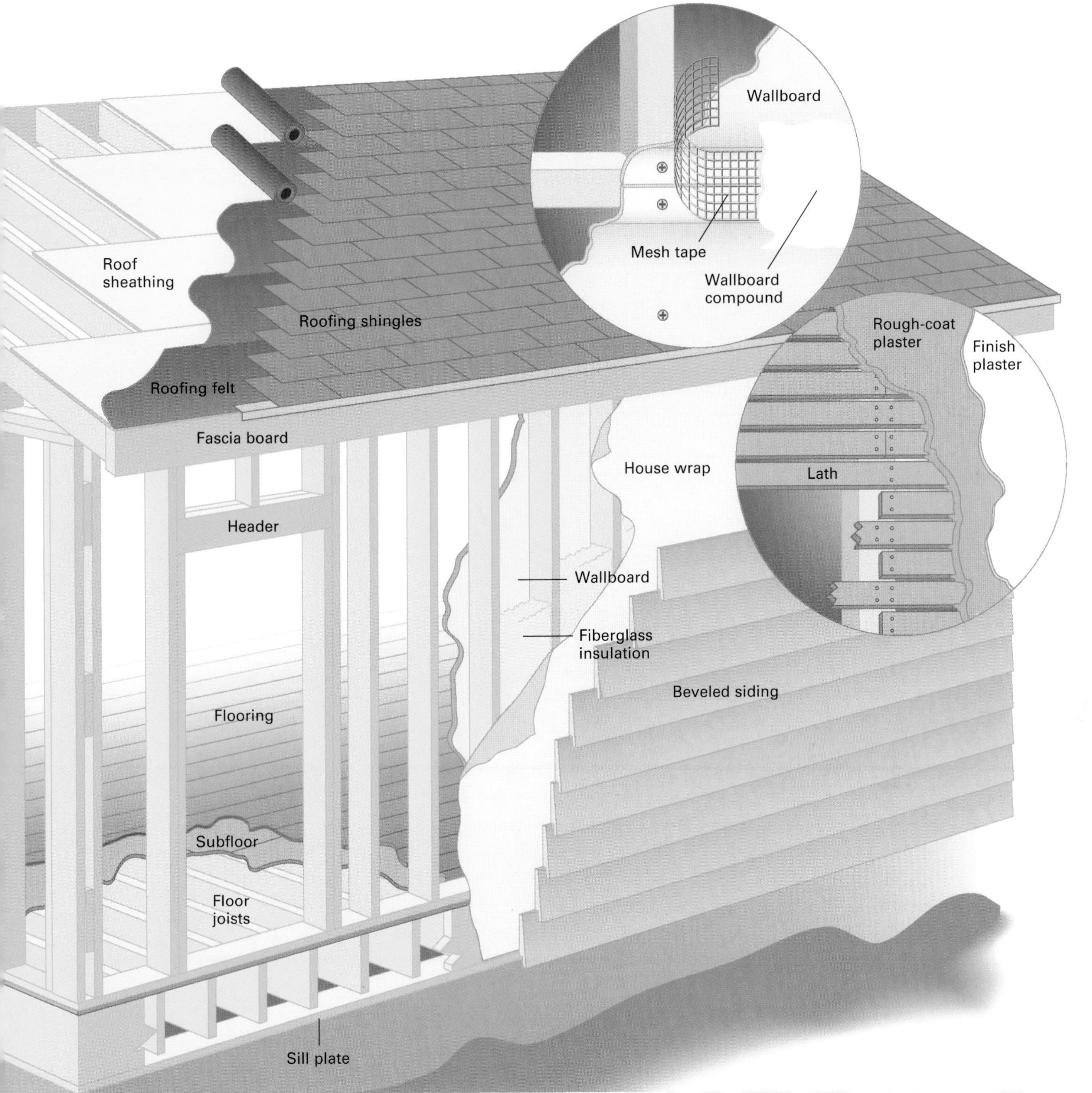

REPAIRING AN OLD HOUSE'S STRUCTURE

Local building departments have strict size requirements for joists and rafters. The framing of an older home may fall short of code. Sagging floors, cracked plaster, and tilted doorways are telltale signs.

If your problems look serious, call in a professional who has experience with repairing house structures—and references to back it up. You will probably not be able to bring your home up to contemporary code, but you can cure those sags. Often the solution is to place adjustable metal posts in the basement. The posts are extended slightly every few weeks until the floor is level.

LUMBER

Wood, said Frank Lloyd Wright, "is universally beautiful to man. Man loves his association with it, likes to feel it under his hand, sympathetic to his touch and his eye." But if you're trying to build something out of checked and twisted lumber, your association may not seem so favorable. Here's how to choose your lumber so it suits the job.

THE NATURE OF LUMBER

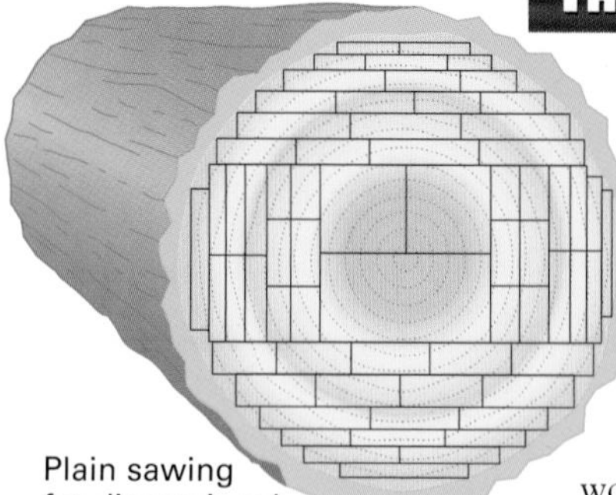

Plain sawing for dimensional lumber

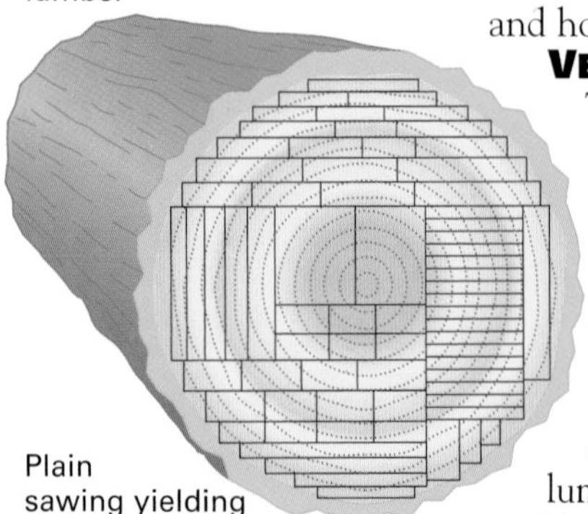

Plain sawing yielding some select lumber

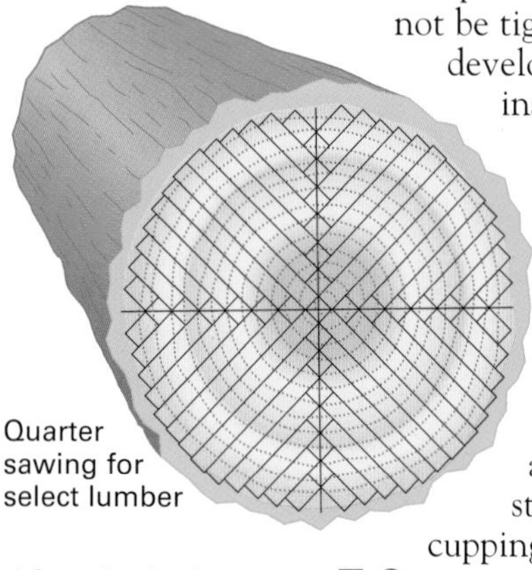

Quarter sawing for select lumber

After the bark is removed, logs are usually plain-sawn to make maximum use of the available wood. Quartersawing is more wasteful.

Pound for pound, wood is almost as strong as steel; yet it's easy to cut and shape. And, it has a warm, natural beauty that no other material can match.

Of course, each piece of lumber was once part of a tree. The characteristics of the wood you buy depend on the type of tree it came from, how it was cut, and how it was handled.

VERTICAL AND FLAT GRAIN: The best lumber comes from old trees, with fewer knots than younger trees, and that have tight rings for a close grain in the lumber. Certain species produce wood that is resistant to warping and rot, while others do not *(see the chart on page 10)*. Much lumber sold today comes from quick-growth trees, so the grain will not be tight and the boards will develop twists if not stored and installed carefully.

There are two basic methods of cutting wood:

■ Plain sawing, in which the boards are cut roughly parallel to the growth rings, produces flat-grained wood, with a pattern of widely spaced wavy lines, V shapes, and ovals. This lumber can be strong, but it will be prone to cupping and warping.

■ Quarter sawing—cutting perpendicular to the rings—produces vertical grain in closely spaced parallel lines. As long as it has few knots, this type is stronger and more stable than plain-sawn (flat-grained) lumber, making it more desirable for finish work. But, if there is a spike-shaped knot extending across much of the width of a board, it will be seriously weakened. Quartersawn lumber tends to be expensive because it often comes from old-growth trees and much of the log becomes sawdust and waste wood.

WOOD MOVEMENT AND MOISTURE: Wood changes with the climate. Freshly cut wood shrinks until it is dry, and dry lumber expands and contracts with changes in humidity. However, given its longitudinal grain, wood can change significantly in width, but hardly at all in length.

Most lumber is air-dried after it is cut. This removes much of the moisture, but leaves enough that wood may shrink, bow, and twist after you buy it. For framing and rough work, air-dried lumber is adequate, as long as you stack the wood flat and fasten it in place before it has a chance to move.

Kiln-drying removes more moisture so the boards are more stable. It is often worth the extra cost, especially when the wood will be used for cabinetry or other finish carpentry.

Wood used for finish carpentry should contain no more than 19 percent moisture, often indicated by "S-DRY" on the lumber stamp. For exacting carpentry, use lumber marked MC-15, meaning it has 15 percent or less moisture content. Cabinetry- and furniture-making call for wood graded MC-12 or drier.

ACTUAL AND NOMINAL DIMENSIONS

After it is cut, lumber is dried, planed, and smoothed, which reduces its thickness and width. The nominal size of a board (for example, "1×4") refers to the size before drying and planing; actual size means the size you actually get.

Nominal Size	Actual Size
1×2	¾" × 1½"
1×3	¾" × 2½"
1×4	¾" × 3½"
1×6	¾" × 5½"
1×8	¾" × 7¼"
1×10	¾" × 9¼"
1×12	¾" × 11¼"
2×2	1½" × 1½"
2×4	1½" × 3½"
2×6	1½" × 5½"
2×8	1½" × 7¼"
2×10	1½" × 9¼"
2×12	1½" × 11¼"

ROT AND TERMITES: Wood has two main enemies—rot and bugs. Rot (even "dry rot") occurs for the most part when wood remains damp for a long time. Boards in contact with the ground or with the house's foundation are at greatest risk; unfortunately, these boards are usually hard to replace. Termites and other wood-eating insects are often attracted to moist wood. They usually live in the ground outside your house, and tunnel in through your structure to get food. "Secondary infestations" occur when there is enough moisture in the wood for them to reside as well as eat there.

Protect against rot and bugs by using pressure-treated lumber wherever moisture may be a problem. It should have a CCA rating (a measure of its preservative content) of at least .40 or be labeled "ground contact." To protect structural wood from damage, take steps to ensure that it can dry out; sometimes just sweeping away dirt can do the trick. You can also brush on sealer that contains preservative and insecticide.

WATCH FOR DEFECTS

If you call the lumberyard and order boards to be delivered, you'll probably get some defective materials. Go there and choose the boards yourself, one by one. Perfect lumber is uncommon. However, you want to make sure your wood does not have problems that will ruin your project. Pick up each board and sight down its length to look for twists, bows, cups, and crooks. Then inspect the surfaces that will be showing for checks, shakes, wane, and knots.

CHECKS: Splits that run perpendicular to the grain are called checks. They are the result of shrinkage; they usually show up near the ends of boards, where the wood dries out fastest. These flaws are a cosmetic—not a structural—problem.

SHAKES: These splits following the grain are a serious concern. They will probably grow larger. Do not use boards with splits that extend halfway or more into the thickness of the board.

KNOTS: A tight knot in the center of a board may actually make it stronger because the wood tissue around it is dense. A large knot at the edge of a board, however, can cause the board to become bent at that point, even if it looks straight when you buy it. Loose knots will probably fall out in time.

WANE: A wane is caused by cutting the board too close to the bark. It is a blemish; boards with wane can still be very strong.

TWIST: These can cause problems. If you use a twisted board as part of a header—over a door frame, for instance—one or more corners will stick out and cause lumps in the wall finish. For studs, joists, and rafters, minor twists can usually be eliminated by installing blocking and by strategic fastening.

CROWN: As you sight down the board, the high part in the middle is the crown. When framing a wall, make all the crowns face the same way. When installing joists or rafters, always put the crown side up. Badly crowned lumber should be rejected or cut into shorter pieces.

BOW: Lumber that's bowed is usually not a problem unless the bow is very pronounced. Bowed studs or joists can be straightened by installing pieces of blocking. In some cases, the bow can be taken out of a board when the finish wood is attached to it.

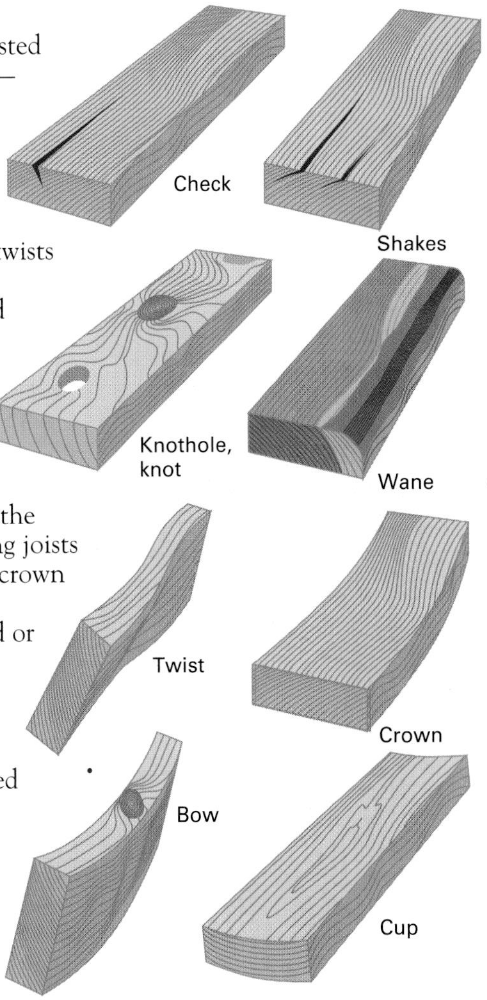

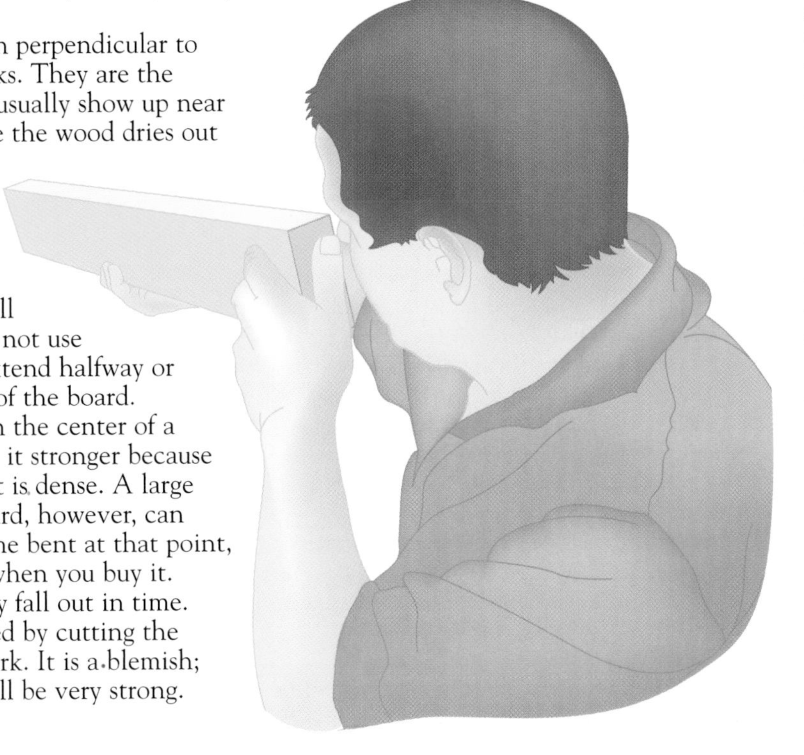

Before choosing lumber, decide which defects will not harm your project, and which are unacceptable. Sight along a board to spot twists, bows, and crowns. Many carpenters set joists crown-edge up for a structural advantage and to let the weight of the floor straighten the lumber.

LUMBER
continued

CUP: Cupped wood does not create a structural problem, but it can look ugly. If the cup is severe, the piece may crack when you fasten it in place. Vertical-grain wood that is not kiln-dried may develop a cup after you buy it.

LUMBER GRADES

There are many grading associations across the country, each with its own set of rules, so a certain grade may mean different things in different places. Some chain stores have their own designations. (For example "appearance board" may refer to very weak hem/fir that will twist severely unless you fasten it almost immediately.) So, the following information is only a general guide.

STRUCTURAL LUMBER: Wood commonly used for framing is usually either Douglas fir or hem/fir. Smaller pieces—2×4s and 4×4s—are graded differently than larger sizes. *Utility* grade is the lowest and is not strong enough for actual framing. Use it for blocking, non-structural partitions, and furring. *Standard* grade is the most common; it is suitable for light framing. *Construction* grade is even stronger and has fewer defects. *Stud*-grade 2×4s are usually somewhere between standard and construction grades in quality and are expressly used as studs. Larger sizes of framing lumber—2×6 and up—have three basic grades. *Number 2* is suitable for most structural purposes; although it may have large knots and be twisted or cracked, it will be strong. *Number 1* has straighter grain and no large knots, so it looks better and is stronger than grade 2. *Structural* or *select* boards are the strongest and are virtually free of knots.

TYPICAL LUMBER GRADE STAMP

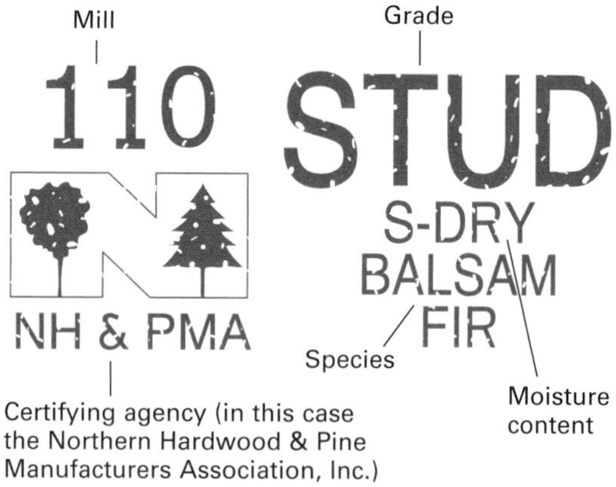

FINISH LUMBER: Grading systems here are more varied. Some associations use a letter system, with A being the highest grade and D the lowest. Others use numbers: *Number 3* is suitable for rough only; *Number 2* has plenty of knots but is good enough for shelving; and *Number 1* is nearly knot-free. *Clear* lumber has no knots and will always be expensive.

Finish lumber is graded mainly for appearance, so the number is not as important as whether it looks good to you. You may

WOOD SPECIES

Softwoods are usually used in rough carpentry, while more expensive hardwoods are more often used in fine woodworking. Here are some of the most common species available in each category:

SOFTWOODS	
Cedar, Cypress	Very light, easily worked, often knotty. Light to dark brown. Not strong, but rot resistant.
Redwood	Stable and rot resistant, easily worked, but with a tendency to split. Cream to reddish brown in color. Stronger than cedar, but not as strong as fir.
Pine	Light, soft, easy to cut, resistant to warping, but tends to shrink. White to yellowish. Not strong.
Hem/Fir	A general designation that includes a variety of types of hemlock and fir. Sometimes tends to shrink and warp. Light in color, fairly easy to cut. Softer than fir and not as strong.
Douglas Fir	Very commonly used for framing. Strong, fairly hard, and moderately easy to work with.
HARDWOODS	
Birch	Strong and fine-grained, resistant to shrinkage and warping. Light in color, hard to cut.
Maple	Extremely strong and hard. Reddish to nearly white. Very hard to cut.
Red Oak	Distinctive open grain, hard and strong, reddish color. Will shrink if not very dry. Hard to cut.
White Oak	Grain not as open as red oak and with fewer variations; golden color. Hard and strong.

HARDWOOD

The price of these slower-growing woods—such as birch, maple, and oak—can be high, so it pays to buy carefully. The more expensive woods are milled to save every possible square inch, so they come in varying sizes. Sometimes they are smooth on only two sides, leaving the edges rough; this is called S2S. You may find it difficult to plane the edges smooth, so ask the lumberyard if they can do it for you.

Hardwoods have their own grading systems. *FAS* (firsts and seconds) will be straight and knot-free. *Select* boards have defects on one side only. *Number 1 common* has tiny, tight knots; *Number 2 common* has larger knots.

choose to save money by buying a cheaper grade and paint it after filling holes and sanding it. If you want a rustic look, you may seek out a lower grade.

METAL FRAMING

Although it may not seem like carpentry, metal framing has some distinct advantages. Steel studs are inexpensive, light, and strong; they won't warp, shrink, or rot; and they save trees. Because they are fire resistant, they are required for most commercial installations.

Steel studs are made of C-shaped, sheet-metal channels with holes for running electrical and plumbing lines. They're available in different weights to satisfy different load-bearing requirements. Tracks are used for the top and bottom plates and for headers.

All connections are made by driving special self-tapping screws, using a drill that has a magnetic screwdriver bit. Use a felt-tipped pen to mark pieces to size and cut with metal snips. Part of the rigidity of metal framing is achieved only after wallboard is installed, using standard wallboard screws.

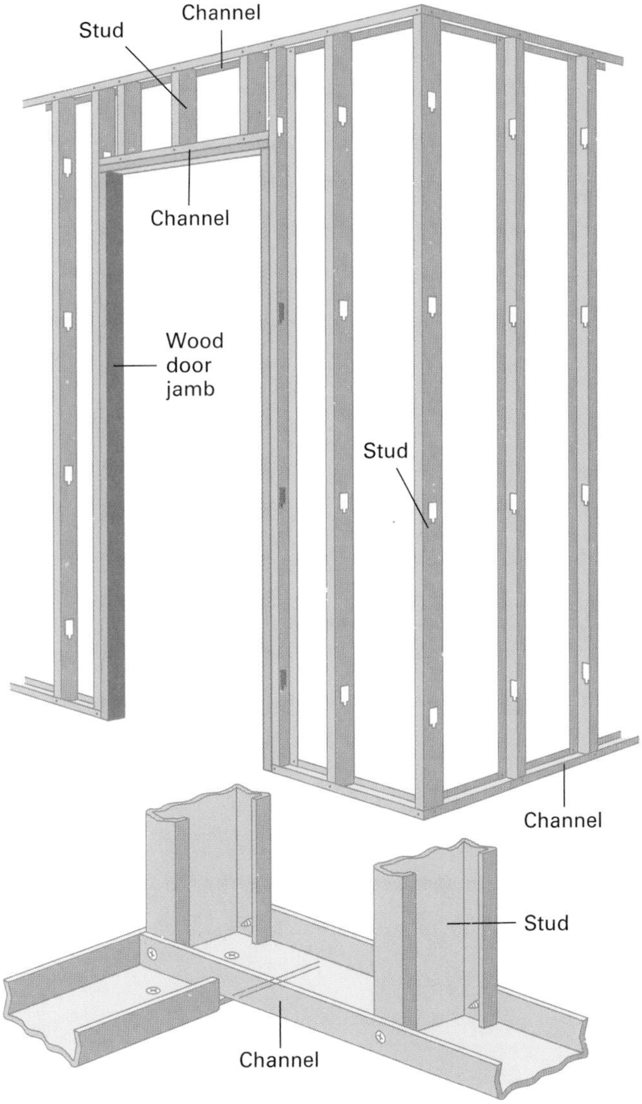

Standard steel framing requires only two types of metal framing pieces—studs and channels (left). To use a channel as a header, cut it so there are flaps that you can bend and attach to the studs.

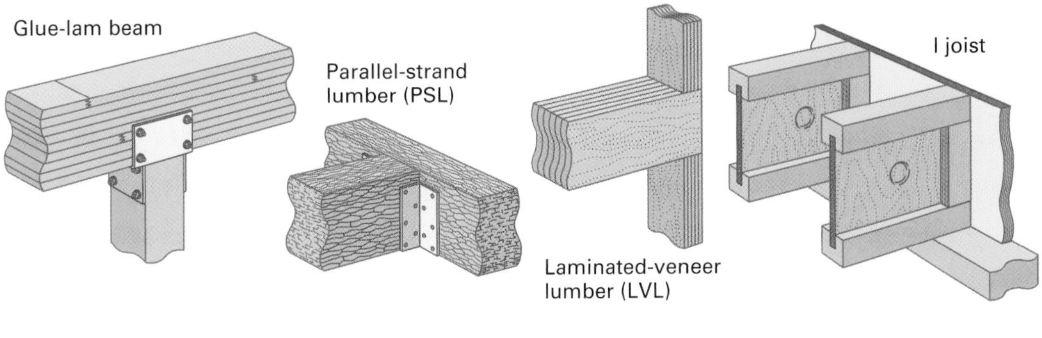

These manufactured-wood structural members are lighter and more stable than their sawn-lumber counterparts.

SHEET GOODS

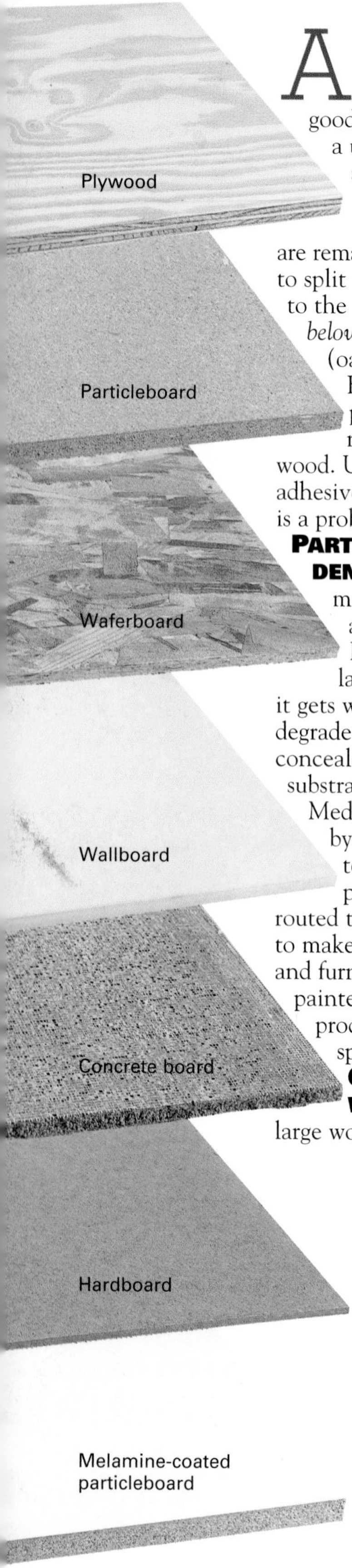

Although they usually lack the grain and sometimes the desirable surface variation of standard lumber, sheet goods make your life easier by presenting a uniform face over a large area—and for a reasonable price.

PLYWOOD: Made by laminating layers of wood veneer, plywood sheets are remarkably stable and are almost impossible to split when you drive fasteners. In addition to the grades of softwood plywood *(see box below)*, hardwood plywood also is available (oak and birch are the most common). Birch is an excellent choice for smooth, painted surfaces; it takes paint more readily and dents less easily than softwood. Use plywood laminated with special adhesives on exteriors and where moisture is a problem.

PARTICLEBOARD AND MEDIUM-DENSITY FIBERBOARD: Particleboard, made of tiny chips and sawdust, can be an inexpensive substitute for plywood. It is dense, heavy, and hard, but it lacks tensile strength. It will swell if it gets wet. A cut edge is ragged and easily degraded. This material works well for concealed portions of cabinets and as a substrate for plastic-laminate countertops.

Medium-density fiberboard (MDF) is made by firmly bonding wood fibers. It is finely textured and more dense than particleboard. MDF can be cut or routed to a strong, crisp edge. It is even used to make paint-grade moldings, door panels, and furniture parts. MDF shelving is an easily painted alternative to 1-by lumber. Neither product holds nails well, and either can split if a fastener is driven near the edge.

ORIENTED-STRAND BOARD AND WAFERBOARD: These are made from large wood chips fused together. Oriented-strand board (OSB) uses layers of chips laid so the fibers in one layer run perpendicular to the fibers of the next layer, making it stronger than waferboard, which has randomly arranged chips. In fact, OSB sheets are as strong as plywood. However, OSB expands and contracts more than plywood, so install the sheets with 1/4-inch gaps between them. Neither OSB nor waferboard holds nails as well as plywood. They swell around the edges if they get wet, so don't use them as underlayment beneath floor or countertop coverings.

WALLBOARD: Made of gypsum sandwiched between layers of heavy paper, wallboard has become the universal choice for interior ceilings and walls. Available in thicknesses ranging from 3/8 inch to 5/8 inch, it comes in 4×8, 4×10, and 4×12 sheets. In addition to standard panels, you can buy specialized panels that resist heat and water damage.

CONCRETE BOARD: For a stable base for tiled walls, floors, and countertops, use concrete board. Made of nylon mesh permeated with concrete, this material cuts fairly easily and is fastened in place with all-purpose screws.

HARDBOARD: This is a high-density fiberboard, used for cabinet backs, drawer bottoms, exterior siding, perforated board, and even doors. The tempered variety is water-resistant. It expands and contracts with cold and heat, so install it with 1/8-inch gaps between sheets.

MELAMINE BOARD: This is particleboard coated with a layer of fairly tough, lightly textured plastic. It can be made into cabinet parts that require no further finishing. The melamine coating seals the particleboard, so it won't swell with moisture unless the coating gets chipped off. Melamine is not as strong as standard plastic laminate, so use wood or plastic veneer to cover exposed edges.

GRADES OF SOFTWOOD PLYWOOD

Plywood faces are usually given letter grades. Most sheets will have two differently graded faces; BC, for instance, has one B side and one C side.

N	A natural veneer face made with select-grade wood. All imperfections have been repaired with wood that closely matches the surrounding surface.
A	Smooth with no knots; all repairs are parallel to the grain, so it is certainly paintable, and able to take a natural finish in undemanding applications.
B	Small, tight knots only, with only tiny splits.
C	Tight knots, small knotholes, small splits.
D	Large knots, large knotholes, large splits, very rough grain.

MOLDING

An architect once said that the primary function of molding is to create interesting shadows. While molding is ornamental and improves the perceived quality of a project, most types have a functional origin, whether it be covering an unsightly joint, giving a door or window something to strike against, or guarding a wall from wear.

USES

In certain areas of the house, molding is just about mandatory to cover up gaps. **Fluted** and plain **screen bead,** though intended to affix screen to wooden screen frames, are handy problem solvers. **Cove molding** not only adds a striking touch, but can also save you the trouble of taping the corner joint where the ceiling meets the wall.

Many older homes have **picture hanger** molding running horizontally on walls near the ceiling; it was originally used to hang pictures on wires, but it has decorative appeal of its own. **Ranch, colonial,** or **fluted casing** and **stop** are almost always needed on windows and doors. Window sashes are separated by **parting stop,** a multipurpose molding that's rectangular in cross section.

Outside corner protects the edges of walls. **Ply cap** is often used as the cap for wainscoting (vertical siding running about halfway up the wall). **Chair rail** performs the same function, but it also looks good as a horizontal band in the middle of the wall, perhaps dividing a painted surface below from wallpaper above.

The edge where the wall meets the floor will require **ranch** or **Colonial base molding,** with **base shoe** or **quarter-round** as well.

Feel free to be creative with moldings. By stacking two or more standard moldings, you can create a unique, richly textured look for a small amount of work. The best way to create is to ask for short leftover pieces at the lumberyard and experiment with them.

SOURCES

Home centers like to tout molding as an inexpensive way to spruce up a room. While it's cheaper than hiring a contractor to make major improvements, trim can be surprisingly expensive, once you add up all the footage. So purchase carefully: To avoid waste, figure exactly how many pieces of each length you will need. Choose cheaper versions where you can *(see box at left)*. If you have a router and a table saw, you may be able to save by milling your own molding.

An older home may have moldings that are no longer made. In many cases, you can use standard moldings (sometimes combining several types) to achieve a similar effect. Some lumberyards can match an old molding. The extra charge may not be as much as you might expect; be sure to call several places to compare prices.

Small decorative pieces, such as rosettes, can dress up a window or door for a small price. A square rosette is usually placed at each corner and then molding pieces butted to them.

INEXPENSIVE MOLDING OPTIONS

Most molding is made from solid pieces of clear pine, so it's pricey. If you plan to paint your molding, consider these less expensive alternatives.

Finger-jointed pine uses small pieces joined together along the length of a piece. It will break more easily than a solid piece, but that is usually not an important consideration with molding.

Make sure the joints are smooth; sand them if not. Primed moldings are made of lesser grade wood but are easier to paint than unprimed pine. You may also want to use moldings made from MDF or laminated particleboard; both are economical sheeting. Plastic foam moldings, found in the paneling section rather than the lumber section of the store, also can save you money. They replace period or hard-to-manufacture moldings once made of wood or plaster. Make sure they can be painted; you may have to prime them first.

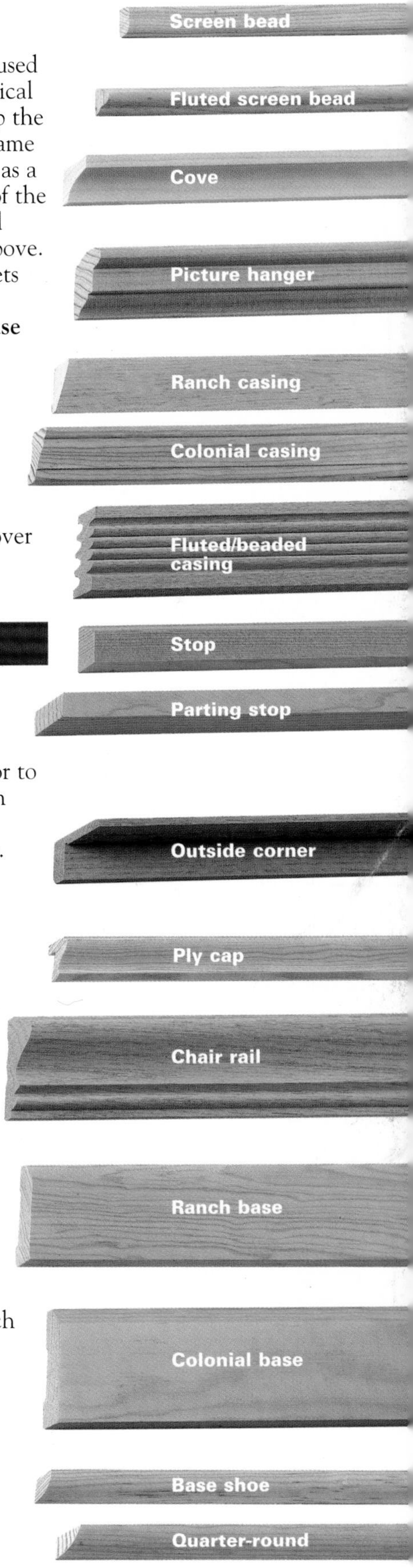

MEASURING AND MARKING

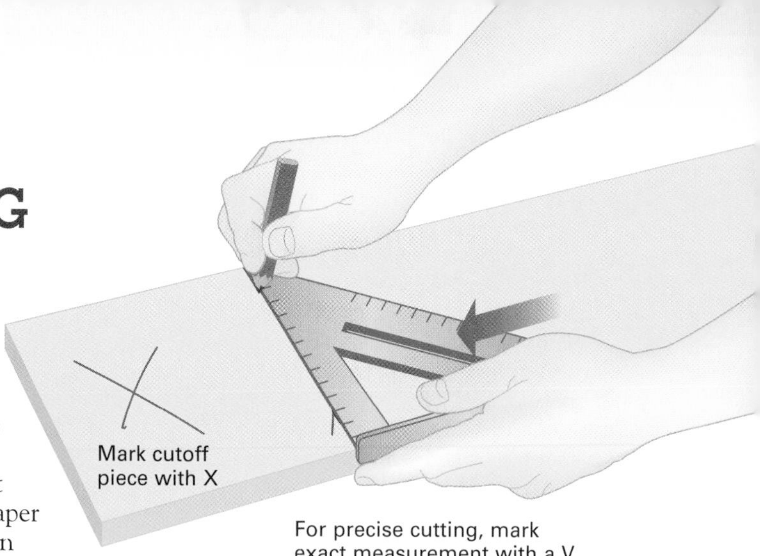

Measuring is the first step in every carpentry project. Usually, it requires no intricate figuring or expensive tools—just common sense and concentration. Because you measure so often in carpentry, you should develop proper measuring habits. Jot measurements down on a piece of paper or scrap of wood. With angled cuts in particular, visualize where the board will go and make sure that you measure along the appropriate edge. Most important of all, apply the adage, "Measure twice and cut once." Double checking your measurements will save time and money.

GET TO KNOW YOUR TAPE MEASURE

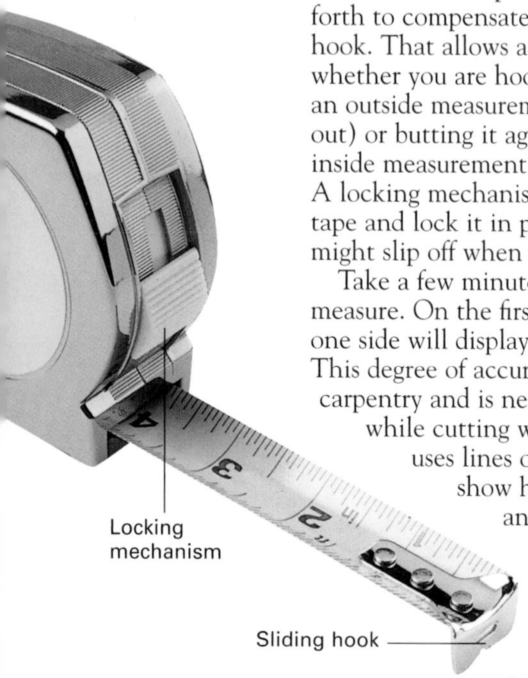

The hook of a tape measure slides back and forth to compensate for the thickness of the hook. That allows accurate measurements, whether you are hooking it onto a board for an outside measurement (the hook will slide out) or butting it against a surface for an inside measurement (the hook will slide in). A locking mechanism lets you extend the tape and lock it in position, useful if the hook might slip off when measuring long spans.

Take a few minutes to study your tape measure. On the first few inches, very likely one side will display thirty-seconds of inches. This degree of accuracy rarely is needed with carpentry and is nearly impossible to achieve while cutting wood. The rest of the tape uses lines of decreasing length to show halves, quarters, eighths, and sixteenths.

Become familiar with the locations of the quarters and eighths markings. ("Quick: Where is the $\frac{5}{8}$-inch line?") Don't try to memorize or write down all the sixteenths; just use "plus" or "minus" to indicate a measurement $\frac{1}{16}$ greater or less than the nearest quarter or eighth inch. For example, jot down "$12\frac{3}{4}$ +" for a measurement of $12\frac{13}{16}$ inches. Learn to read your tape measure right-side up; even experienced carpenters mistake a "6" for a "9" by looking at it upside down.

Tape measures can differ. A tape measure used by a fellow worker might read as much as $\frac{1}{8}$ inch more or less than yours. So, when you cut a board to fit a space, measure both the board and the space with the same tape.

MARKING STRAIGHT CUTOFFS

Hook the tape and slide the tape case several inches past the measurement you want to mark. (Make sure the hook itself has caught the end of the board, not the little grommet that holds the hook.)

Using a sharp pencil, mark a V so its tip is at the precise location for the cut line. This is more reliable and accurate than drawing a short line because you may forget which end of the line marks the spot.

The saw blade will remove about $\frac{1}{8}$ inch from the board, turning it into sawdust. This opening is called the saw's *kerf*. Draw a large

WHY A CARPENTER'S PENCIL?

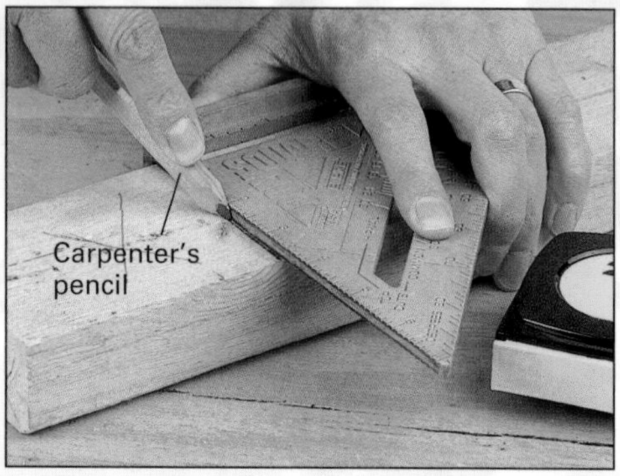

A traditional carpenter's pencil is flattened, giving it a large lead that is rectangular rather than round. Many people find them clumsy to use, but there is a reason many carpenters prefer them. A standard pencil will give you a sharp point, but it will grow dull quickly. A carpenter's pencil, if sharpened not to a point but to a sort of chisel shape, will allow you to make many more precise lines if you hold it so you are marking along the sharp edge.

X on the side of the V that will be waste. Always saw on the waste side of the line so that the kerf doesn't shorten your finished board. Place the pencil point on the tip of the V, and slide the square up against it. Draw the cutoff line, using the square as a guide. If you will be crosscutting a board into several pieces, you may be tempted to mark them all at the same time and then cut. But this will cause some boards to be a little shorter than others because of the saw's kerf. You could add ⅛ inch to your measurements to take the kerf into account, but it's safer to measure for each cut individually.

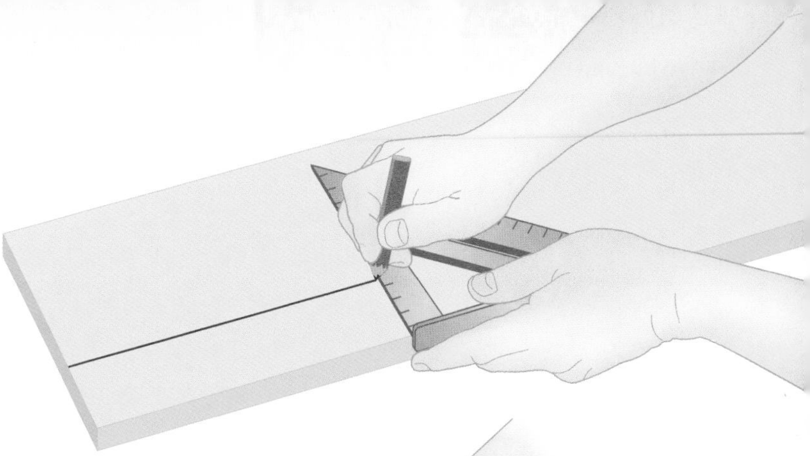

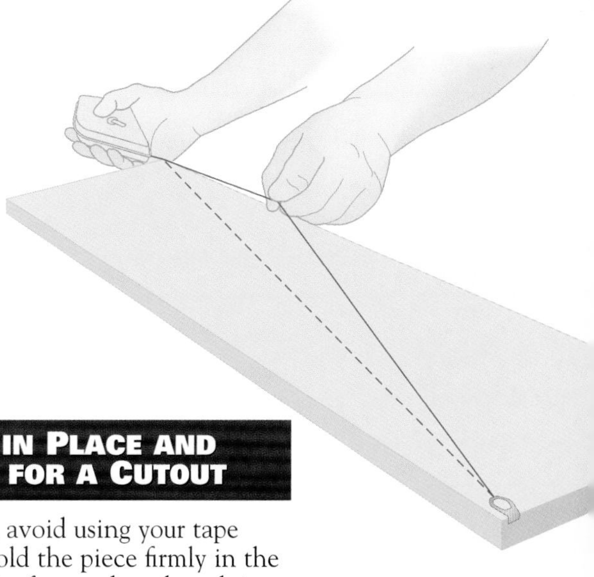

To make a pencil line parallel to the board's edge, set your pencil against a square and draw it toward you (above). Or, snap a chalk line (right).

Marking Rip Cuts

Unlike crosscuts, which slice across the grain of a board, a rip cut runs parallel to the grain. If the cut will be parallel to the edge of the board, scribe a line by using a square and a pencil. Hold the square against the board's edge and place the pencil tip against it at the correct distance from the edge. Keeping the square firmly against the edge and the pencil tip firmly against the square, slide both along the board. Don't press too deeply with the pencil, or the grain will lead you astray.

If the rip cut will not be parallel to the edge, or if you find it difficult to scribe a parallel line, use a chalk line. Make a V-shaped mark at each end of the board. Hook the line to one end; pull the string taut to the V at the other end. Pull the string straight up a few inches, and let go.

To mark cuts in sheet goods, use a chalk line. Or, make a V mark at each end of the cut, and use a straightedge as a guide. If you will be making a lot of crosscuts in sheet goods, it helps to have a drywall square (*see page* 5). Hold the square snugly on the edge and guide it to your V mark. Spring clamp the square in place and draw the cut line.

Marking in Place and Marking for a Cutout

Whenever possible, avoid using your tape measure. Instead, hold the piece firmly in the place where it will be fastened, and mark it. Not only is this more accurate than using a measuring device, but it also makes it less likely that you will cut the wrong end.

To mark for a cutout or notch, measure in two directions. You can probably measure for length by holding and marking in place. With the piece still in place, use a tape measure to find out how deep the cutout must be (*see below*). Transfer that measurement onto the board. Draw a clear X for the waste; it's easy to get confused. Use a square to mark two straight lines.

Put boards in position when marking cuts—you'll lower the probability of mistakes.

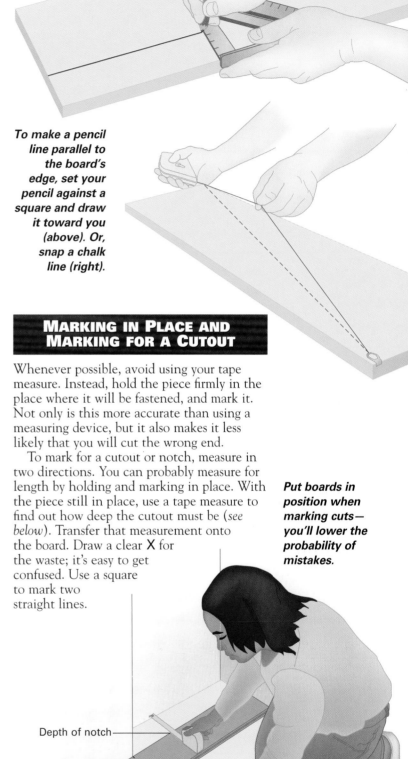

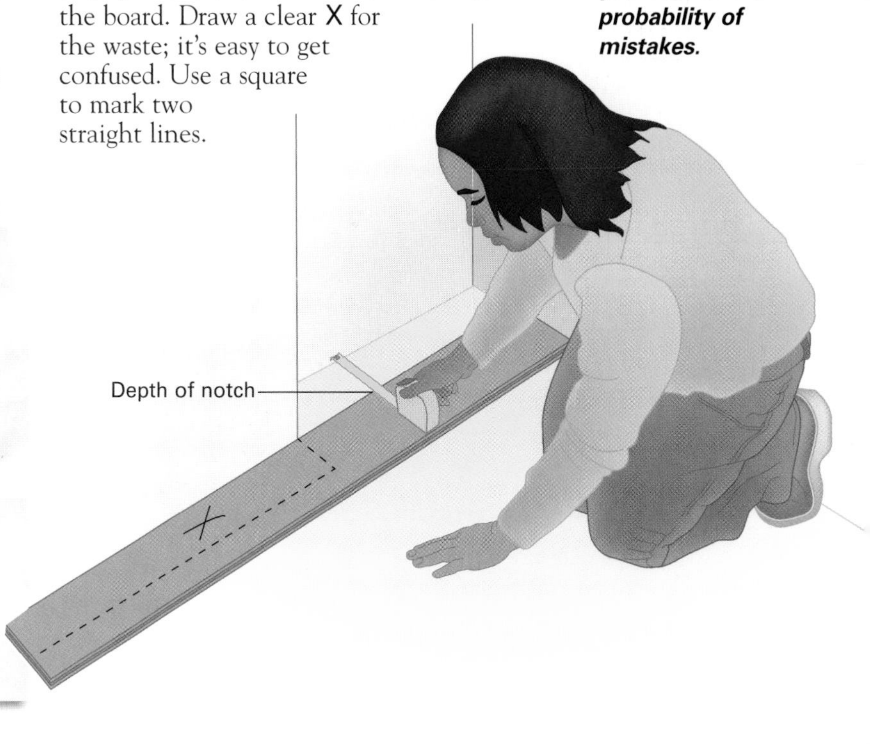

Other Marking Tools

Even a carpenter's pencil will soon wear down if you are drawing lines on rough plywood or marking for layout on a concrete floor. When possible, use a chalk line. If the lines do not have to be accurate within an eighth of an inch, a yellow carpenter's crayon will do the job.

Some people don't trust pencils because the lines change in thickness as the pencil is used. Instead, they use an awl or a knife. These will produce precise lines, but they may be difficult to see.

SQUARING AND LEVELING

Nearly every carpentry project requires that at least some of the component parts be cut or positioned at precise 90-degree angles. And most installations need to be either level (horizontal) or plumb (vertical). Squaring and leveling skills are essential.

Never assume that the walls or floors of your house are square or plumb. Even if they were built correctly, normal settling of the foundation may slightly skew walls and floors. In rare cases, things may be so out of skew that a square and plumb addition will look crooked in relation to them. But, it is usually best to build your projects square and plumb. Attempting to follow the house's faulty lines usually makes the installation more difficult.

T-BEVEL

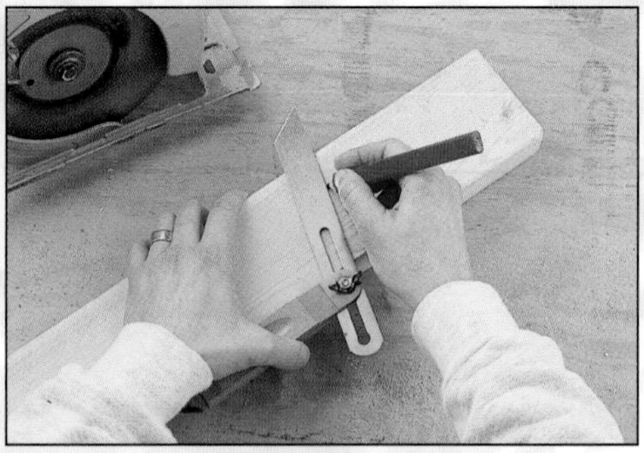

Use a T-bevel when you need to capture and transfer an angle other than 90 or 45 degrees. Loosen the wing nut and press the tool into the angle you want to duplicate. Check that the handle and the blade rest against the work all along their lengths. Tighten the nut, and check to see that the blade did not move while you tightened it. Handle the tool carefully when using it to mark for a new cut—bumping it can alter the angle.

CUTTING SQUARE

Check all your board ends for square before cutting or using them. It's not unusual for about 5 percent of the boards to be out of square. If it isn't square, mark and cut it square or use the other end.

Don't assume that your power saws are cutting squarely. Check them regularly to see not only that they crosscut squarely but that the bevel of the cut is square as well. Check by simply holding a square against a cut board. For greater precision, cut a board with the tool, flip it over, and see if the saw will cut exactly the same line. Circular saws often have bevel gauges slightly out of whack, and this is easy to correct. Table saws, radial arm saws, and power miter boxes are more difficult to adjust. But if you can get them correctly adjusted, projects will go smoothly and quickly.

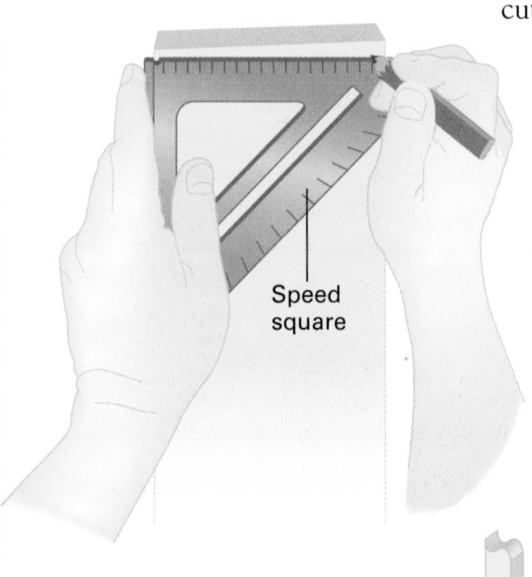

SQUARING PROJECTS

Use a framing square for small installation projects. Set it in place, and check to see that both the blade and tongue rest against the work all along their lengths.

For larger projects, use a piece of plywood or some other sheet good as a square. Any two adjacent factory edges will form an exact right angle.

On very large installations use the 3-4-5 method. Measure along one edge exactly 3 feet,

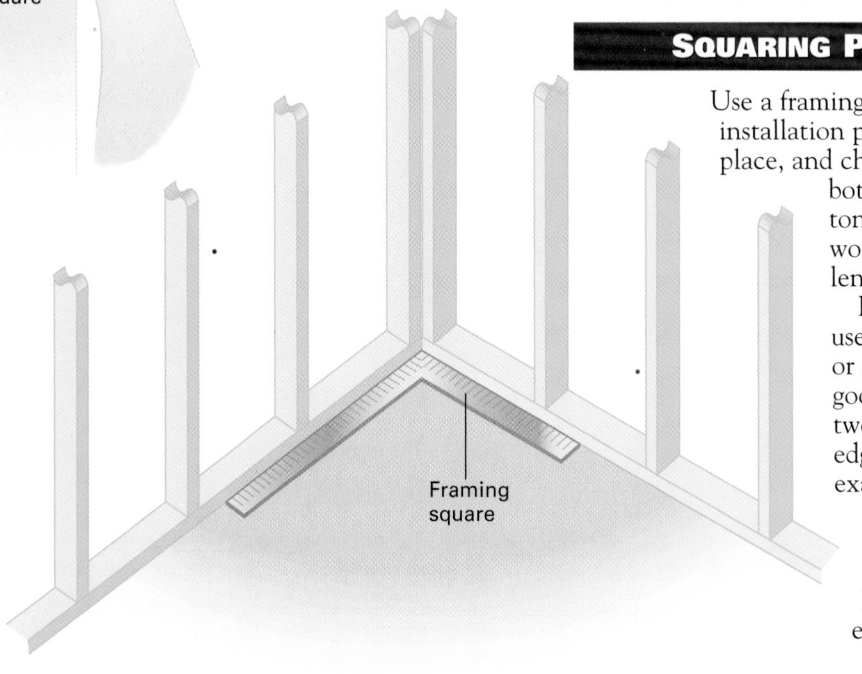

Trust your tools, not your luck, to verify that corners are square.

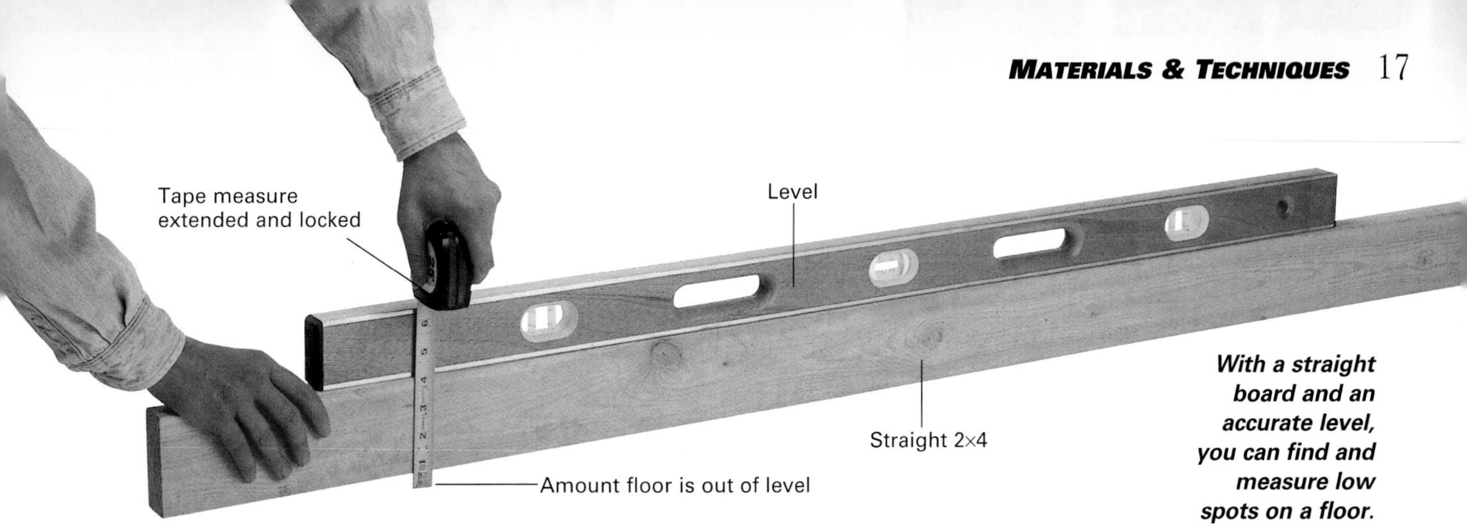

With a straight board and an accurate level, you can find and measure low spots on a floor. Then drive shims between flooring and supporting joists to level the surface.

and make a mark. Then measure along the other edge, using precisely the same starting point, and make a mark at exactly 4 feet. If the distance between these two marks is exactly 5 feet, then the work is square.

PLUMB AND LEVEL

It is often necessary to check an installation for both plumb (perfectly vertical) and level (perfectly horizontal). Or, you may need to check for plumb in two directions—the front and side of a kitchen cabinet, for example. This is especially important for a doorway because if the opening is not plumb in both directions, the door may open or close by itself.

Begin with a reliable tool. Check your level regularly; it can get knocked out of alignment. Set it on a fairly level surface, note where the bubble is in the vial, then turn it over. If the bubble is in exactly the same place, the level is accurate. Some models allow you to adjust the vial. If only one of the vials is inaccurate, cover it with tape.

Test for plumb by holding a level against the vertical surface and checking the vial. Sometimes a wall or board is warped, so that one area is level while another is not. Check at several points.

When installing a cabinet or shelf, you can often set a level on top of the unit, raise or lower the unit until the bubble is centered, and scribe a mark on the wall showing the exact position you want. To test for level over a long span, set the level on the middle of a long, straight 2×4 set on edge. When checking an entire floor, move the board until you find the high point of the floor. You can measure from there to find out if other parts of the floor are level.

A torpedo level is very handy in tight spots. When checking shelves or cabinets for plumb against a wall that is not plumb, loosely fasten the unit in place, then insert shims above or below until the unit is plumb.

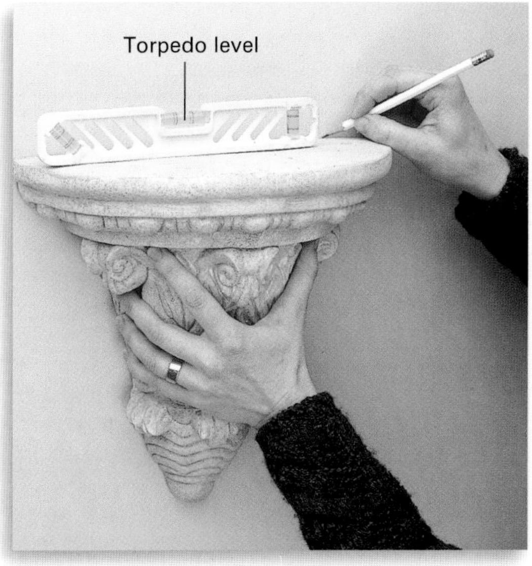

Use a torpedo level for leveling or plumbing small objects where a carpenter's level would be cumbersome.

LINE, WATER, AND LASER LEVELS

In addition to a level and a board, consider these tests for level over long distances.

- **A LINE LEVEL** is basically a vial with two hooks. Attach it in the middle of a taut line to turn the line into a level. Line levels are inaccurate if the hooks get bent, so test yours regularly: If the bubble is in the same place when you reverse it, it is accurate.
- **A WATER LEVEL** has two calibrated transparent tubes attached to a garden hose filled with water. It employs the principle that water seeks its own level. Use it to check level around corners or over distances as long as the hose.
- **A LASER LEVEL** projects a pinpoint beam of light, so you can make level marks wherever you point it. Some models even project horizontal lines. It needs to rest on a stable surface and often requires a tripod.

CUTTING WITH A CIRCULAR SAW

The circular saw is the carpenter's workhorse. If you have done much handsawing, you'll appreciate how effortlessly a circular saw cuts through lumber. It can crosscut, rip, miter, and bevel much faster than a handsaw. It can easily make plunge cuts in the middle of a board. With the right blade, a circular saw will cut almost any material, including concrete and steel.

These basic blades will equip you for most carpentry projects.

CHOOSING A SAW

A standard carpenter's circular saw uses a $7\frac{1}{4}$-inch blade, which is large enough to cut 2-by lumber at a 45-degree angle. Smaller models, designed for cutting paneling, are lighter and a bit easier to use but are not as versatile. Framing carpenters use heavy worm-drive saws to cut thick lumber for hours and hours, but most homeowners find them too heavy and awkward for smaller projects.

Amperage, rather than horsepower, is an accurate measure of a saw's power. If this information is not given on the saw's box, look for a metal label attached to the saw. A circular saw rated at 10–13 amps is powerful enough for any job you are likely to encounter around the home. If the saw has ball bearings, it will run more smoothly.

Choose a saw that feels comfortable in your hand. Most of the time it will be resting on the lumber you are cutting, but it should not be uncomfortably heavy. Make sure you can easily see the gunsight notch and the blade as you work. A plastic housing does not mean that the saw is of low quality; but better saws often have long, rubbery cords while cheaper models have short, stiff ones. The saw's base plate should be at least $\frac{1}{16}$ inch thick and should be easy to adjust for blade depth and angle.

PREPARING TO CUT

Normally, it takes less than a minute to prepare for a cut with a circular saw. But it is important to have the blade correctly aligned and the board adequately supported, or else your work will be not only sloppy but dangerous as well.

CHECK AND SQUARE SAW BLADES

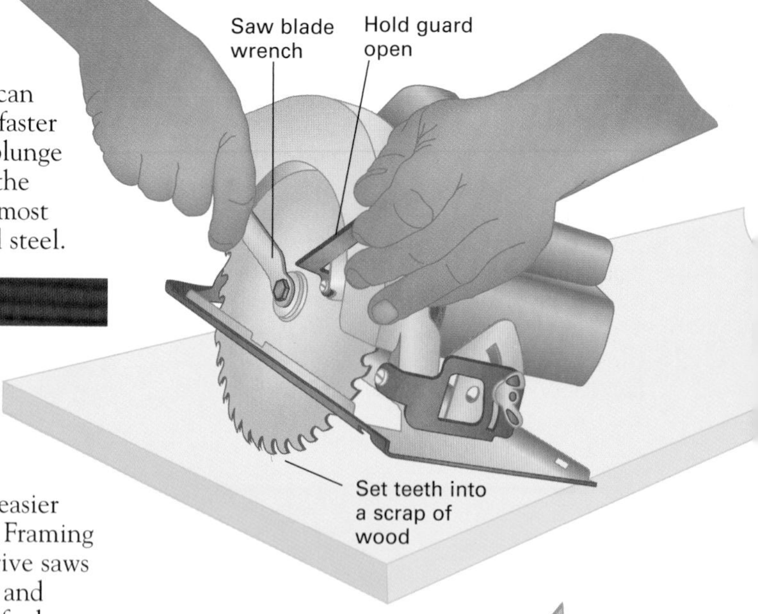

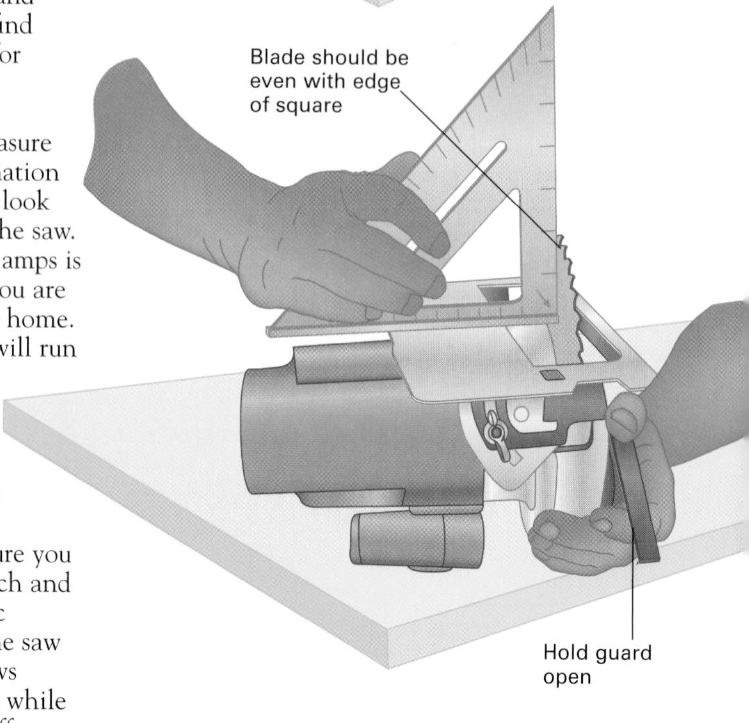

ADJUSTING THE BLADE: The calibrated bevel adjustment gauge on your saw is seldom trustworthy. To accurately square up the blade, unplug the saw and turn it upside down. Retract the guard, and hold a speed square against the blade and the plate. Position the square between the teeth, which point a bit to the left and right. Adjust the bevel so the blade lines up with the square. Test your adjustment by cutting through a piece of 2-by lumber. Flip one of the two resulting pieces over, and press one cut edge against the other cut edge. If the blade is square, they will line up perfectly. If your bevel gauge is not accurate, scratch a new line on it so you will be able to adjust quickly in the future.

Before cutting, check that the saw blade is at the correct depth—about 1/4 inch below the bottom of the board you're cutting. A blade set at this depth will make a cleaner cut than a blade set way below the board. Also, the lower you set the blade, the greater the possibility of kickback (*see box below*).

Become familiar with the kerf of your saw blade—the width of the cut it will make. An average blade will remove about 1/8 inch. A plywood blade will remove less, a carbide-tipped blade will remove more.

SUPPORTING THE WORK SAFELY: By supporting the board or plywood correctly, you'll not only reduce the chance of the blade binding, but you'll also make cleaner cuts.

If the piece of waste will be short, support the board on the non-waste side, and let the waste just hang over. It will simply fall away when the cut is completed.

If the waste side is long, you can't just let it fall away: It will splinter and crack away from the cut because of its weight. Support the work in four places, two on the waste side and two on the other side (*see below*). Be sure that the board to be cut does not bend in the middle due to the weight of the saw.

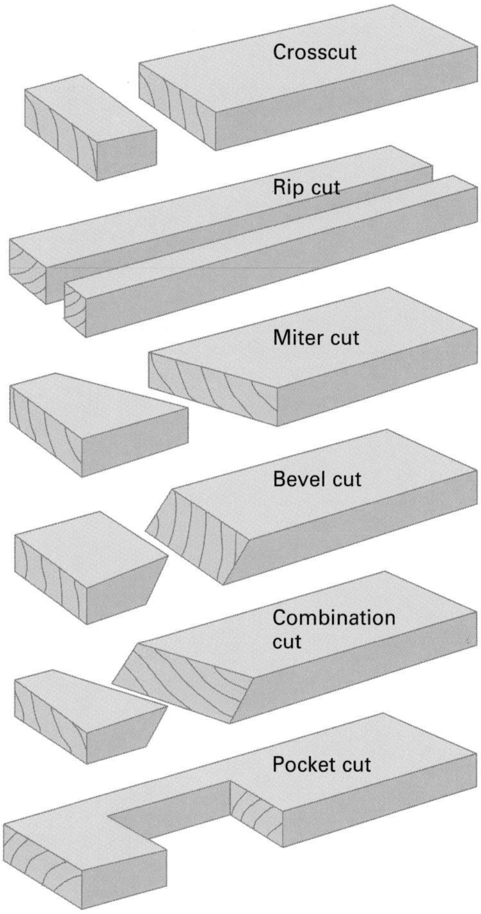

No matter what kind of saw you use, these are the six basic cuts you need to know.

SAFETY VS. KICKBACK

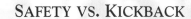

When the teeth on the rear of the blade catch on a board, a circular saw will kick back out of its cut line, ruining the cut and endangering the carpenter. Here's how to avoid kickbacks:

■ Don't try to change directions in mid cut or the blade will grab. If your cut is starting to veer off in a wrong direction, stop the saw, back up, and start again. Don't run the saw as you back it up—that can also cause kickback.

■ Keep your blades sharp. If you have to push hard to make a cut, chances of kickback are great.

■ Be sure the work is supported correctly. If the board bends down in the middle, that will cause the board to grab the blade. If a heavy piece of waste falls away, it can also grab the blade.

■ Sometimes a twisted board, or one with a certain type of grain, will grab the blade suddenly. This happens seldom, but be prepared for it.

■ Take other safety precautions, as well. Never wear long sleeves or have any other piece of clothing that could come near the blade as you cut. Never bring your face close to the blade as you cut. Keep the power cord clear of the cutting area.

CUTTING WITH A CIRCULAR SAW

continued

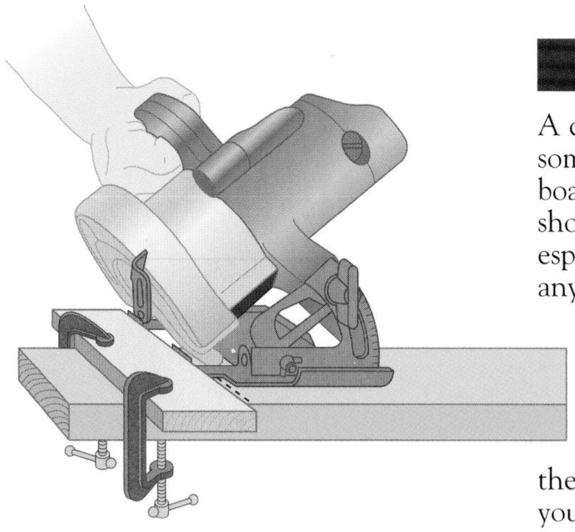

For a bevel cut, adjust the base plate to the desired angle. The bevel guide may be inaccurate, so cut scrap pieces and test them before making the final cut.

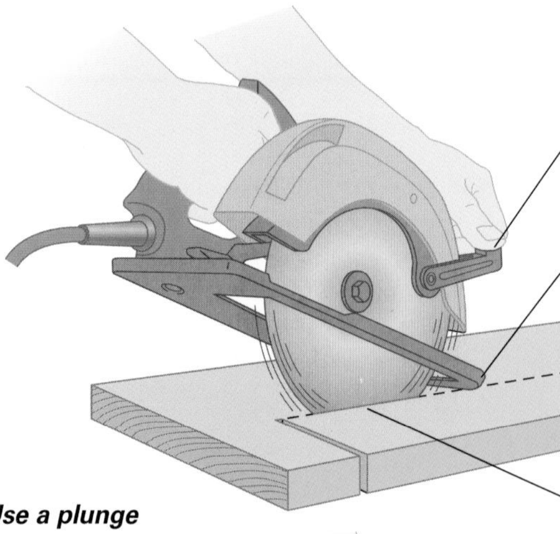
1. Hold guard open
2. Rest front of base plate on board
3. Lower blade into the wood

Use a plunge cut to complete a pocket cut.

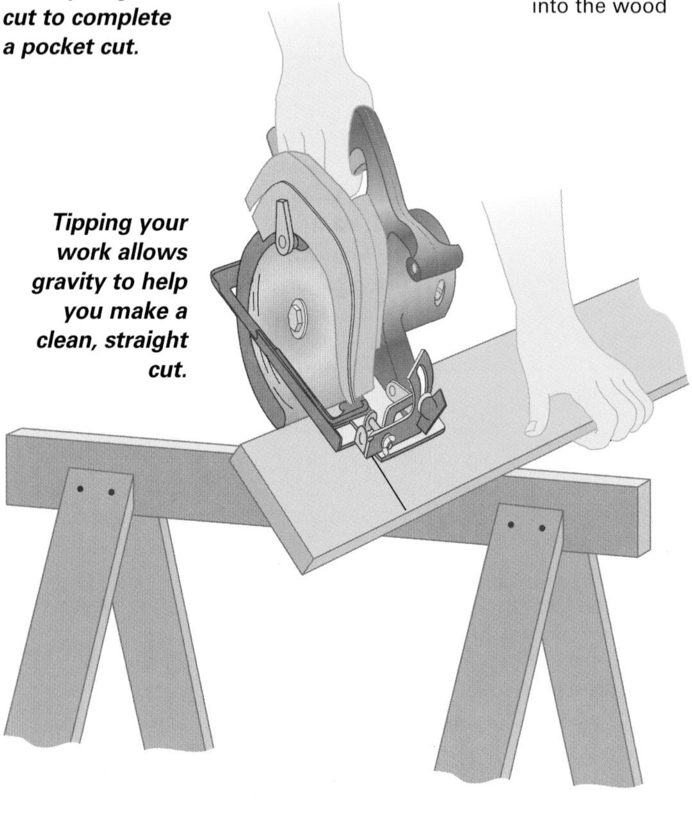

Tipping your work allows gravity to help you make a clean, straight cut.

MAKING THE CUTS

A circular saw cuts upward, which causes some splintering on the upper face of the board. Therefore, the least desirable face should be in contact with the base of the saw, especially when cutting plywood. (As with any saw, splintering is minimal when you are cutting with the grain.)

Don't cut too slowly, making little turns every few inches to keep the blade near the cut line—you'll end up with a gaping, wavy cut line. And don't force the saw to move too quickly into the board—you'll strain the motor and likely miss your cut line. Instead, try to develop a smooth, fairly rapid movement that doesn't require a lot of force.

Some carpenters align the cut line with the saw's gunsight notch as they cut, while others prefer to look at the blade. For cuts that must be dead-on accurate, use the blade—especially when you want to follow a fine pencil line. When making long cuts where a straight cut is more important than a closely accurate cut, use the notch. For example, when cutting underlayment or plywood marked with a chalk line, use the notch as your visual guide.

CROSSCUTS: Place the tip of the base plate on the board, and align the blade with the cut line. Make sure you are on the correct side of the line so the kerf is eaten out of the waste side. Do not let the blade touch the wood until the motor is running at full speed. Feed the saw into the cut, using a smooth motion. Keep the base plate resting on the board as you cut. Once the cut is completed, release the trigger and wait for the blade to stop spinning before lifting the saw.

With practice, you'll make accurate freehand cutoffs. But if the cut needs to be precise, use a guide. The simplest is a speed square: Start the cut, slide the square into place against the saw's base plate, and finish the cut. For a more secure guide, start the cut and stop the saw; square up and clamp a short board along the base plate and finish the cut.

Many carpenters find it easier to crosscut while tilting the board. Gravity makes the cutting easier, and the scrap is more likely to fall away without splintering. This takes practice. Make sure you rest your work on a steady base and can hold the lumber firmly.

POCKET CUTS: Sometimes you need to start a cut in the middle of a board for a notch or other opening. To make a pocket cut (also called a plunge cut), rest the front of the base plate on the board and retract the blade guard. Find a way to retract it so that you are comfortable and there is no danger of the blade grabbing your sleeve.

With the blade just above the board, start the saw and slowly lower it into the wood. When the base plate rests firmly on the work, move the saw forward (never backward) to finish the cut. Because the blade is round, the cut will be longer on the visible side than on the bottom; you'll need to complete it with a handsaw or saber saw.

RIP CUTS, CUTS ON SHEET GOODS: Most circular saws come with a rip fence, a metal guide that fastens to the base plate. This will enable you to cut a fairly straight line parallel to the board's edge, as long as the piece to be cut is not too wide.

If the board is too wide to use a rip fence, or for long cuts on sheet goods, clamp a guide in place. You can make a two-piece jig like the one shown *right*, or just use a single straight board. Measure the distance between the outside edge of the base plate and the saw blade, and position the guide the same distance from the cut line. Be careful to keep the kerf to the waste side of the cut.

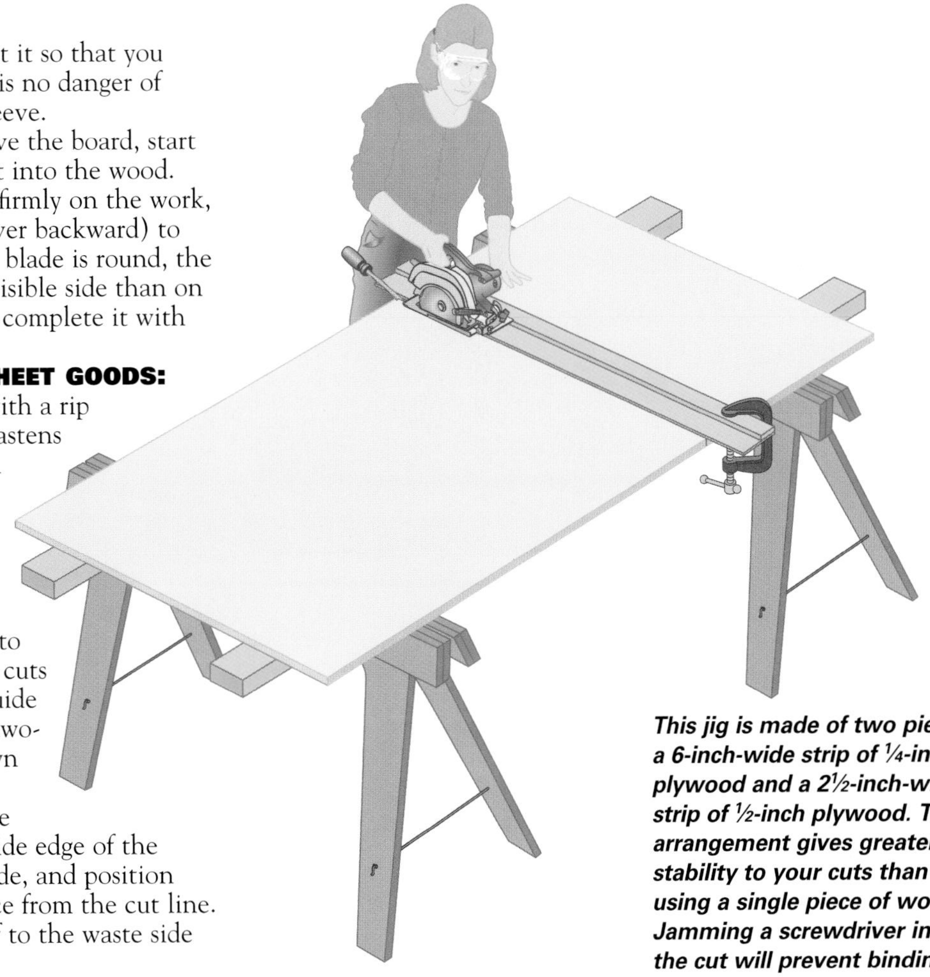

This jig is made of two pieces, a 6-inch-wide strip of ¼-inch plywood and a 2½-inch-wide strip of ½-inch plywood. This arrangement gives greater stability to your cuts than using a single piece of wood. Jamming a screwdriver into the cut will prevent binding.

MAKING A SAWHORSE

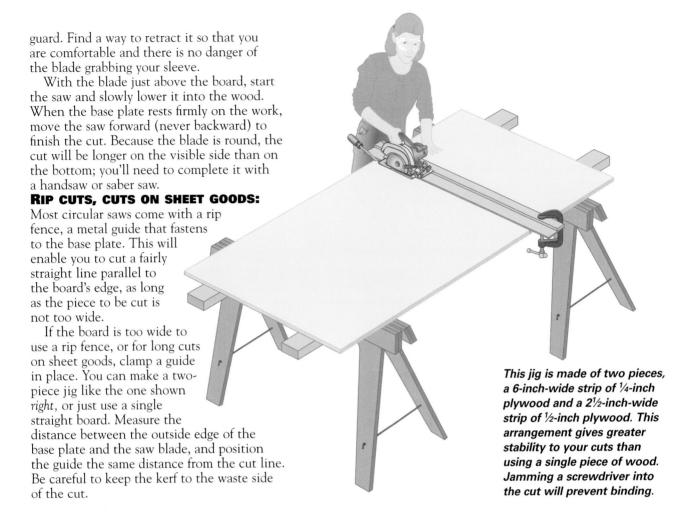

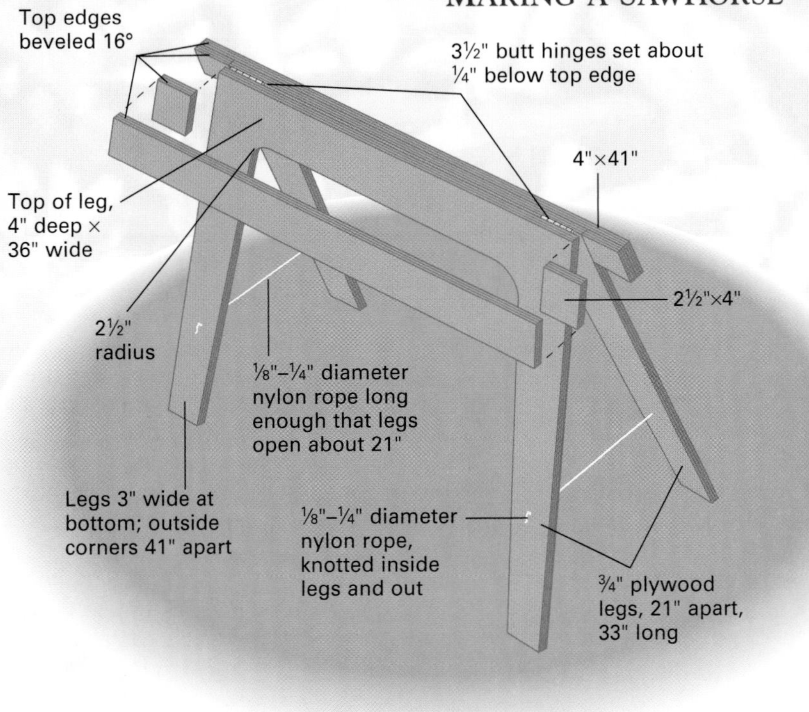

Here is a handy sawhorse you can build yourself. It will be stable enough for most carpentry work (though it is not designed to be stood on), and it folds away for easy storage. It is economical as well: You can cut all the pieces out of a single sheet of 4×8, ¾-inch plywood.

Cut all the pieces according to the dimensions shown. Use a saber saw for the curved inside corners of the leg pieces. Set your circular or table saw at a 16-degree bevel to cut the top edges of the side pieces. Attach hinges to the two leg pieces, using ¾-inch screws.

Fasten the side pieces and the block pieces with 1¼-inch all-purpose screws, making sure their tops will be flush with each other. Drill holes in the legs just large enough to accommodate the cord. Attach the cords, making knots that keep the legs about 21 inches apart.

MITER CUTS BY HAND

Crisp, tightly fitting joints in moldings give a job a professional look. And you don't have to buy expensive tools to get that look. You can get precise results with good hand tools.

Make a miter joint by cutting two pieces, each at half of the final joint's angle. To make a 90-degree joint, for example, cut two pieces at 45 degrees; to make a 45-degree joint, cut two pieces at 22½ degrees.

CHOOSING A TOOL

Mitered pieces must be cut precisely. If the angle or bevel strays even half a degree, the joint will have noticeable gaps. That's why your miter box must be in good shape.

A cheap plastic or hardwood box will be limited to 45- and 90-degree cuts in narrow boards—which will take care of most molding projects. As long as the backsaw is straight and fits into the miter box's groove tightly, the results will be acceptable.

Other hand miter boxes use a bow saw, which looks like a hacksaw, in a metal frame. This type costs more, but it allows you to cut wider stock, adjusts for a variety of angles, and makes a truer cut. It is also lightweight, so many people find it easier to use.

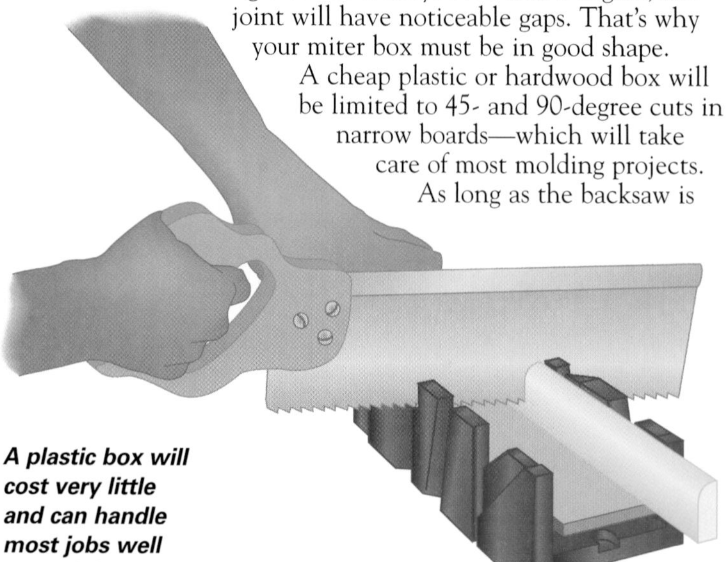

A plastic box will cost very little and can handle most jobs well enough for painting.

MAKING THE CUTS

The most difficult part is getting precise measurements. Hold the board in place and mark it, whenever possible, using a sharp pencil or even a knife to make the mark. Be sure to mark the point where you will begin the cut; this varies from molding to molding.

When you make your measurement mark, also draw a light line indicating the direction of the cut. Some situations can be surprisingly confusing. To be sure you are cutting in the right way, experiment with scrap pieces, cutting them and holding them in place.

For a plastic or wood box, rest the molding on a scrap of 1-by lumber so you can saw completely through it without damaging the box. Hold the molding firmly against the far side of the box. Double-check to make sure you are cutting in the right direction, and place the saw teeth lightly against the cut line to get a precise location.

Saw with an easy motion. If you have to push hard, chances are good that the molding will slip and the cut will stray off course.

Once the cut is made, trim away any frayed edges with a utility knife. There's no harm in cutting away a bit too much, as long as it's on the unseen side.

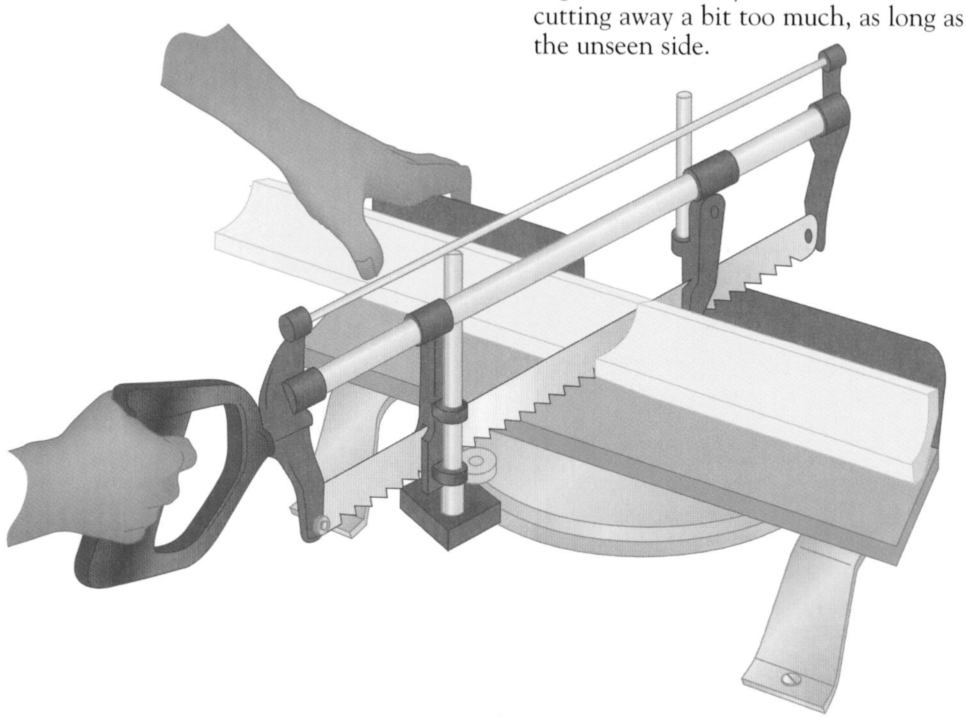

For more precision and greater ease of operation, purchase a miter box with blade guides and adjustable settings. This type has interchangeable blades, so you can use it for cutting wood or metal.

POWER MITER CUTS

Though a quality hand miter box can produce a great looking job, nothing can match the sense of control and precision that you get from a chop saw. It zings out cuts that look like they've come from a factory.

CHOOSING A SAW

A power miter box, commonly known as a chop saw, can cut more than moldings. It will zip through 2-by stock as well, making quick work of framing cuts. (Make sure your power miter is large enough. For example, a 10-inch saw cannot make a 45-degree cut in a 2×6.)

When shopping for a chop saw, look for a retractable blade guard that works smoothly. It shouldn't bind on the piece being cut, and it should lift out of the way easily to give you a clear view of your cutoff mark.

Some chop saws can make compound miters—cuts that miter and bevel at the same time. Unless you plan to frame something complicated, such as a gazebo, you probably will not need this feature.

With a 40- to 60-tooth carbide blade, you will be able to cut both framing lumber and delicate moldings. Purchase a high-quality blade because it will last for a long time.

MAKING THE CUTS

Careful measuring and marking are the keys to all miter cutting. Make sure you know which way each cut should go (*see page 22*).

A chop saw is small and portable, so it doesn't have much of a table. Set the saw on a stable surface, and fasten it in place with screws through the feet if you will be doing heavy work. If the piece to be sawn is long, support it at the other end; you shouldn't have to squeeze hard to hold it in place.

CHOP SAW SAFETY

This is a powerful saw with a large blade that is often very close to you, so take special care.

- Keep the blade guard in good shape. If it starts to stick, oil it or have it repaired. Never remove it.
- Keep it on a stable surface, and make sure the work is well supported. If you have to wrestle with the board while cutting, or if the saw wobbles, you're asking for trouble.
- Don't wear long sleeves or any other clothing that can come close to the blade.
- Wear eye protection.

TABLE SAW, RADIAL ARM SAW, OR CHOP SAW

Choose power tools that complement one another without duplicating too many functions.

For example, most shops do not need a table saw, a radial arm saw, and a chop saw. However, if it's in your budget and you have room in your shop, a table saw and a chop saw will cover your needs perfectly. The chop saw makes quick work of crosscuts, while the table saw makes long cuts and dadoes with ease.

A radial arm saw handles crosscutting and ripping, but often with a bit less precision and a bit more awkwardness than a table saw or chop saw.

However, quality can make a difference. A powerful and stable radial arm saw will do all jobs better than a poor-quality table saw or chop saw.

SLIDING COMPOUND MITER SAW

A chop saw is limited to crosscuts on fairly narrow stock. You may want to spend more money and purchase a sliding miter saw. This saw can handle boards up to 12 inches wide and can cut bevels, miters, and compound angles. Many also allow you to set the depth, so you can make dado cuts (*see page 37*). The sliding miter saw can handle most of the crosscutting chores of a radial arm saw, with the added advantages of compact size, portability, and rapid angle adjustment.

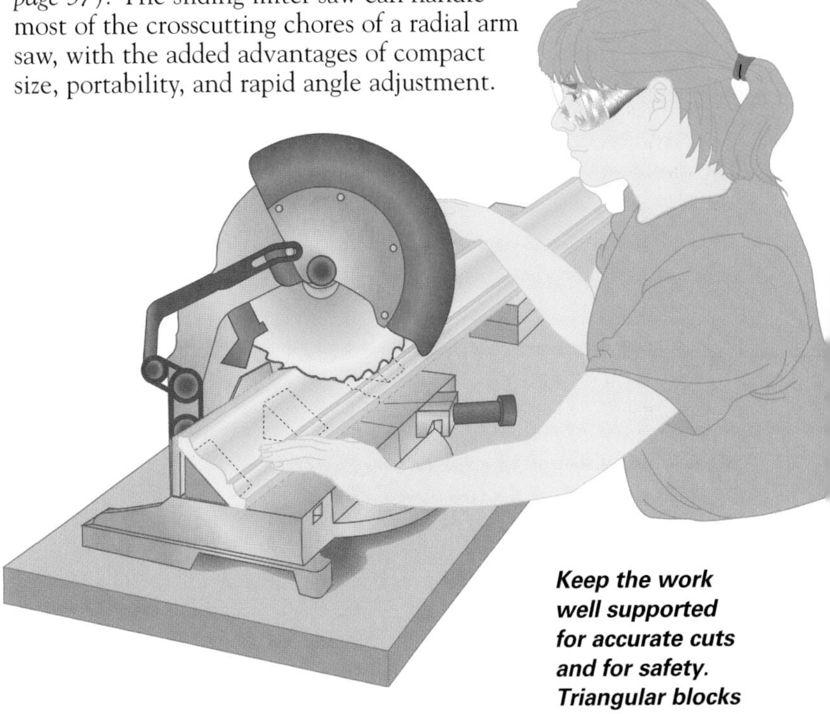

Keep the work well supported for accurate cuts and for safety. Triangular blocks hold this piece of crown molding in place so it imitates its position when installed.

TABLE SAWS

A high-quality table saw will be the king of your wood shop. It works best when ripping boards to width, but with a few accessories and jigs, it also performs accurate crosscuts and makes joinery positively fun.

CHOOSING A SAW

Most saws work by moving through the board; a table saw stays stationary while the board is pushed across it. With a sturdy table saw, you can cut large boards by yourself.

Check the table with a straightedge to make sure that it is perfectly flat. More importantly, examine the fence, which is an essential part of the tool. It should move easily to any position on the table without binding, it should lock into position securely, and it should always remain exactly parallel to the saw blade. See that the blade turns without wobbling. A belt-driven saw will last longer and produce cleaner cuts than one with direct drive.

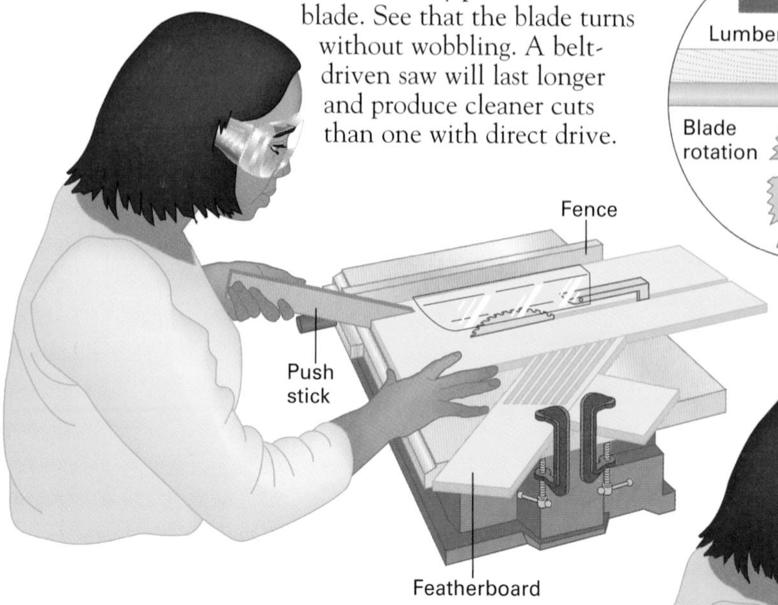

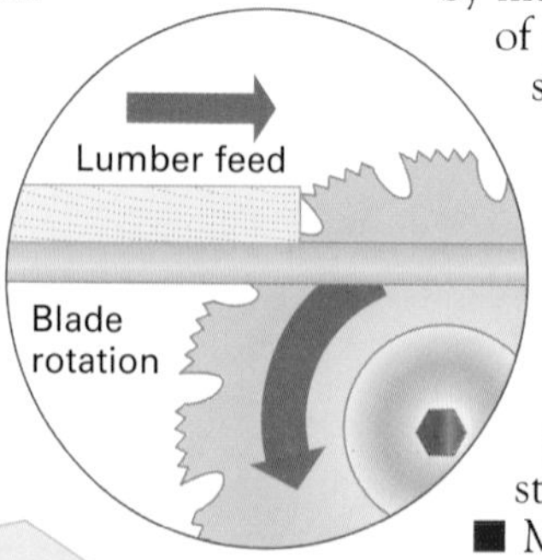

USING THE SAW

Though expensive, carbide-tipped blades save money in the long run because they last longer. A combination-tooth blade can handle almost any job and save you from constantly changing blades. Choose a thin-kerf rip blade or a plywood blade if you specialize in fine cuts.

■ Make a simple push stick by notching one end of a piece of 1×2 and rounding off the other end. To ensure against kickback, make a featherboard *(see below)* from a piece of 1×6. Cut one end to 60 degrees, then cut a series of slots ¼ inch apart. Once clamped in place *(see below left)* it will hold your work against the fence as you make a rip cut.

■ Set the blade so it protrudes above the board by the height of a saw tooth. For a rip cut, be sure the fence is parallel to the blade by measuring at the front and the rear of the blade. Position the board or sheet so it sits flat on the table and you can slide it freely all the way through.

■ Start the motor and let it reach full speed before pushing the board through. Push the board against the fence at all points as you work. Use a push stick as you reach the end.

■ Make crosscuts using a miter gauge, which slides in the groove of the table. Screw a piece of 1-by lumber to its face to provide more support. Adjust the gauge to make angled cuts. Hold the board on only one side of the cut; if you hold both sides, it may bind.

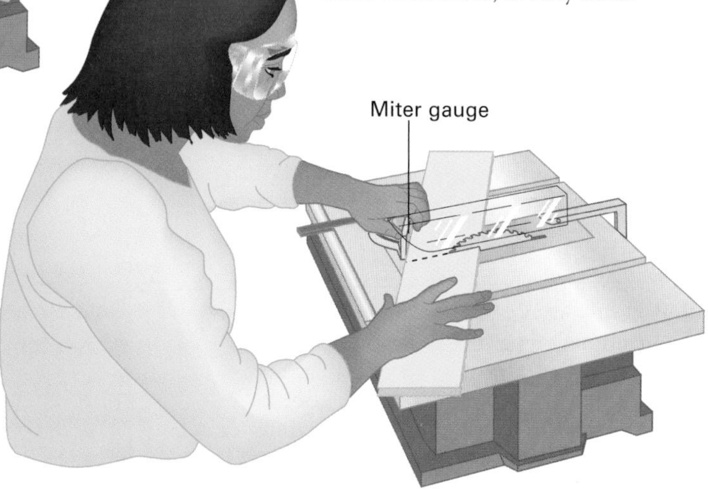

Use a featherboard to help hold your work in place as you make a rip cut on a table saw (above). A miter gauge adjusts to make an angled crosscut (right). The best dado cutters use a pair of saw blades and a set of chippers (below). Stack them together to make grooves for your desired thickness. An adjustable dado wobbles as it spins (below right).

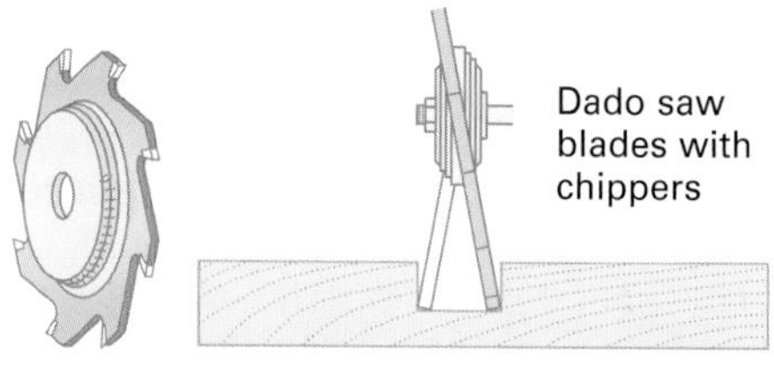

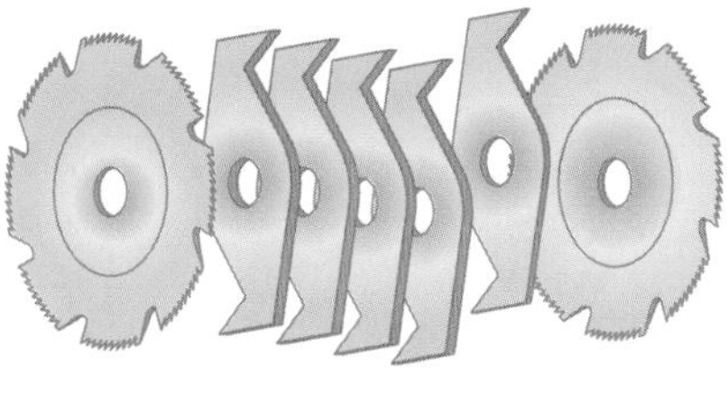

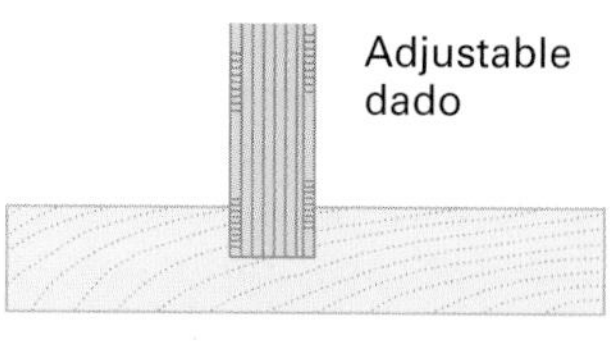

RADIAL ARM SAWS

While a table saw works best for ripping, a radial arm saw is in its element when crosscutting. If it is a quality tool and the table is set up accurately, you can also make precise rip cuts.

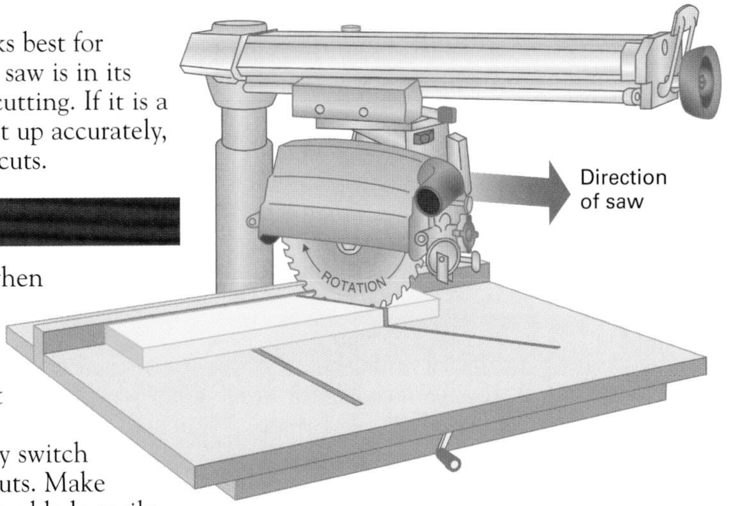

A radial arm saw is ideal for making dadoes and grooves. Test on a piece of scrap wood to see that the blade is raised to the correct height. Make a series of cuts and clean out the notch with a chisel, or use a set of dado blades.

CHOICES

A good saw will not wobble when the motor is running. When you pull the motor to make a crosscut, the assembly should glide smoothly without wavering. Look for ease of adjustments so you can quickly switch from crosscut to bevel or rip cuts. Make sure you can raise and lower the blade easily.

The table—made of particleboard or plywood—should be flat and even, and the fence must be perfectly parallel to the blade for rip cuts. Expect to change the fence fairly often—a straight piece of 1×2 is all you need—and to replace the table every couple of years.

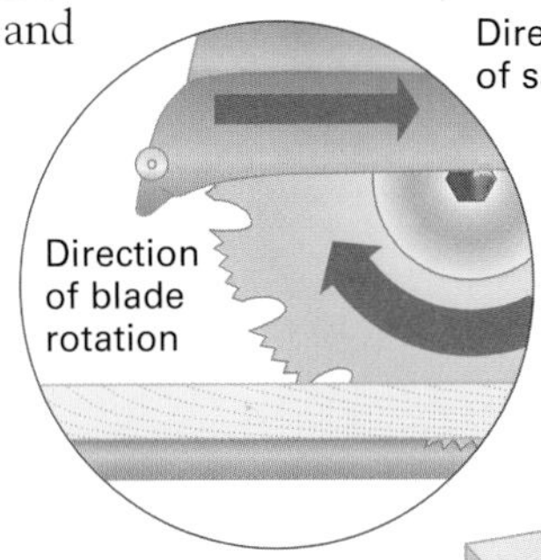

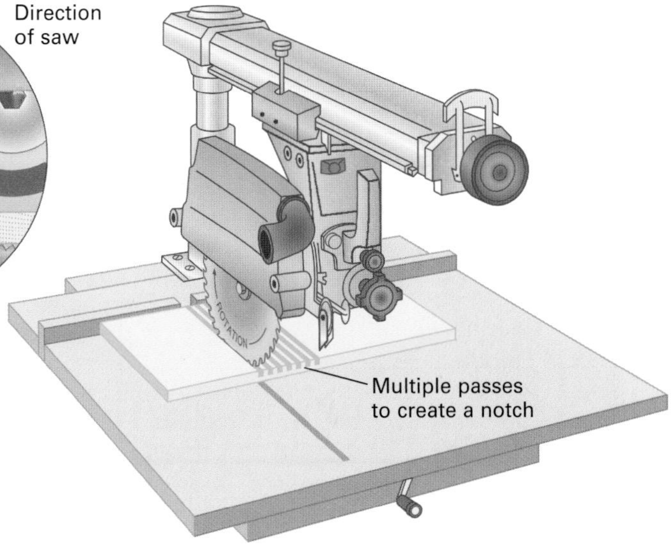

TECHNIQUES

Use a framing square or a piece of plywood with two factory edges to make sure the saw crosscuts squarely. If it is not perfect, you will thank yourself later for taking time to adjust the saw. This may involve tweaking a series of allen-head bolts; the saw's manual will give instructions. Cut scraps to see that your 45-degree cuts are accurate, as well.

■ For all cuts, it is important to clean away the wood chips and even sawdust that collects where the fence meets the table. If the board does not butt against the fence all along its length, your cut will be inaccurate.

■ To make a crosscut or miter cut, set the board firmly against the fence. If it is long, provide support at the board's end. The support should be at the correct height, so the board sits flat on the table. Hold your hand well away from the blade as you pull the saw.

■ Whenever you make a bevel cut, you must raise the blade first. For a rip cut, start with the blade above the table or the blade may bind. Start the motor, then lower the blade.

■ Rip cuts may go slowly, so be patient. And be careful: If the board gets twisted slightly, the saw may kick it back with bullet-like force. Position the anti-kickback assembly, and stand to the side.

■ If the saw binds, turn the motor off to keep it from overheating, and pull the board back an inch or so. If it does overheat, it will automatically shut off. Wait a few minutes, then push the reset button.

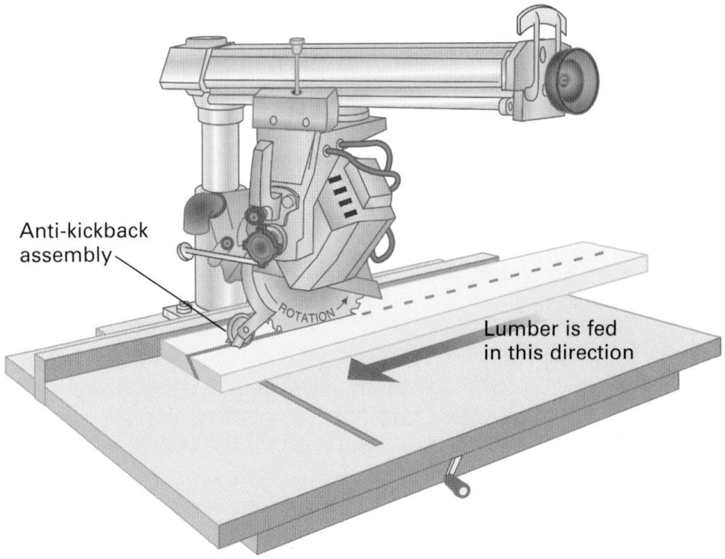

When ripping, take the time to position the anti-kickback assembly correctly because the saw may throw the board backwards with great speed. Stand to the side instead of directly behind the board to avoid being hit.

CONTOUR CUTS

Saber saws cut curves cleanly. Work slowly and watch closely.

Projects that call for curved cuts may seem daunting. You may wonder who could make such fancy lines with your meager set of tools. You can. The truth is, most contour cuts can be done with simple equipment, and require more patience than carpentry skill.

CHOOSING TOOLS

To make a few cuts through 1-by lumber or plywood, an inexpensive saber saw will do. However, many cheaper tools have base plates that swivel under pressure. So make sure that the blade is square to the base plate and that the base plate is held firmly in place. (You may need to bear down extra hard on the adjustment screw.) You will need to cut slowly.

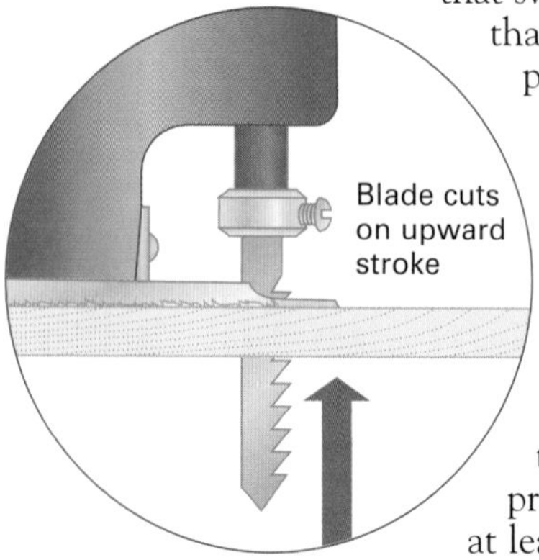

You can quickly learn to make smooth contour cuts with a saber saw. Always place the best side of your work down; the blade cuts up, leaving a ragged edge on the upper side of your work.

To do a lot of contour cutting, or if you need to cut through hardwood or 2-by lumber, or if you need to make accurate curved cuts that are also beveled, choose a professional-quality tool. It will pull at least three amps, run on ball bearings, and have a base plate that is easy to make firm. Have plenty of saber saw blades on hand because they break easily. The more teeth per inch a blade has, the smoother it will cut.

For scrollwork on small boards, a bandsaw is best to ensure cuts are perfectly square to the face of the board. An 8- or 9-inch model will cost about the same as a high-quality saber saw. (A heavy-duty bandsaw with a fence and miter gauge can also crosscut and rip.) A bandsaw is the usual first power tool for children as young as 8 because it requires little strength and it poses no danger of serious injury.

MAKING THE CUTS

The hardest part of contour cutting may be drawing the lines. Usually, an ornate curved configuration can be made using a series of partial circles of various diameters. Experiment with a compass on a piece of paper.

SABER SAW: If you need to start a cut in the middle of a board, drill a starter hole large enough for the blade to fit through.

The main challenge is to keep the saber saw blade from wobbling.

- Use clamps to keep the board stable as you work, and allow plenty of room beneath the cut line for the saber saw blade.
- As you cut, press downward on the board with more pressure than you use for pushing forward, to ensure that the base plate remains flat on the board.
- Every few seconds, blow away the sawdust so you can see the cut line.
- Push the blade slowly; you can feel it if you're forcing the blade. If the blade produces smoke, you're moving too fast.
- Avoid sharp turns, which can break blades.
- If you veer off course, back up an inch or so and cut again, rather than try to make a sudden correction.

COPING A PIECE OF MOLDING

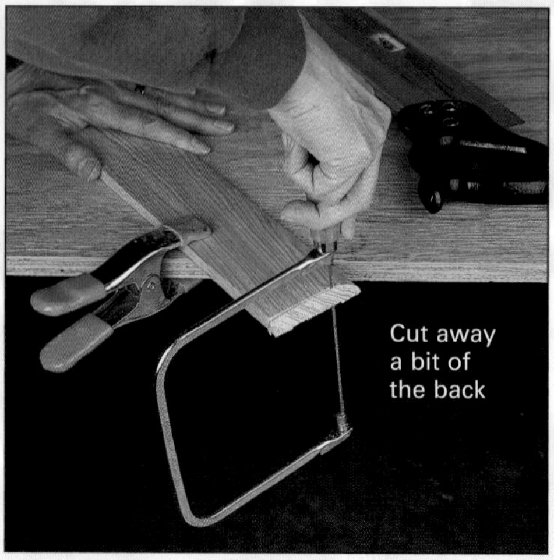

When making an inside corner with curved molding, coping will ensure a tight fit even if the walls are not square. Cut the first piece of molding at a straight, 90-degree angle, and fit it tightly against the adjoining wall. Miter-cut the second piece to 45 degrees. Then use a coping saw to cut away the wood behind the face of the miter cut. Cut off a bit more than necessary, since the back will not show. When possible, cut the coped end first, hold the molding in place, and mark for the cut on the other end.

BANDSAW: Here, the trick is often to position the board so it doesn't bump into the saw's arm as you work. This may be difficult on larger boards.

■ Hold the board flat on the table with both hands, and move it gently into the blade.

■ Maintain an even pace and a smooth turning action for curves that do not waver.

■ Avoid binding the blade. Don't try to correct a cut by making a sharp turn.

■ If you need to back out of a cut, turn the saw off and wait for the motor to stop. Back out carefully to avoid twisting the blade.

COPING SAW: This saw has a fine-cutting blade that can be turned while the frame remains still, so you can make tight turns. It works best on lumber no thicker than an inch. Because it has no base plate, it is difficult to make a cut that is perpendicular to the face of the board.

■ Before cutting, determine where you will position the frame.

■ To reposition the blade, loosen the handle and then move the levers at either end.

■ For cuts on the inside of a board, drill a hole in the center of the cut.

■ Remove the blade, slide it through the hole, and reattach.

■ Have plenty of replacement blades on hand; they snap easily.

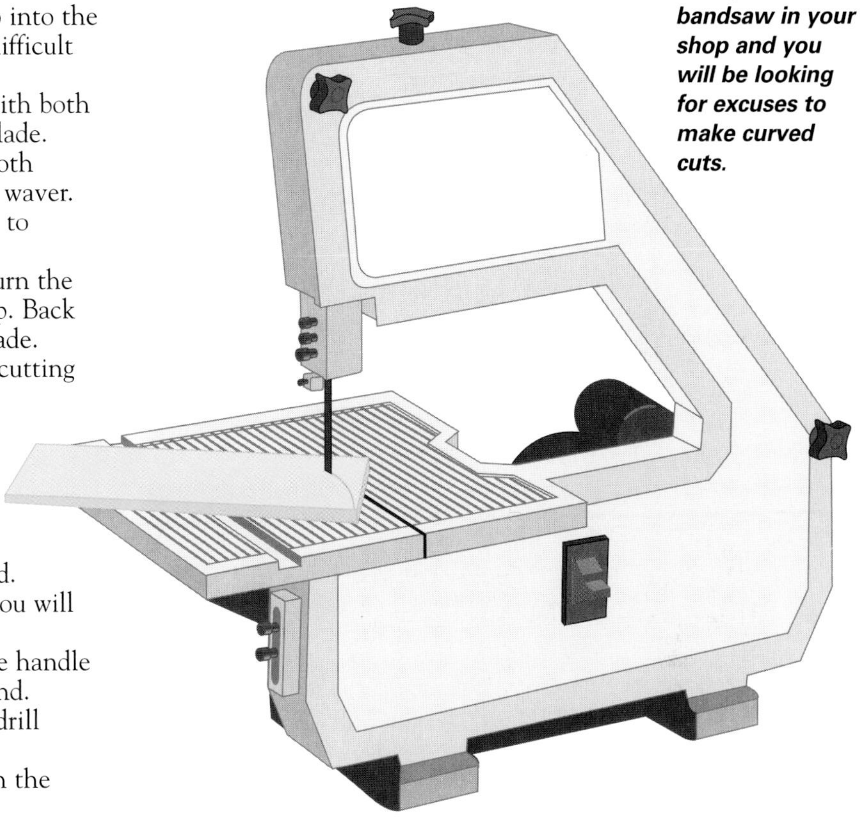

Set up a bandsaw in your shop and you will be looking for excuses to make curved cuts.

HOLE SAWS

When faced with a hole too large for a drill bit to manage, as when you are installing a lockset on a door or cutting holes for pipes, use a hole saw rather than wrestling with a saber saw. One system allows you to attach various-sized hole saws to a single starter bit. If you don't plan to bore holes of different sizes, a single-sized unit may save money.

Measure and mark for the center of the hole only. (Make sure your hole saw is the right size; don't confuse radius and diameter.) The starter bit will protrude from the hole saw a little. Hold the hole saw perpendicular to the wood and push into the hole with steady, medium pressure. If the going gets rough or the saw heats up, the teeth may quickly become dull, so take it easy.

If the board is thicker than the hole saw, you may need to stop and clean the cut wood from the inside of the saw before proceeding. Stick a nail into the side slot, or poke through a hole in the back of the saw.

To keep from splintering the other side of the board when you break through, drill just until the starter bit pokes through, then drill from the other side.

HANDSAWS

Carpenters once had massive right arms because they used a handsaw all day. Today a circular saw does most of the work for us, but a handsaw still has a place in every carpenter's toolbox. It can reach into the corners of a notch and make cuts flush with an adjoining surface. It is sometimes preferable for small projects because it doesn't throw sawdust around the room.

PRO TACTICS

Pull saw to get started

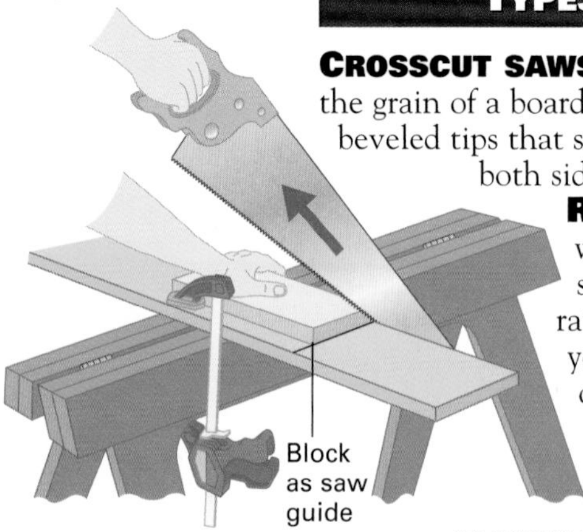

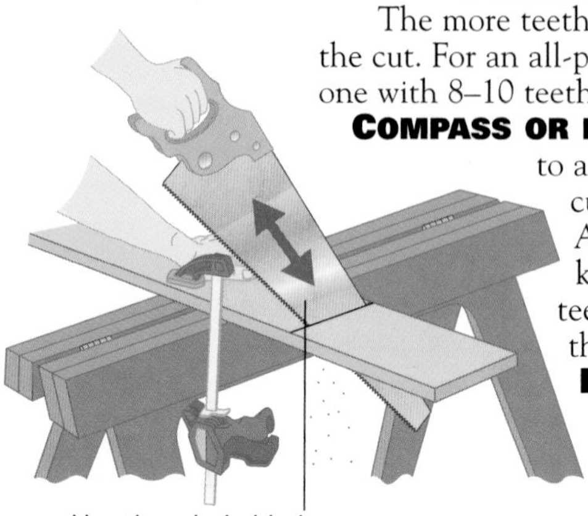

Use the whole blade with full, smooth strokes

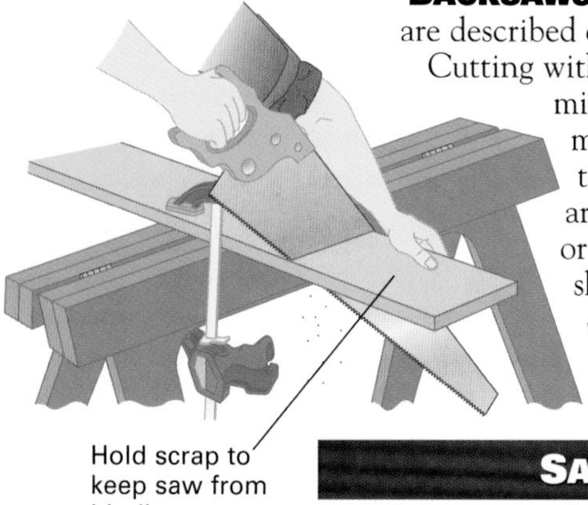

Hold scrap to keep saw from binding

TYPES OF SAWS

CROSSCUT SAWS are meant to cut across the grain of a board. They have teeth with beveled tips that score the wood fibers on both sides of the cut.

RIPSAWS, designed to cut with the grain, have teeth sharpened straight across rather than beveled. If you won't be doing a lot of hand-sawing, buy a saw with a combination blade, which will do a good job of cutting with or across the grain.

The more teeth, the smoother and slower the cut. For an all-purpose handsaw, look for one with 8–10 teeth per inch (tpi).

COMPASS OR KEYHOLE SAWS taper to a point and are handy for cutting in tight spots. A drywall saw is like a keyhole saw but has wider teeth so it can cut quickly through drywall.

HACKSAWS have interchangeable blades and are useful for cutting metal or hard materials like ceramic tile.

BACKSAWS AND COPING SAWS are described on pages 22 and 27.

Cutting with a dull handsaw is a miserable experience. You may have to spend some time looking, but there are still hardware stores or individuals who will sharpen blades in most communities. If not, buy a new saw when the old one becomes dull.

SAW TIPS

Hand sawing takes practice. To get the hang of it, draw a series of perpendicular lines on a piece of 1×6. Square the lines completely around the board so you can see whether your cuts are straight up and down. Then saw off slices, one after another. The first few will probably go astray, but after a half-hour of practice, you should be pleased with your progress.

- Hold the saw loosely—don't squeeze it.
- Hold a square-cut scrap against the cut line as a guide, or gently press your thumbnail against the saw to keep it from wandering.
- Begin with light, smooth strokes. Don't push down on the saw—a sharp blade cuts with its own weight. (Experienced carpenters often will say, "Let the saw do the work.")
- Avoid quick, short strokes: Use the whole blade. Trying to correct a cut midway through the board will cause the saw to bind.

With practice, you can set your course truly at the beginning and sail through the cut without struggling. As you near the end, reach across with your free hand to support the waste piece, so it won't fall and splinter.

JAPANESE HANDSAWS

These have teeth pointed backwards, toward the user, so the saw cuts on the pull stroke. Their thin blades have long, razor-sharp teeth, which cut quickly and leave a smooth surface with very little splintering. The teeth are difficult to sharpen, so they are sold with replaceable blades.

The *ryoba* saw has teeth on both sides of the blade, one for crosscutting and the other for rip cuts. It is very flexible, but it makes straight cuts because the teeth grab only on the upswing. The *dozuki* saw is rigid and is used for small precision cuts.

Hybrid saws combine a Western-style body with the teeth of the Japanese style. These saws have a short, stiff blade that cuts on the push stroke. The teeth cut very aggressively and quickly. The cut is coarse, so they are usually used for rough work.

SANDING

Many carpentry projects take hours of painstaking work to produce but still look sloppy because the sanding wasn't done properly. Don't expect stain or even paint to cover up minor imperfections; they usually accentuate them instead.

HAND SANDING

In most cases, sandpaper lasts longer and sands more smoothly if it is attached to a block. You can simply staple it to a piece of wood, but tools that have a little flexibility work better. A drywall sander with a handle (rather than the kind that attaches to a pole) is excellent for large wood surfaces as well. It uses specially sized sheets of sandpaper that can be changed quickly.

■ Have smaller blocks for sanding in corners.
■ Often the best way to get into a tight spot is to use a scrap of sandpaper and your finger.
■ Before putting a sheet onto a sanding block, make sure the block's bottom is smooth; any debris can cause the paper to tear.
■ Attach sandpaper tightly; loose paper rips.
■ Unless you need to shave down a lot of wood, always sand with the grain.
■ Use light, long strokes. Short strokes can lead to a wavy surface, and pushing too hard may clog up the sandpaper.
■ Edges should be rounded off at least slightly, to make them less sharp and to prevent splinters. Determine how much rounding you want to do, and be careful not to oversand at any point.
■ Use a sanding block that is somewhat spongy so the sandpaper can round the corner rather than chamfering it.
■ Hold the block at a 45-degree angle, and sand with long strokes, using a slight rocking motion.

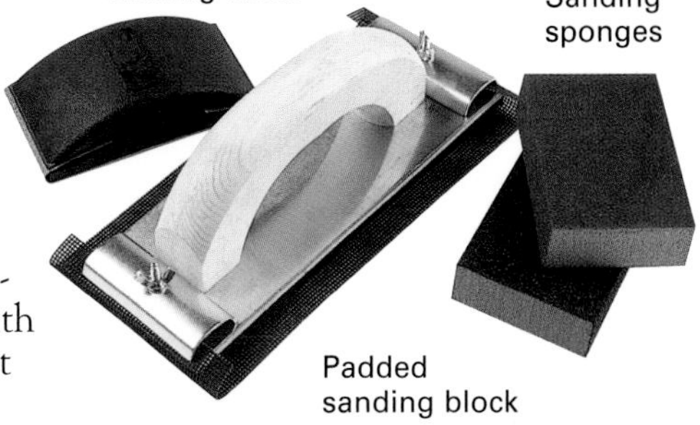

POWER SANDING

For heavy-duty sanding of fairly large surfaces, a belt sander is the right tool. Work carefully, however, because it is very easy to gouge wood if you press down or stay in one spot for a few seconds.

■ Always sand with the grain, and let the weight of the sander do the work.
■ You can use vibrating, random-orbit, and detail sanders without worrying about sanding with the grain. They work slowly—often more slowly than hand-sanding. Don't use them on large areas because they can easily produce dips in the surface.
■ For a high-quality surface, it is almost always necessary to finish with a hand sanding, using long strokes and fine paper.

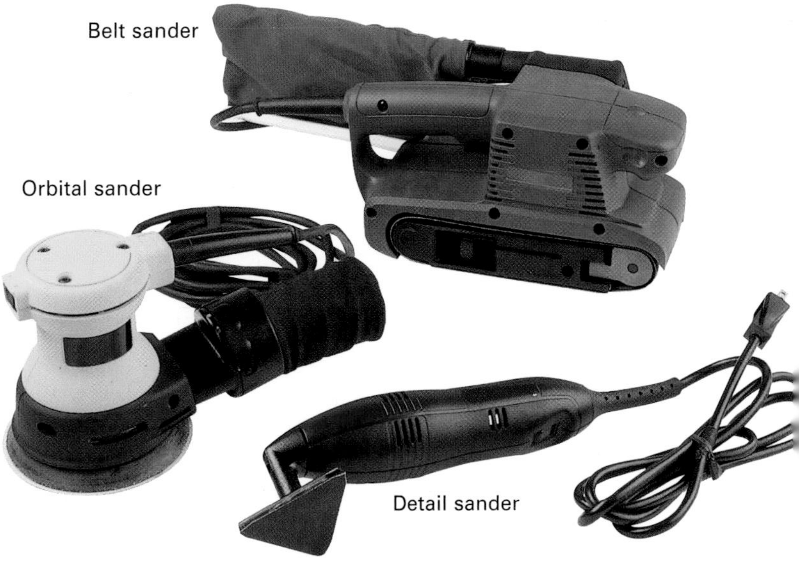

A full range of sanders will let you tackle any finishing job. Use the belt sander with a deft touch; it can gouge your work. Use an orbital sander on flat surfaces. A detail sander gets into hard-to-reach spots, such as the gap between stair balusters.

STEP DOWN GRITS

Whether you are sanding by hand or using a power sander, sand three times, and use a finer paper for each step, working your wood down to a finer and finer finish. Many projects start with 80-grit paper, step down to 120-grit, and then finish with 240-grit. Brush away the dust after the sanding.

If you think the first sanding feels smooth enough, you'll detect a subtle but real improvement with the second and third sanding. Only wood that has received three sandings can achieve a furniture-like surface once it is stained and finished.

SHAPING AND CHISELING

Somewhere between cutting and sanding are chiseling and planing—time-tested techniques for shaving wood to fit. Some practice with these tools will help you achieve smooth-looking results.

KEEPING TOOLS SHARP

There is no substitute for a sharp plane or chisel. Choose chisels and planes with high-carbon tempered steel; they hold their edges longer than cheaper tools. Though sharpening may be a chore, you save time and aggravation in the long run if you consistently hone the edges of all your tools.

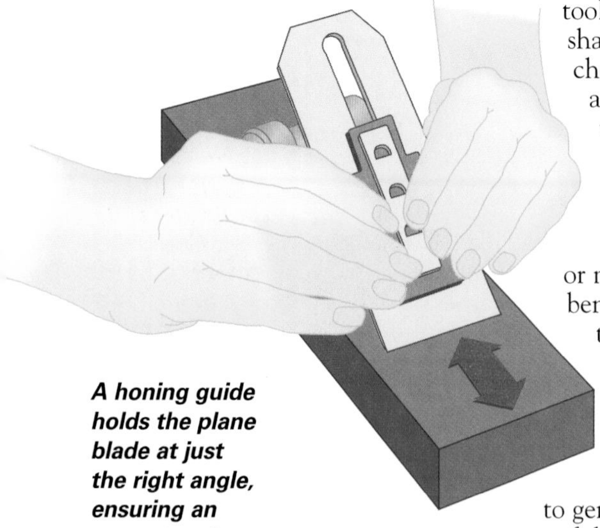

A honing guide holds the plane blade at just the right angle, ensuring an accurate edge.

If a tool is dull or misshapen, use a bench grinder or a file to bring it close to sharp. Be careful to maintain the original beveled angle. Don't press hard enough to generate heat or the temper of the edge will be lost and the blade will quickly become dull.

Use a two-sided whetstone for sharpening and then honing a plane blade or a chisel. To sharpen by hand, lightly oil the rougher (sharpening) side of the stone, and brace it on a flat surface. Press the bevel of the blade against the stone, and grind by moving the tool back and forth. Press gently; tip the tool slightly so you do not grind the entire face of the bevel.

Turn the tool over and rest the flat side on the stone. Here, you want to remove burrs only. Oil again, if needed, and use circular motions as you press gently.

After sharpening, turn the stone over and repeat to hone the edge to razor sharpness.

PLANING

Use a rasp or rasping plane to shave wood roughly; these inexpensive tools require no special skills. But for a straight, smooth finish, nothing beats an old-fashioned plane.

Planes range in size from a palm-held block plane to a 20-inch jointer plane, and a fine woodworker will have a collection of them. For most projects, a small block plane and a mid-sized jack plane are all you need. Use a straightedge to check the bottom; it should be nearly perfect. Also, see that the blade cap fits tightly to the blade. Use a file to true the edge of either the blade cap or the sole. Hone the blade razor-sharp before you use it.

■ Set the blade cap about 1/16 inch behind the cutting edge.

■ Adjust the depth of the cut by turning the depth adjustment nut, sighting down the sole until you see the blade protrude slightly.

■ Test on a scrap of wood, and make fine adjustments. If the blade cuts more on one side or if it makes a score mark, move the lateral adjustment lever until shavings come from the center of the blade.

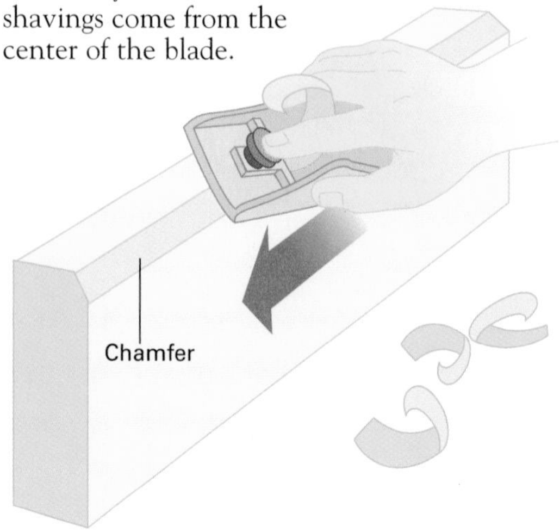

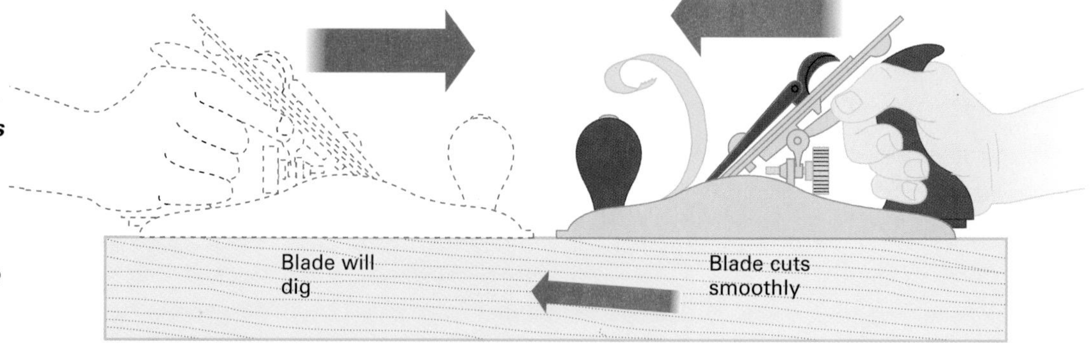

Hold the plane at the correct angle (usually 45 degrees) when beginning to chamfer (above right). Changing the angle of the chamfer once you have begun is difficult. Plane with the grain as it runs upward ahead of the plane (right); otherwise the plane will gouge the surface.

■ Always plane with the grain; that is, the grain should run upward ahead of the plane. If you plane toward a grain that runs downward, the blade will dig into the wood and produce a rough surface, perhaps even tearing out splinters. You may have to change directions in the middle of some boards in order to plane with the grain consistently.
■ Start the stroke by applying downward pressure to the front of the plane. As you get to the end of the board, shift pressure to the rear to prevent the end from rounding off.

CHISELING

Use chisels to chip waste wood from notches, to trim joints, and to mortise for door hardware. Two chisels—say, one with a ½-inch-wide blade and one with a 1-inch-wide blade—will enable you to tackle most jobs. You may want to designate one "junk chisel" for demolition and rough work, and keep other chisels in pristine condition for fine work.
■ For most chiseling jobs, start with the chisel bevel-side down (against the wood). Tap with a hammer to chop down about ⅛ inch, and pry up to remove the waste.
■ Pay attention to the grain of the wood; prying up may cause you to splinter out more than you want. Often it's better to chisel both sides, and then pry.
■ When fine cutting, such as shaving a joint to fit, keep the flat side of the chisel down (against the board).
■ Most light cuts can be made with hand power alone: Place the butt of the chisel handle in your palm, lock your elbow against your body, and make the cut by shifting your weight; use your whole body to push.

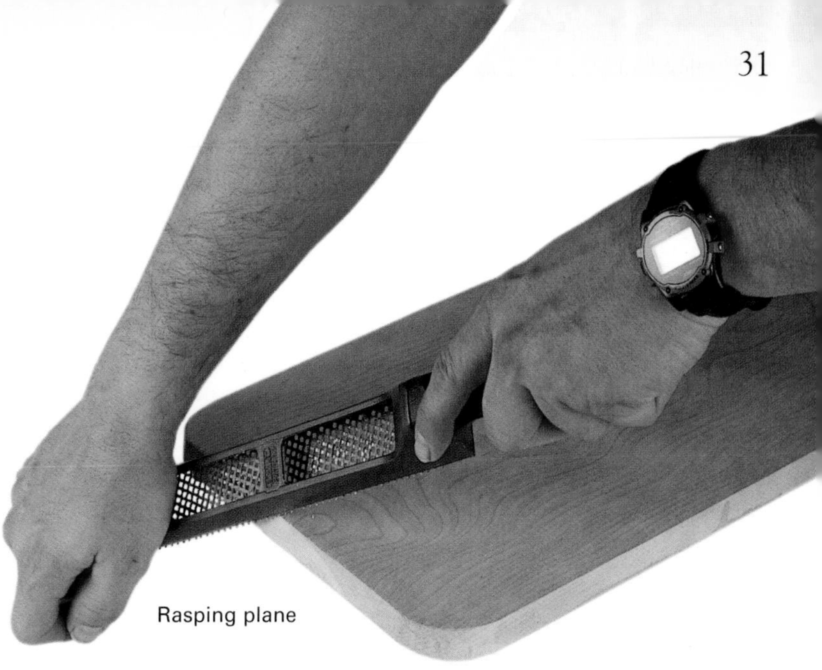
Rasping plane

Use a rasping plane for rounding edges. While it makes a rougher cut than a plane, it works equally well when used with or against the grain.

CHISELING A MORTISE

If you buy a prehung door, chances are you'll probably be spared this chore because the mortises for the strike and hinges are precut. But if you buy a specialty or replacement door, you'll need to do it yourself.

To cut a strike mortise, first cut the lockset hole and drill the hole for the strike mechanism, using the template provided with the lockset.

Push the strike into the hole. Holding it firmly, cut around the strike with a utility knife. Remove the strike; cut again until the knife cut is ⅛ inch deep. (Be careful not to let the grain pull you off track.)

For a hinge mortise, fasten the hinge in place, then cut around it with a utility knife. Once an outline is incised for the strike or hinge mortise, use a sharp ¾-inch-wide chisel to cut away a small amount of wood at a time.

Work with the grain so you don't cut too deeply. Make the bottom of the mortise smooth and even, so the hardware lies flat. If you cut too deeply, shim with cardboard.

DRIVING NAILS

Toenailing

A journeyman carpenter drives a nail with relaxed, fluid motions to avoid "smiles" or "frowns" indented into the board. With practice, your nailing technique can become just as smooth and consistently accurate.

TOOLS FOR NAILING

Select a hammer that fits you and your specific job. The handle should feel comfortable, and the hammerhead should be firmly anchored.

- For most interior projects, choose a **16-ounce** curved-claw hammer with a smooth bell-shaped head face.
- For light demolition work, or if you have a lot of framing to do, **20-ounce** hammers with straight claws will work more efficiently.
- For drywall, be sure to buy a special **drywall hammer.**
- A 5-pound **baby sledge** is essential for heavy demolition.

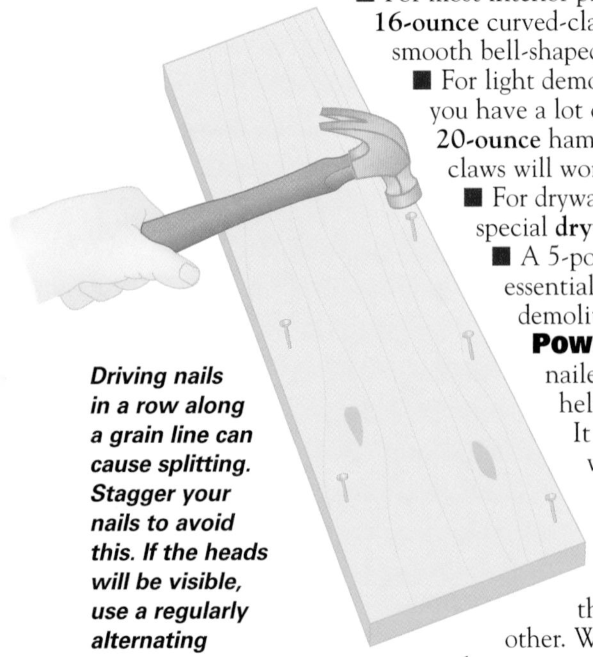

Driving nails in a row along a grain line can cause splitting. Stagger your nails to avoid this. If the heads will be visible, use a regularly alternating pattern.

POWER: A pneumatic nailer can be a great help on a large project. It drives nails quickly without marring the wood, and it allows you to hold a board in one hand while you shoot the nail with the other. With one of these tools, you can trim out a room in a third of the time it would take to drive and set nails, and the result will be neater.

However, pneumatic nailers are expensive and bulky. You will need a compressor, a hose, and a nailer compatible with the type of nail you want to drive. It may make sense to rent rather than buy; be sure the rental agency gives you instructions.

To attach furring strips or sleepers to concrete, brick, or block, a nail gun offers the quickest method. This tool is literally a gun, using 22-caliber cartridges and special nails. Use it with care.

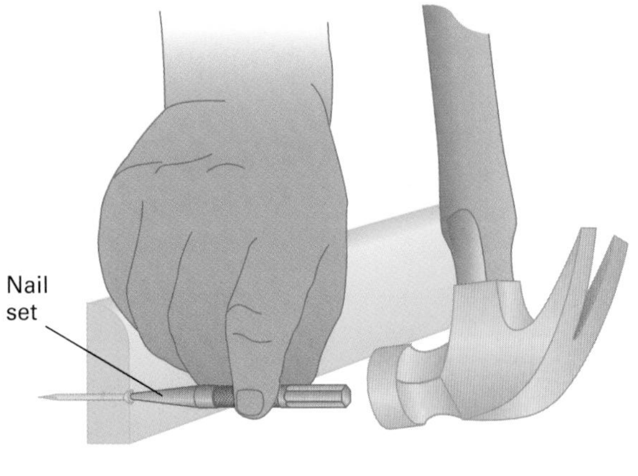

Using a nail set for the last blow prevents marring the surrounding wood with the hammerhead. For finish work, set the nail head below the surface and fill the hole with wood putty.

NAILS

The length of nails is designated by the term *penny*, or *d* (which stands for *denarius*, an ancient coin; it referred to the cost of 100 nails of a given size).

A nail's holding power depends on how much of its surface is in contact with the wood. So, the longer and thicker a nail is, the better it holds. However, if a thick nail causes a board to split even slightly, it will have almost no holding power.

Common nails are the heaviest and thickest. They hold well but are hard to drive and may split the wood. **Sinkers** are thinner than common nails and are the easiest to drive. Cement-coated or vinyl-coated sinkers have a thin coating of adhesive that makes them easier to drive and increases their holding power. They are the best type nail for framing and rough carpentry.

Finishing nails have slender shanks and small, barrel-shaped heads that can be driven below the surface of the wood with a nail set. Use them for trim work, for paneling, and wherever you don't want the heads to show. **Casing** nails are heftier versions of finishing nails and provide more holding power. **Brads** are miniature finishing nails, used for attaching thin, fragile pieces.

RUST: Use a rust-resistant nail where a nail head will be exposed to moisture. Galvanized nails are the most common type. Hot-dipped galvanized (HDG) nails are more reliable than electro-galvanized (EG). But no galvanized nail provides insurance against

The Importance of Pilot Holes

Once split, not only is a board unsightly but the nail that caused the split has lost nearly all holding power. Small splits almost certainly will grow in time. So, save time and long-term disappointment by drilling pilot holes wherever there is the possibility of splitting. This includes anytime you are driving a nail or screw within a nail's length of the end of a board. When attaching hardwood, drill a pilot hole for every nail. Choose a drill bit that is slightly narrower than the nail. Test by drilling a hole and driving a nail; it should be snug enough so it takes some hammering to drive it in. When attaching hardwood, the drill bit should be very close to the same thickness of the fastener; for softwood, it should be thinner.

rust; the coating often flakes off. Aluminum nails will not rust, but they bend easily. Stainless-steel nails are the best choice and are often worth their high price.

SIZE: In most cases, a nail should be about three times longer than the thickness of the board to be fastened. For example, when attaching a 1-by board, which is $\frac{3}{4}$ inch thick, use a nail that is about $2\frac{1}{4}$ inches long. To fasten 2-bys for framing, use 16d nails. If a nail must go through dead space or drywall, increase the nail's length by that distance.

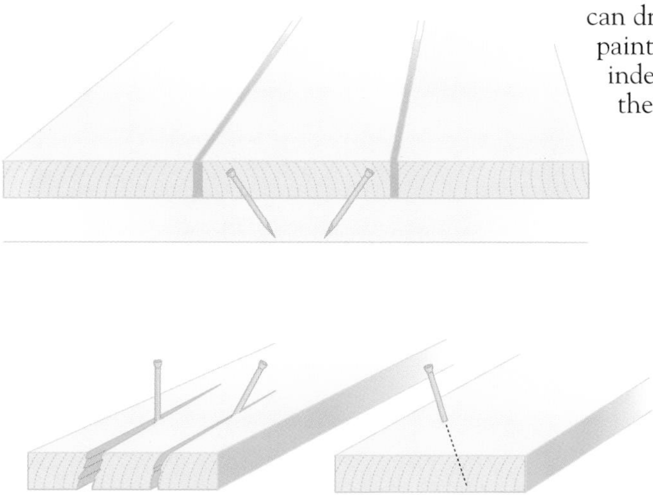

For stronger fastening, "skew" nails by driving them in at opposite angles. Nailing against the grain is less likely to cause splitting.

Specialty fasteners include spiral-shanked **flooring** nails and ring-shanked **wallboard** nails. Use **masonry** or **cut** nails to attach wood to concrete, block, or brick.

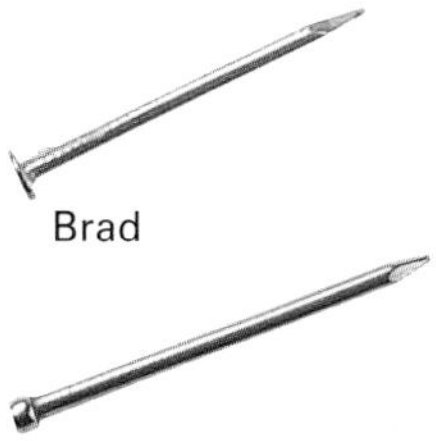

Brad

3d finishing

Driving Nails

Practice on scraps before assembling boards that you really care about; beginners often make mistakes, and a dented board is nearly impossible to fix.

TECHNIQUE: Hold the nail near the head, and push it against the wood so it will not wander. Give the nail a light tap or two so it can stand up by itself. Then move your hand out of the way and drive the nail home.

Don't grip the hammer handle tightly. Use a smooth stroke with a snap at the end. Swing from your shoulder, not your elbow, and allow your wrist to flex a bit, providing the final snap. Keep your eyes focused on the head of the nail at all times.

NAIL SET: To avoid denting the wood, don't try to drive it all the way flush, using the hammer alone. Once it is nearly driven home, use a nail set for the last blow. To save time, you can drive a number of nails nearly flush, then use the nail set to complete driving them all.

FINISH: For a finished look, always set the nail heads below the surface, fill with wood putty, and sand smooth. This can be tedious but is well worth the effort. Don't fool yourself into thinking that you can drive the nails perfectly flush and then paint over them. The nail heads will leave indentations or bumps, and they may rust.

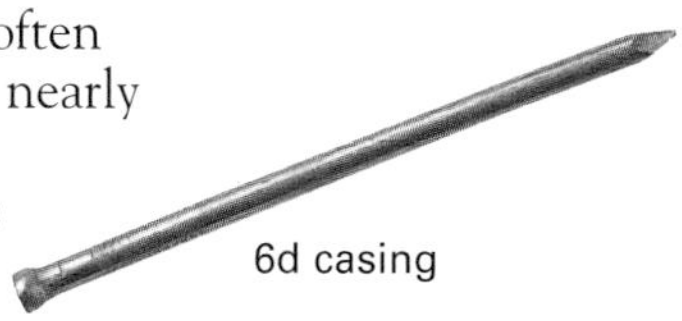

6d casing

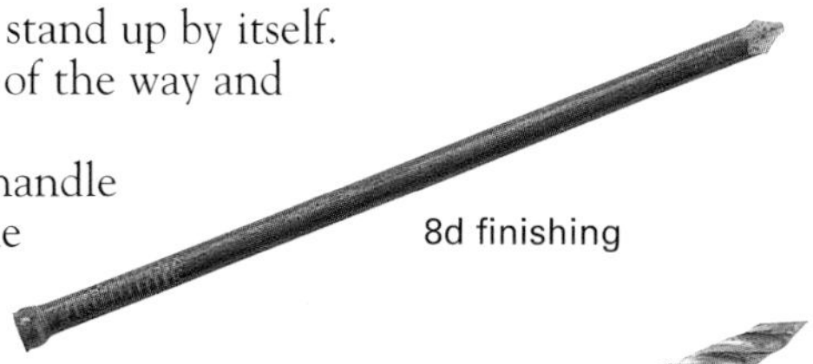

8d finishing

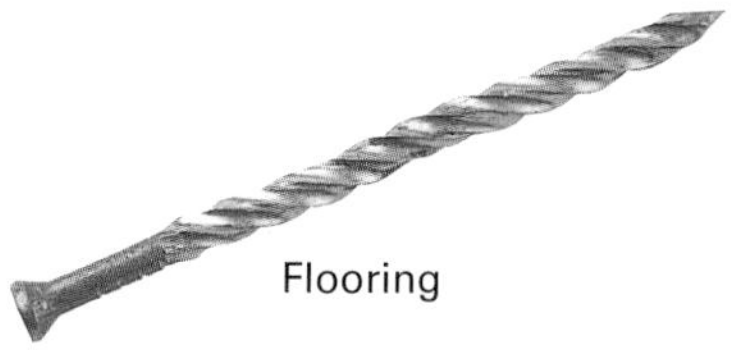

Flooring

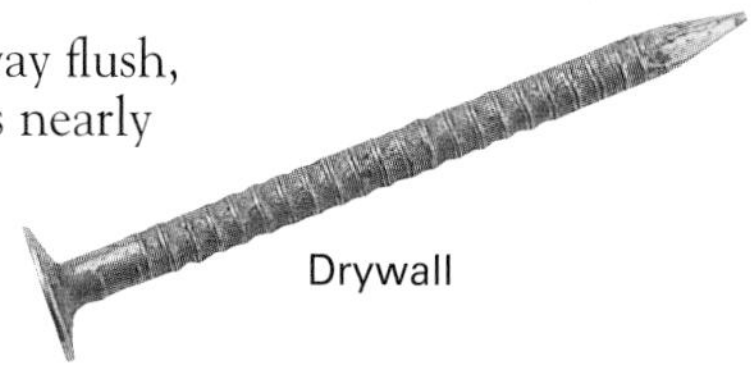

Drywall

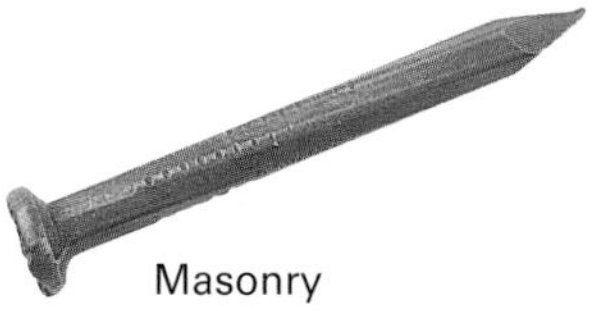

Masonry

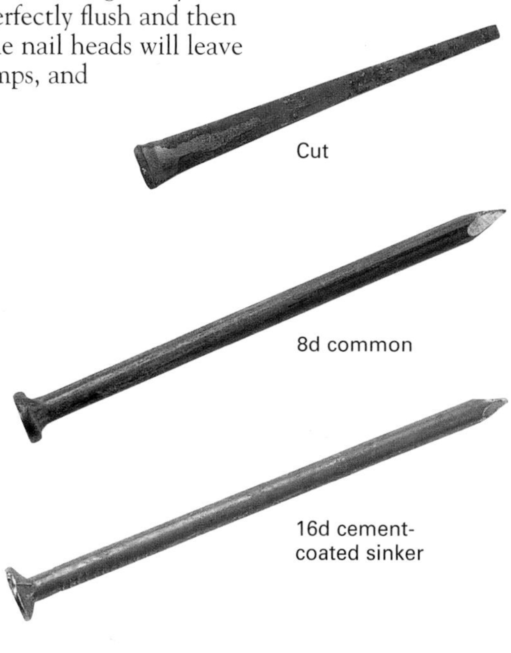

Cut

8d common

16d cement-coated sinker

DRILLING AND DRIVING SCREWS

Clearly, screws fasten more firmly than nails. They also are easy to remove without damaging the surrounding area; nails aren't. Using screws was once more costly and time-consuming than nailing, but many screws are inexpensive these days. And with the right tools, you can drive them quickly.

DRILLS AND BITS

A high-quality drill equipped with sharp bits will help many carpentry jobs go smoothly.

PERFORMANCE OPTIONS: Choose a drill that is variable-speed and reversible. It should have a 3/8-inch chuck, pull at least 3.5 amps, and rev up to at least 2,500 rpm. If you need to run the drill constantly for hours at a time, get a contractor-grade model.

For heavy-duty jobs (such as mixing mortar or drilling holes for electrical work), use a ½-inch drill. It runs slower but is more powerful.

CORDLESS: A good cordless drill will reward your investment. You will find yourself using it often, and you'll love how it saves you the hassle of dealing with cords. Make sure it is powerful enough, however. A 12-volt model will handle most jobs; drills with lower voltage may fail to completely drive screws.

A cordless drill will run slower than a corded drill, but that usually is not a problem.

BIT STYLES

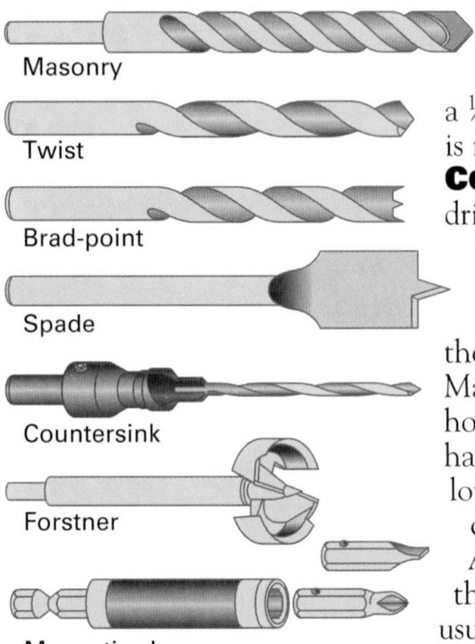

A QUICK FIT

One of the quickest ways to upgrade your carpentry armament is to buy a magnetic sleeve and several sizes and types of bits to fit in it. Slip this tool in your variable-speed, reversible drill and you can drive screws as quickly as you can pound nails. Because it's magnetic, you can fit the screw head on and shoot with one hand.

Most all-purpose screws require a #2 Phillips bit, so buy several of those. You will need a #1 Phillips bit for trim-head screws. Buy #1 and #2 slot ("regular") bits as well, and perhaps square-head bits of various sizes. (Square heads are the least likely to strip out when being fastened.) These screws are cheap, so keep plenty on hand.

If your drill has a keyless chuck, you will be able to drill pilot holes and then drive screws very quickly.

CHUCK KEY: If you need a chuck key to change bits, attach it to the drill or cord so you can reach it easily and it won't get lost. Keyless chucks make quick work of changing bits. Some people find it difficult to tighten the chuck, however, so their drill bits often come loose as they work. Newer drills with keyless chucks use special drill bits with hex heads that can be tightened without much effort.

If you need to make a lot of holes in concrete, buy or rent a hammer drill, which pounds as it drills.

BITS: Not having the bit you need can set back the work day, so assemble a good basic collection. Start with a set of high-speed twist bits, from 1/16-inch to 1/4-inch. Buy extras of the smallest sizes because they are easily broken and lost. (Copper-colored "titanium" bits last longer, especially if you will be drilling through metal, but are more brittle.) Brad-point bits make cleaner holes than standard twist bits.

To make larger holes, spade bits are the least expensive option, but they become dull quickly and usually make rough holes. If you are making holes that will be visible, a Forstner bit is worth the price. Unlike a spade bit, a Forstner bit can make angled or overlapping holes.

For holes larger than 1½ inches in diameter, a hole saw is best. This has a starter bit that protrudes beyond the hole cutter, allowing you to start the hole easily (*see page 27*).

To drill through concrete, masonry, or stucco, use a carbide-tipped masonry bit.

BORING HOLES

To keep the drill bit from wandering when you start drilling, first push the bit into the surface. If the surface is hard, first tap a small hole with an awl or a nail set.

Start the drill and press gently. Do not change direction once you have begun drilling or you can easily break the bit. If the drill is straining, pull it out to remove trapped sawdust. You may need to clean particles from the bit. If the bit jams, put the drill in reverse and pull out gently, without twisting.

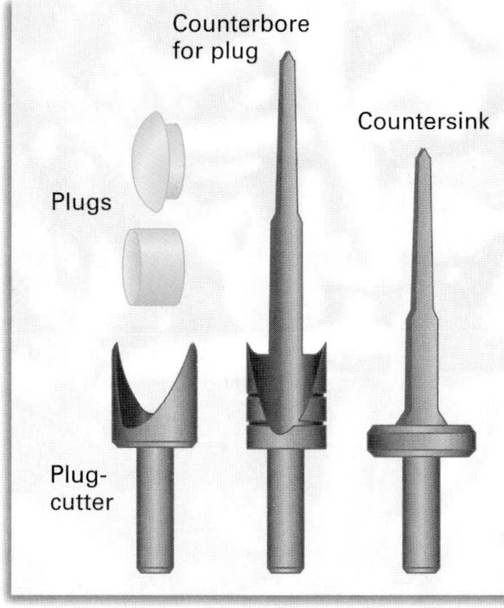

COUNTERSINKING SCREWS

Often the most attractive option is to let the screw heads show. Use a countersink bit and drive a flat-head screw exactly flush with the face of the board. Or, let the head stick out a bit: Install a round-head screw or a flat-head screw with a trim washer.

If you want to hide the screw head, you have two basic options. The simplest is to drive trim-head screws slightly below the surface of the wood, fill each hole with wood putty, and then sand lightly. The correct color of putty can blend well with its surroundings.

For a more elegant appearance, counterbore and plug. Use a combination bit with counterbore (not countersink) for the pilot hole, and drive the screw below the face of the board. Use a plug-cutter bit to cut a series of plugs out of a like-colored scrap piece of wood. Drip a little glue in the hole, then tap the plug in. Sand the plug smooth.

ANGLES: You'll often need to drill a hole at a near-perfect, 90-degree angle to the surface. For instance, if a pilot hole for a hinge screw is not straight, the screw head will not sit flush and the hinge will not close properly. It takes practice to eye-ball a perpendicular hole; to be accurate, purchase a drill guide.
DEPTH: To stop drilling at a certain depth (for instance, so you will not poke through the other side of the board), make a simple depth guide by wrapping a piece of electrical tape around the drill bit. When drilling with a spade bit or a hole saw, avoid making splinters when you poke through the other side. Drill until you are just starting to poke through, then drill from the other side.
METAL: If you are cutting through metal, have a small container of oil on hand. Dip the bit frequently so it is oiled all the time you are drilling. Don't press hard, and don't allow the bit to overheat; stop as soon as you see or smell smoke. Drill a small hole first, then switch to the larger bit and drill again.
MASONRY: Drill into concrete or brick with a masonry bit. If you have many holes to drill, rent or buy a hammer drill. Don't allow the bit to overheat. A spray of window cleaner will keep the bit cool and bring debris out of the hole. Have an extra bit or two on hand because they easily burn out.

DRIVING SCREWS

If driving a screw is a struggle, you may be in danger of splitting the wood. When in doubt, drill a pilot hole first.
BY HAND: Choose a screwdriver with a head that fits snugly into the screw head; if it fits loosely, it could easily strip the head. Hold the screwdriver handle with one hand. With the other hand, hold both the screw head and the tip of the screwdriver so they clasp together. Insert the screw tip into the pilot hole, or push it into the wood so it sticks. Remove your fingers from the screw before driving the screw. If the screw is not sinking into the wood, apply more pressure.

If the screw is difficult to drive, unscrew it and drill a larger pilot hole. Or, rub the threads with soap or a candle to make them slide more smoothly.
POWER DRIVING: Place the screw head on the bit and hold it in place as you guide the screw tip into the hole. Push firmly as you start the drill, increasing speed once the screw begins sinking into the wood. Pushing too gently can cause the drill bit to come loose, which can strip the bit and the screw head.

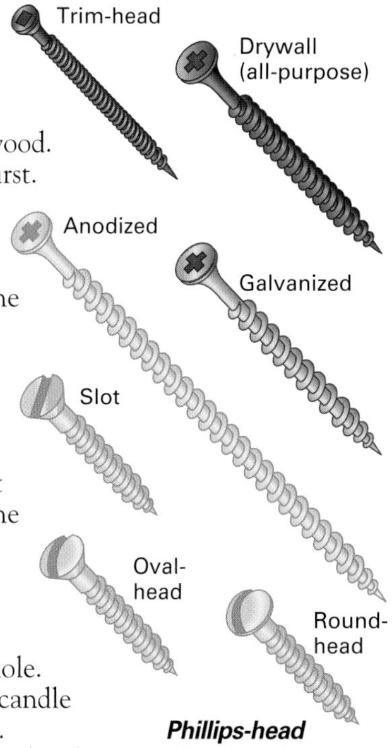

Phillips-head (+-pattern) screws work best for power driving; slotted screws have a cleaner look. Fasten to concrete with one of the devices below.

MASONRY FASTENERS

Expansion shield

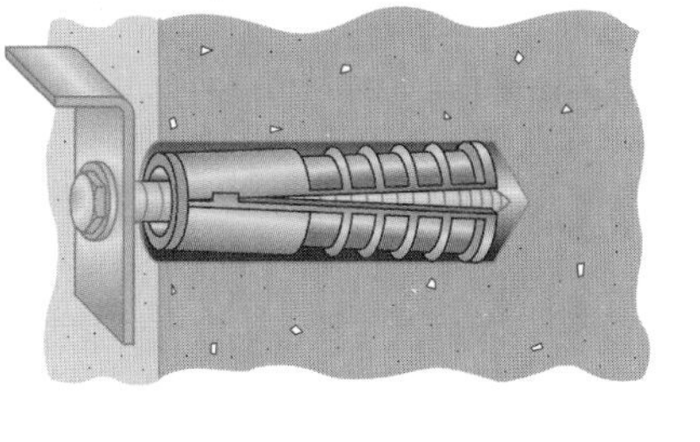

Anchor bolt

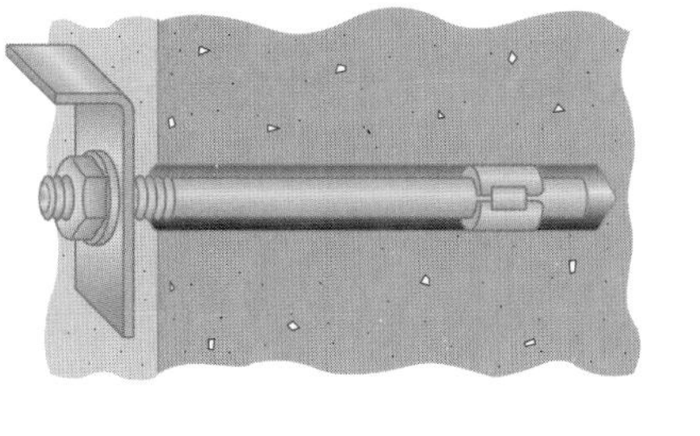

Hex-sleeve anchor

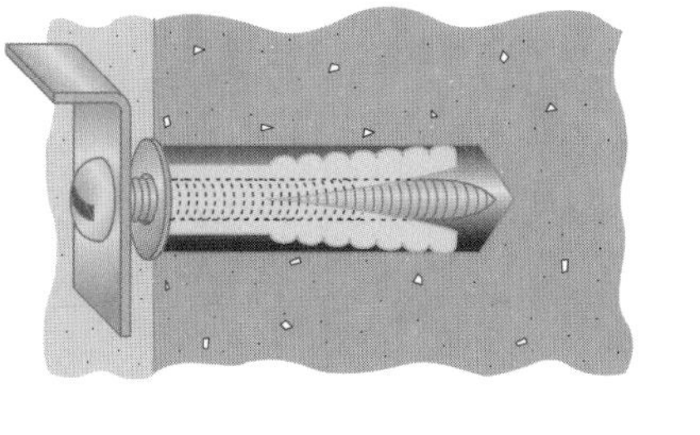

QUICK JOINTS

When speed is more important than appearance, use one of the joints shown here. A fine woodworker may cringe to look at them, but these quick joints are strong and they're easy to make. You'll find them especially useful for utilitarian projects, such as building garage shelves, mending a wooden screen door, or reinforcing a garden gate.

Plates and angle brackets make quick work of refastening pieces that have come apart, such as the bottom of a window sash. For a more permanent and attractive repair, use dowels or biscuits (see pages 38–39).

HARDWARE OPTIONS: Reinforce butt joints with metal mending plates and angle brackets. These fasteners can sometimes temporarily hold pieces together while you drill holes for dowels (*see page* 38).

Begin by dry-fitting the pieces, placing them on a flat surface. Make sure your worktable or floor is even and free of debris.

Because these fasteners will be attached near the ends of boards, drill pilot holes before driving any screws. Wrap tape around the drill bit as a depth guide, if you need to prevent drilling all the way through. Also, make sure the screw is short enough so it will not poke through.

Set the plate or brace in place, and tightly attach one of the screws so the metal piece will stay in position. Then drill pilot holes and drive the other screws. You can center your pilot holes perfectly, or err on the side of pulling the boards a bit tighter.

Plywood can also be used for reinforcement because it will not crack. Cover as much of the area as possible with the plywood, then drill pilot holes and drive a grid of screws. Again, be sure your pieces are lying perfectly flat while you work.

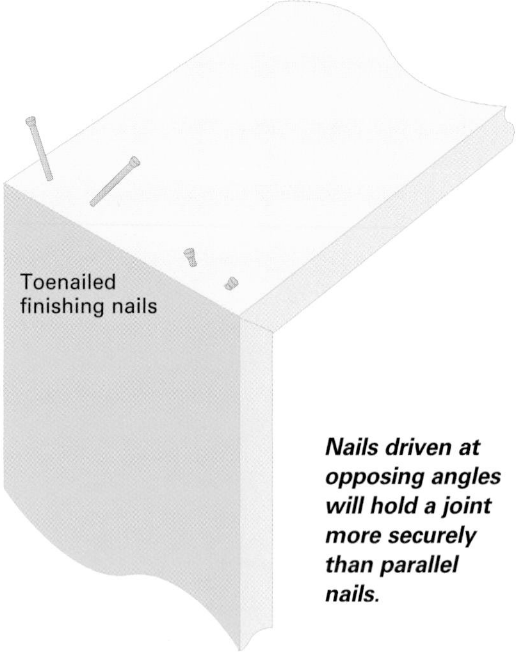

Nails driven at opposing angles will hold a joint more securely than parallel nails.

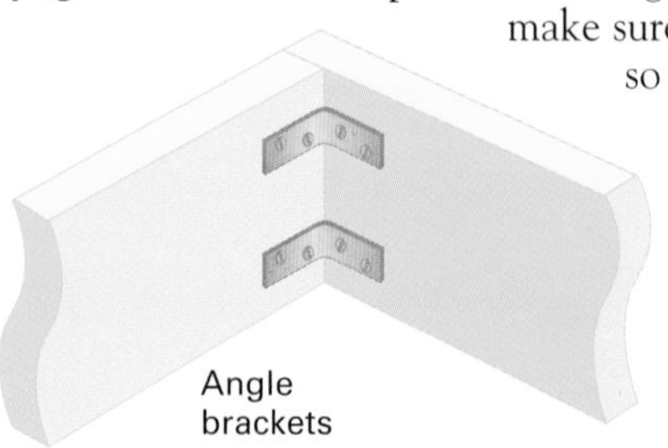

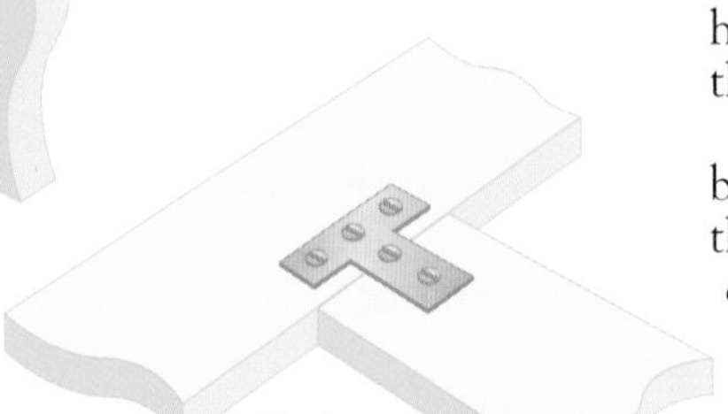
T-plate

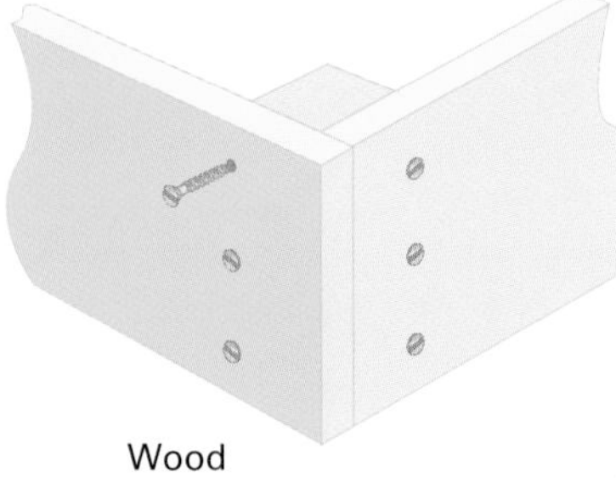
Wood block

Angle brackets

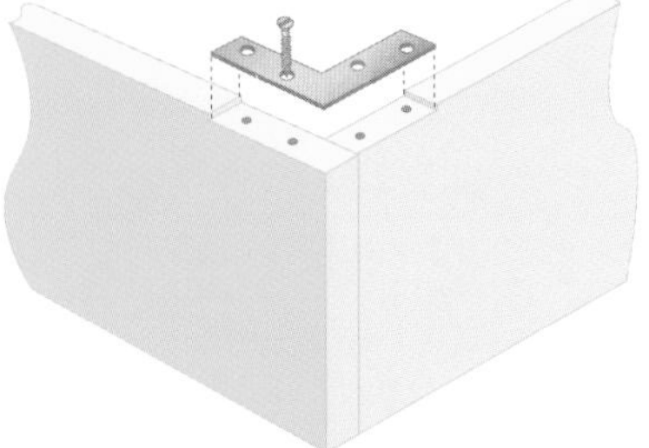
Flat corner iron

REINFORCING A MITER JOINT: Miter cut the two pieces to the same bevel. (Two 45-degree cuts join to make a 90-degree angle; two 22½-degree cuts make a 45-degree angle.) Dry fit the pieces, using a square to see that the angle is correct, and closely examine the joint for any gaps. Sometimes you can fix a bad joint by sanding one or both cuts, but often the best solution is to start over again.

Wood glue will help hold the joint together, but only if the pieces don't keep getting shifted around. So, apply it at the last possible moment.

Hold the pieces together on a flat surface. A miter clamp (*see page* 40) makes it easy to hold the pieces while you work. Drill pilot holes at angles so they are skewed, and drive small finishing nails. Set the nails carefully—it is easy to crack the wood this close to the end of a board. Use trim-head screws for a more secure fit.

JOINERY

You may think that tight, long-lasting, and attractive joints can be made only by a professional carpenter or in a factory. But with patience and some basic tools, you can make joints of near-furniture quality.

Woodworking is a lot more pleasing if you set up your work area carefully. You will need a flat, even surface—preferably a table, because working on the floor can get tiring—that is large enough for your project. Buy wood that is straight and free of cups and cracks. Stack it neatly so it doesn't warp. Make sure your power tools are adjusted so they cut perfectly.

DADOES, LAP JOINTS, AND RABBETS

Making woodworking joints usually involves cutting one or both pieces partway through so they fit together snugly. The simplest joints—lap joints, dadoes, and rabbets—call for a groove or notch cut in one or both of the boards.

A *dado* is a partial cut across the grain of a board, somewhere in the middle of the board. The dado joint is made when the butt end of another board is inserted into the dado cut. This provides excellent support for the lateral board, and is often used for shelving. A *rabbet joint* is like a dado, but it is made at the end of the notched board instead of in the middle.

Lap joints use wider notches, producing a surface with no protrusions. For a *half-lap* joint, notch both pieces; for a *full-lap*, notch only one piece. Do not notch more than one-third of the thickness of the board for a full-lap or it will be weakened.

MARKING: Lap and dado joints require precise notches or grooves so the adjoining board will fit snugly. (A rabbet need not be as precise.) Whenever possible, use the board to be joined as a template for marking. Use a sharp pencil or a knife to draw the lines.

For dadoes, first mark square lines indicating the bottom of each cut. Mark the top with a scrap of the same-sized lumber as a template, or measure precisely. For lap joints, hold the pieces in position and mark. Mark the depth of the cut as well.

CUTTING BY HAND: You can make a joint without power tools if you're careful; the tricky part will be cutting straight down. Don't attempt this with a standard handsaw, which flexes. Use a straight, rigid backsaw.

Firmly clamp a board to the side of the backsaw to act as a depth guide. It must be parallel to the blade and placed above the teeth at the desired depth of the cut. Test with a scrap piece to make sure it cuts to the right depth. Practice cutting straight down, perpendicular to the face of the board.

Saw at the cut line(s) first, taking care not to cut outside the area. It may help to use a speed square to guide the blade at first. Then make a series of cuts, ⅛ inch or so apart, then chisel out the interior.

CUTTING WITH POWER TOOLS: You can make accurate dado cuts with a circular

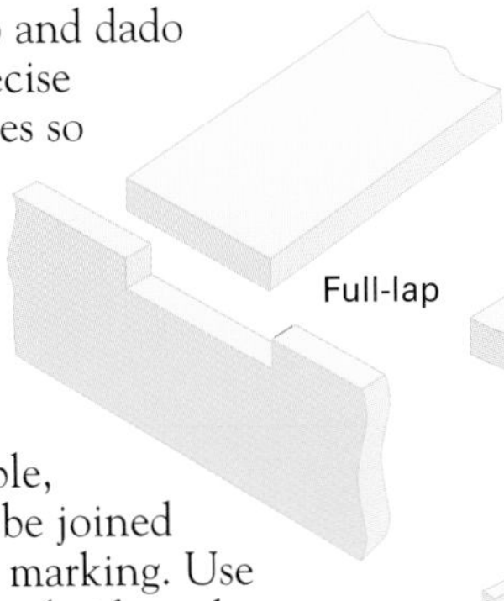

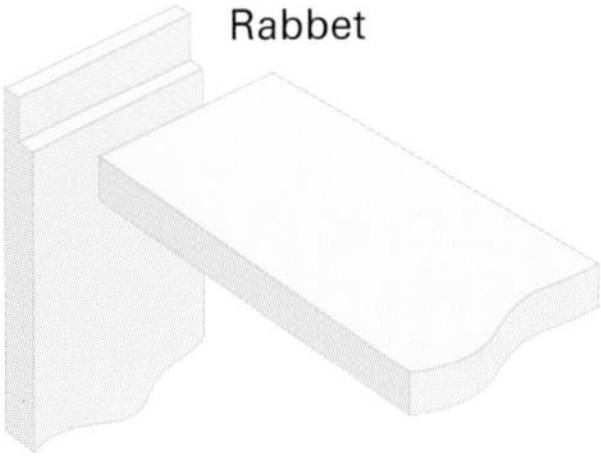

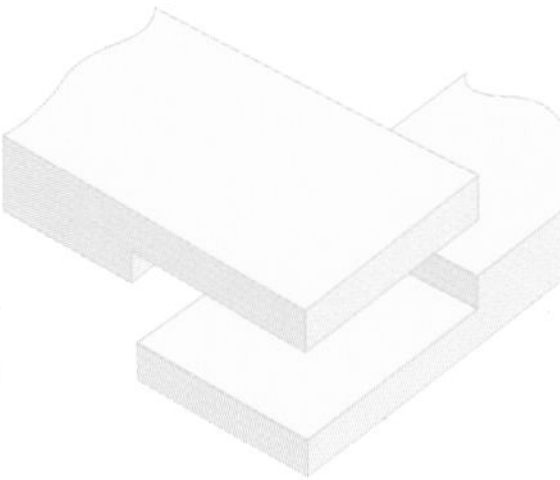

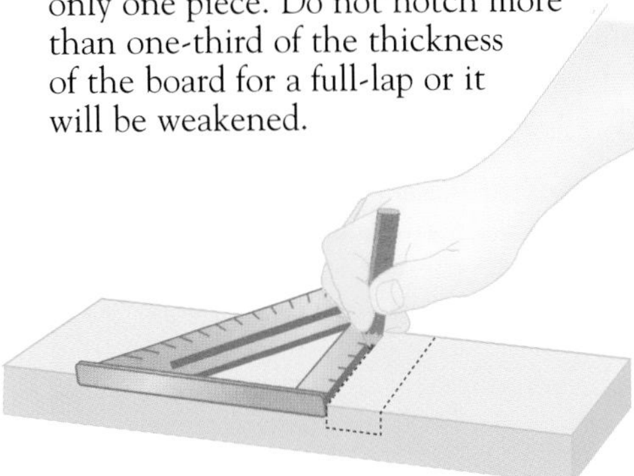

Make precise marks for the width and depth of the dado cut.

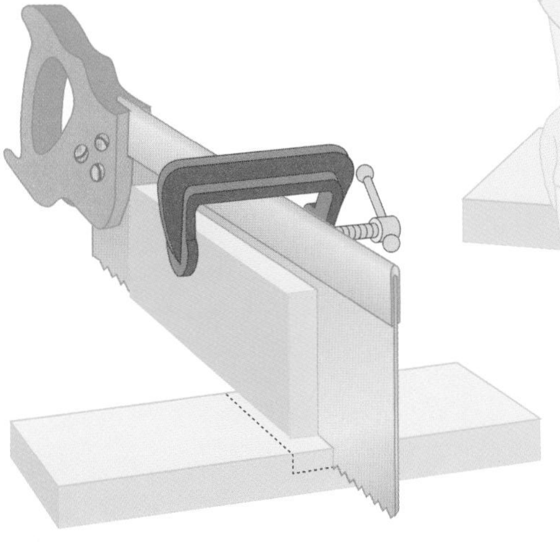

Clamp a simple depth gauge to a backsaw or handsaw to saw the cut lines and to make a series of cuts in the middle. You can also use a circular saw, table saw, or radial arm saw.

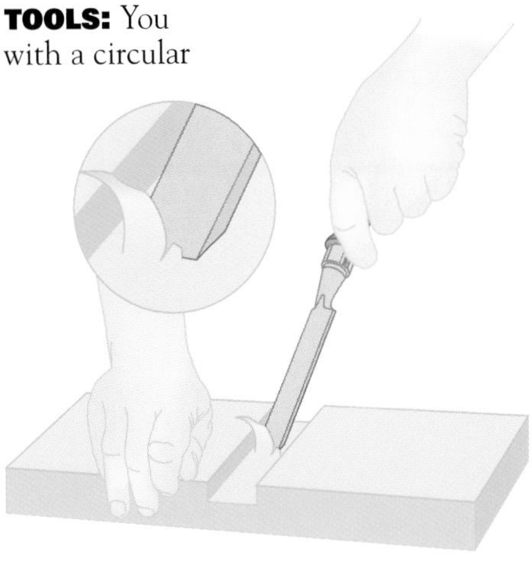

Hold the chisel bevel-side up to remove most of the waste. Then turn it over to smooth the bottom (inset).

JOINERY
continued

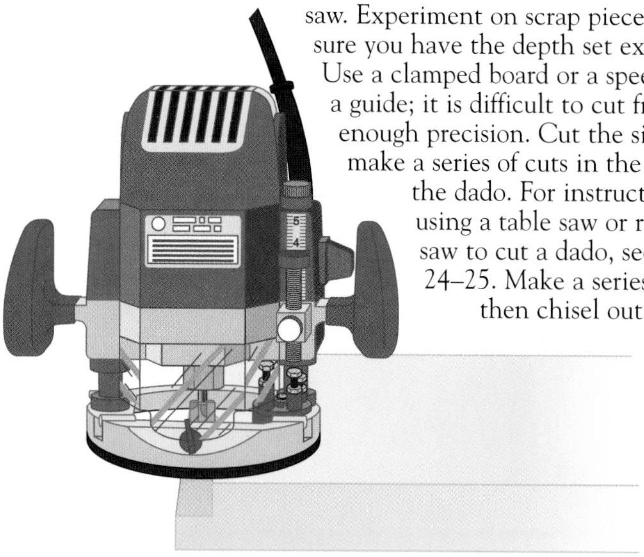

saw. Experiment on scrap pieces to make sure you have the depth set exactly right. Use a clamped board or a speed square as a guide; it is difficult to cut freehand with enough precision. Cut the sides, then make a series of cuts in the interior of the dado. For instructions on using a table saw or radial arm saw to cut a dado, see pages 24–25. Make a series of cuts and then chisel out the middle, or use a dado assembly to cut out the whole area.

A router is a great tool for making partial cuts. It is difficult to control when working freehand, so always use a guide, or set the router on a router table.

Make accurate router cuts with an edge guide like the one shown, or use a clamped straightedge. You do not need a guide with a rabbet bit; just hold it against the end of the board.

CHISELING OUT THE WASTE: With the bevel facing up, position the blade on the edge of the board to make an accurate cut across the width of the dado, and tap gently with a hammer. You will not need to be so careful in the middle because it will not show. Clean away most of the waste, then turn the chisel bevel-side down to smooth the bottom of the cut. Remove a little more than needed.

ASSEMBLING THE JOINT: Dry-fit the pieces. Once you know that they will fit together well, squirt some woodworking glue on both pieces. For lap joints, just clamp and allow the glue to dry completely. For dado and rabbet joints, you can also drill pilot holes and then drive nails or trim-head screws.

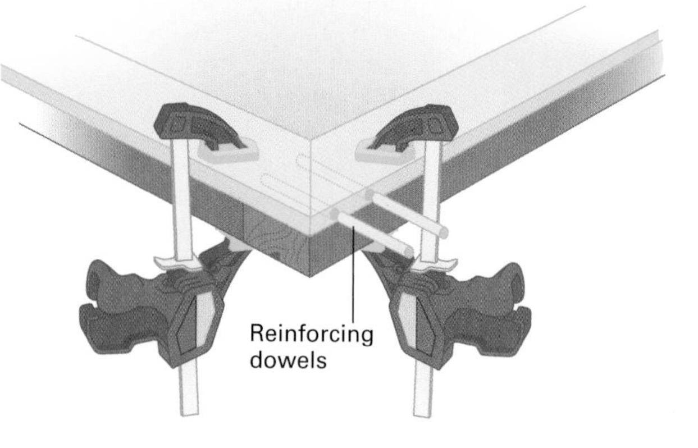

DOWEL JOINERY

This is a way to make very strong joints without expensive tools. There are two basic techniques.

DOWEL REINFORCEMENT: The easiest way to make a dowel joint is to hold the pieces securely, bore holes through them both completely, and drive a dowel through each hole.

Position the two pieces exactly as you want them to be joined; once they're doweled, you will not be able to make adjustments. Either clamp them in place, as shown *below left*, or join them temporarily, using nails, screws, or other fasteners. It's important to prevent them from moving while you drill.

Use lengths of dowel no more than half the thickness of the boards you are joining. Using a drill bit of the same diameter, bore a hole completely through the first piece and well into the second piece. It may take practice before you can drill accurately enough so that you do not poke through the surface of a board. A doweling jig *below* will ensure accuracy. Squirt glue into the hole, tap in the dowels, and cut their ends flush. Sand smooth.

BLIND DOWEL: With this technique, the end of the dowel is not visible. Use fluted dowels to give the glue room.

Use a doweling jig, which ensures straight holes, to drill holes in the first piece. Place a metal dowel center in each of the holes, and mark for the holes in the second piece by accurately positioning the jig and pressing down. Drill these holes, again using the jig. Squirt some glue into all the holes, tap the dowels into the holes of the first piece, and tap the second piece into place. Wipe away any excess glue, and clamp tightly until the glue sets.

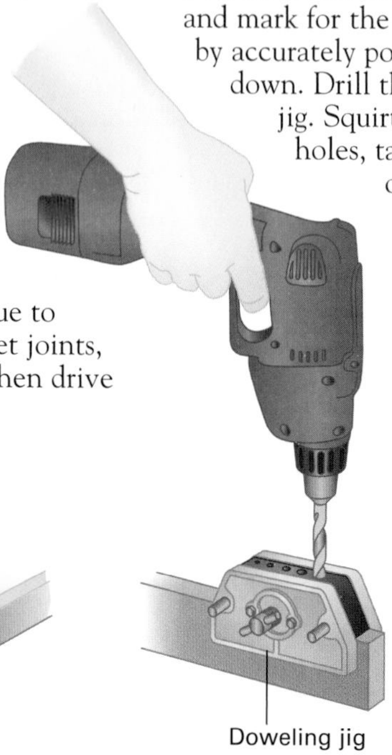

A jig ensures straight, precise dowel positions.

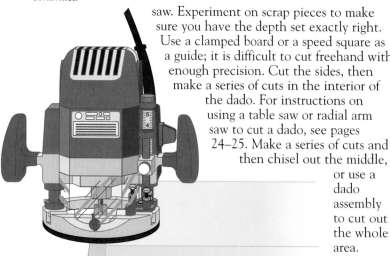

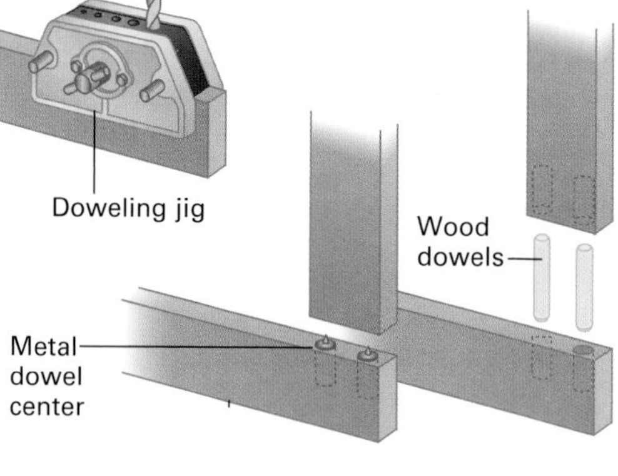

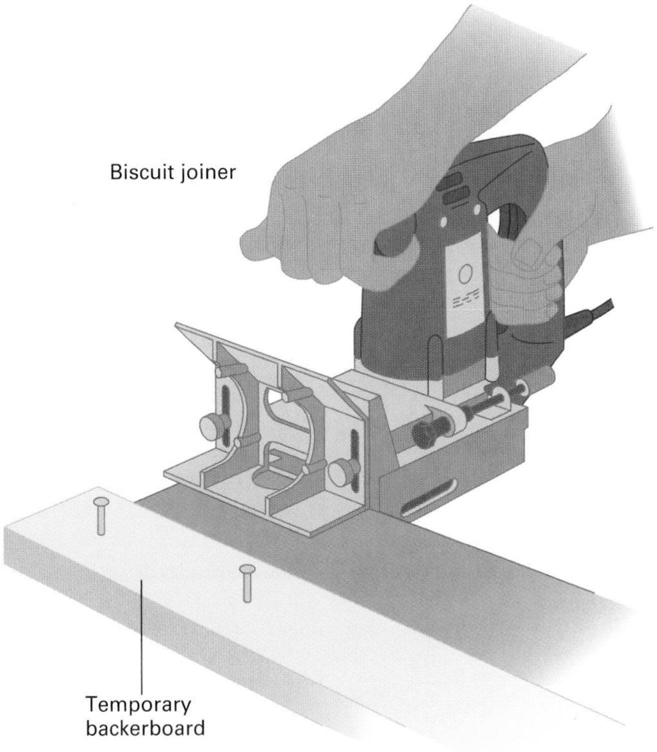

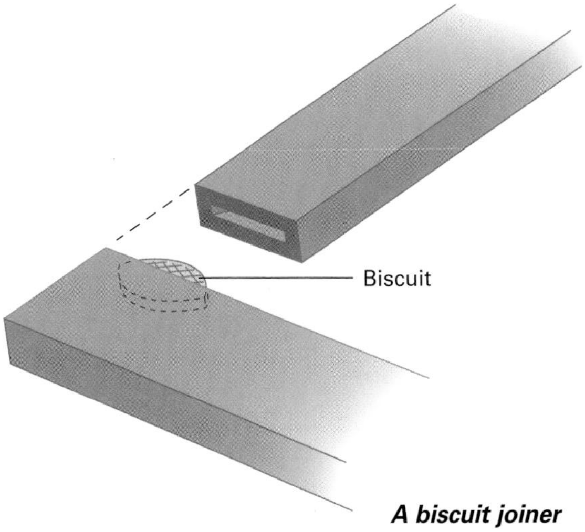

A biscuit joiner makes incisions for the waferlike disks, or biscuits, that fasten low-stress joints.

USING A BISCUIT JOINER

This tool makes it easy to form tight, accurate joints. While this type of joint has some give to it that makes it easier to line up your boards, biscuit joints are not as strong as dado or dowel joints.

Place the boards together, aligned as you want them to be joined. (Biscuit joints work well for corners or for joining boards together side by side, as you might when making a tabletop.) For each biscuit, mark a short line that extends from one board to the other.

Set the joiner to the correct depth so that the biscuit (there are several sizes) will fit easily. Attach a temporary backerboard to your bench to push your boards against as you use the biscuit joiner. Cut an incision at each pencil mark. The tool has a guide line that makes this easy to do, and you do not need to be precise.

Squirt glue into each incision, insert biscuits into the incisions on one board, and clamp the boards together. This can be difficult if you are working with long boards or are using many biscuits for one joint. If so, have a helper hold one end while you push the pieces together in consecutive order.

Wipe away excess glue. Clamp firmly until the glue has set.

MORTISE-AND-TENON AND DOVETAIL JOINTS

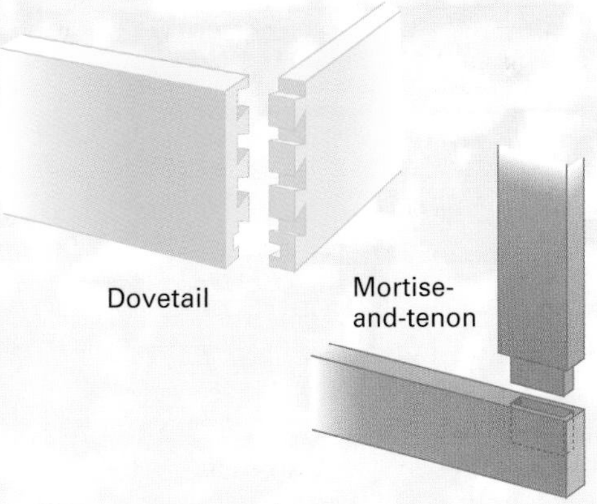

For furniture-making or where appearance is important, you may want to test your skills on these more complicated joints.

A dovetail joint is useful for attaching boards at right angles, when making a drawer, for example. If you have a router and a dovetail jig, it's time-consuming but not very difficult. With careful layout and a sharp backsaw and chisel, it can be done by hand.

A mortise-and-tenon joint requires precise cutting, drilling, and chiseling. It is not much stronger than a blind dowel joint or dowel reinforcement.

GLUING, CLAMPING, AND CAULKING

Sometimes the best way to join wood is without fasteners. Attaching with adhesives is not difficult, but you must have the right tools and materials and a little know-how.

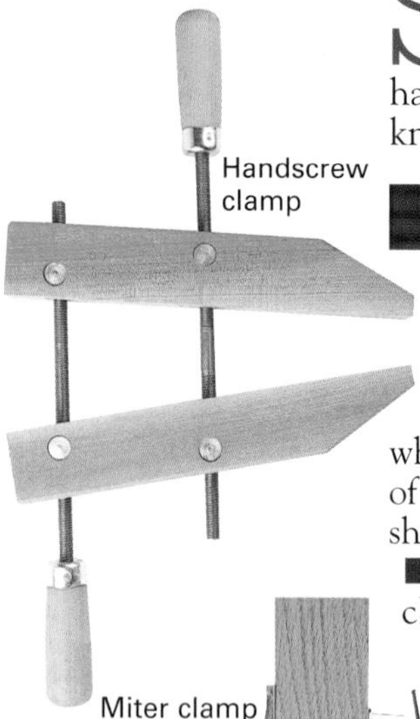

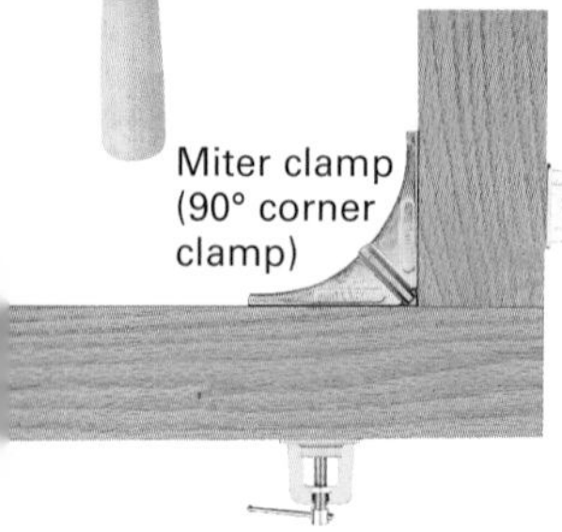

CLAMPS

Standard carpenter's glue is quite strong, if the pieces it joins are held firmly together, without moving, until the glue has completely hardened. Always use clamps when fastening with glue. Having a variety of clamps on hand will help make your wood shop efficient and enjoyable.

■ **SQUEEZE CLAMPS,** like giant paper clips, have spring-loaded jaws. Only the larger ones have enough holding power for glued joints, but they work well for temporarily holding things—such as a straightedge guide for a saw—in place.

■ **C-CLAMPS** are inexpensive and useful for joints that are not wide. Be careful to protect your wood with scrap blocks because they can dig in and cause dents.

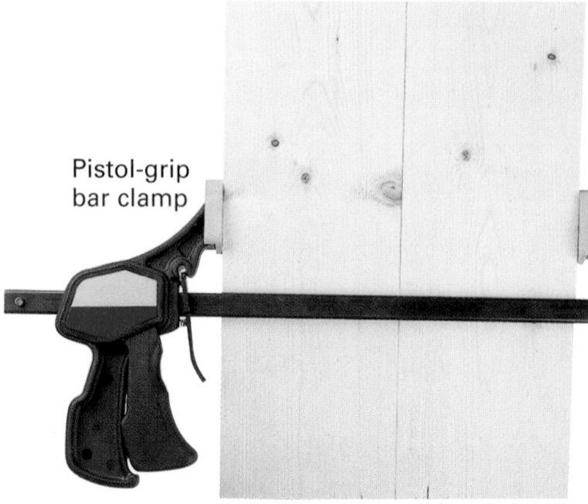

■ **MITER CLAMPS** hold two boards—either miter cut or butt jointed—at a perfect 90-degree angle while you fasten them with nails, screws, or dowels.

■ **BAND CLAMPS** are handy when repairing furniture with several joints that have become separated.

■ **HANDSCREW CLAMPS** (also called Jorgenson clamps) not only join together pieces at odd angles but do so without denting the wood.

■ **PISTOL-GRIP BAR CLAMPS** use trigger action to grab wide boards quickly; you'll find many lengths.

■ **PIPE CLAMPS** work similarly but can't be attached as quickly; they extend as long as the pipe they are slipped onto.

CLAMPING TECHNIQUES

Always set up the job ahead of time, with all supplies at hand. Dry-fit the pieces and adjust your clamps so that you will be able to complete the work quickly after the glue is applied. When you dry-fit, be sure to use enough clamps so the joint will be tight all along its length.

Clamps can dig into a board and damage it, so place pieces of scrap wood or cardboard wherever there is a chance of denting. You should clamp firmly, but there is no need to apply tremendous pressure. Usually a firm squeeze or twist with one hand will provide enough grip without putting you in danger of bowing or cracking the wood.

Once the joint is clamped, wipe away the excess glue and examine the joint closely. Make any necessary adjustments right away, then leave the pieces alone until the glue sets.

ADHESIVES

Many adhesives used in woodworking are stronger than wood. So a well-glued joint under extreme stress may fracture along the grain of the wood rather than along the seam of adhesive.

WOODWORKING GLUE: Yellow-colored wood glue with aliphatic resin is stronger and sets up more quickly than white glue. It remains slightly flexible, so joined pieces can move or expand and contract a little. Fast-drying types can adhere in 10 minutes, but wait a day for maximum bond.

POLYURETHANE GLUE: This extremely strong adhesive resists moisture, making it

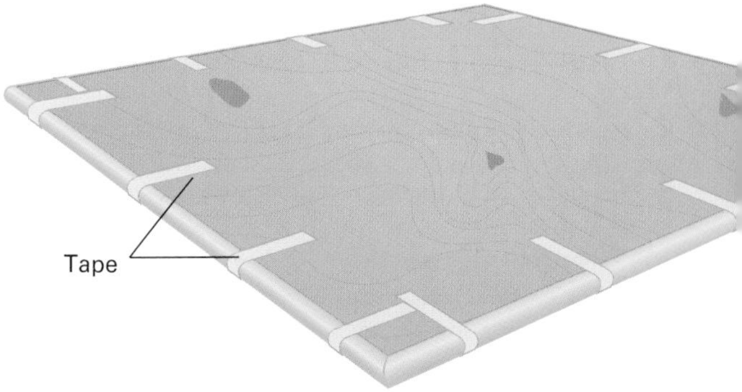

Thin edging like this could be glued and nailed, but that would leave you with nail heads to set, fill, and sand, and the filler would be visible. For a clean appearance, apply glue and tape the pieces in place. Use plenty of glue on a plywood edge; it will soak it up like a towel.

Getting a Clean Bead

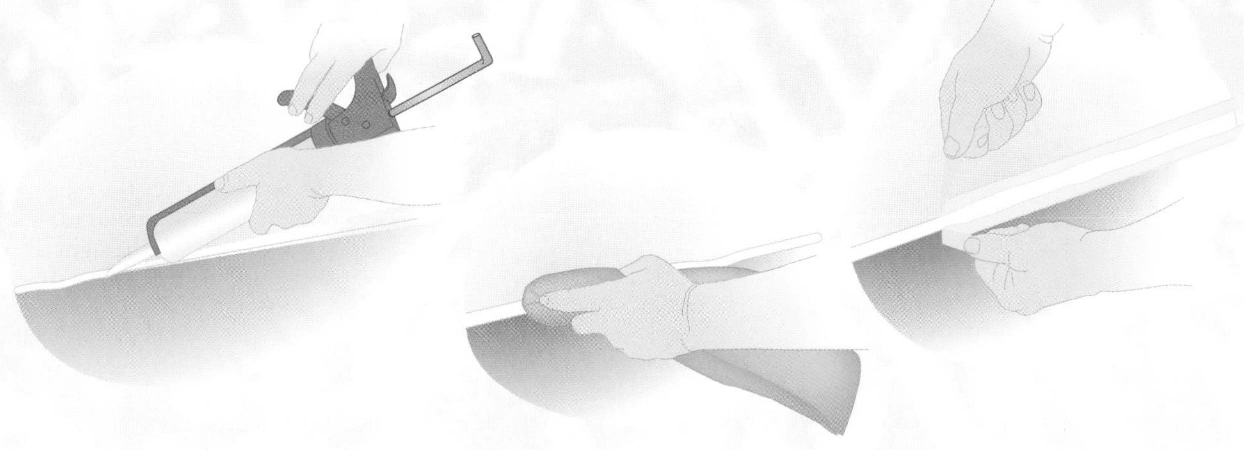

To make a basic caulk bead, cut the tip at an angle; some types require that you must also poke through the tip to rupture seal. Clean the surface and get in a comfortable position. Squeeze the trigger gently and pull the tube toward you in a smooth motion. Practice your technique.

If the bead is not smooth enough, wipe with a rag dampened with water or mineral spirits, depending on the caulk. Compress the rag into a smooth ball, and wipe the bead smooth. When excess caulk builds up, clean the rag or fold it a different way and form a new ball.

Here's the deluxe bead: Before caulking, carefully apply masking tape to both surfaces, revealing enough space for your caulk bead. The tape must be straight. Apply the caulk so it overlaps onto both pieces of tape. Pull the tape away at a consistent angle.

ideal for outdoor projects. It requires 24 hours to set up. When it comes into contact with moisture, it will foam up, filling gaps. Polyurethane glue can form a fairly strong bond even if the pieces are not clamped.

Contact cement: This is best for gluing sheets together—for example, applying plastic laminate to particleboard to make a countertop. Cut the laminate larger than needed. Apply the cement to both surfaces, and allow it to dry. Then carefully place the laminate; once in place, it cannot be budged. Use a router or a file followed by a sanding block to trim the edges of the laminate.

Construction adhesive: Apply with a caulking gun, or buy it in a can and apply with a notched trowel. Its thick consistency allows it to adhere to vertical surfaces. Attach the pieces soon after applying the adhesive, or it will "skin" over and no longer stick.

Epoxy resin: This will bond most anything with superior strength and it's very resistant to moisture, but it is expensive and time-consuming to use. Mix the two parts together, and throw away any of the mixture that you do not use.

Cyanoacrylate ("super") glues: Use this to bond small items that are not porous; it is not practical for wood projects. Apply a few drops and hold the pieces together for a couple of minutes. Although it bonds immediately, most products take 24 hours to reach full strength.

Totally Tubular

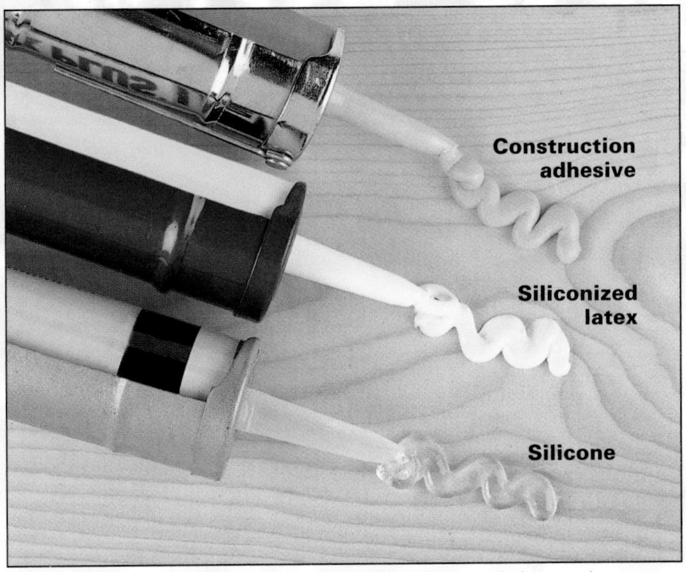

Construction adhesive can easily glue all sorts of things, but you can help it to work even better by using clamps to hold the joint firmly until the bond has set. Siliconized latex caulk is better for most carpentry and wall-repair projects; it is longer lasting and easier to wipe than plain latex caulk. Silicone caulk is more expensive and it forms a rubberlike surface that is very durable. Be sure the surface you apply it to is clean and dry because silicone caulk lacks the sticking power of latex.

DEMOLITION AND REMOVAL OF FASTENERS

Remodeling projects begins with demolition, whether it is taking down cabinets or tearing out walls. Don't just rip into it; with the right tools and techniques, you can minimize mess and destruction and save yourself a lot of work.

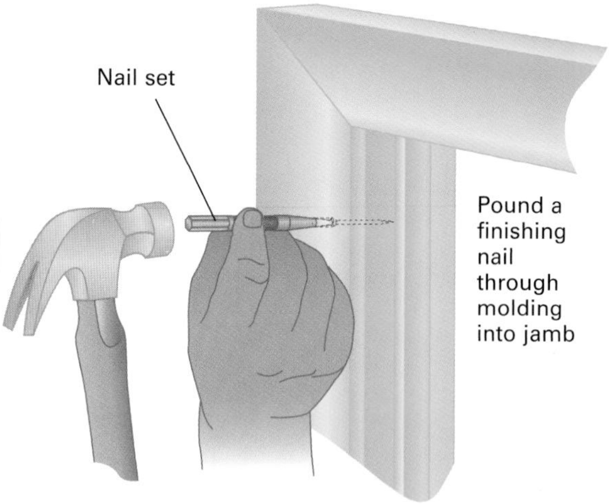

DISASSEMBLING

Often removing a fastener or board neatly is also the quickest and easiest way.

PULLING NAILS: If a nail head is sticking up even a little, shoehorn it up farther by tapping with a flat pry bar and hammer. (A flat bar will make less of an indentation than a crowbar.) If the nail head is sticking up far enough, slip a block of wood under the hammerhead. This prevents dents in the board and acts as a fulcrum to give you better leverage. Sometimes you can pop nails out a bit by tapping or prying out the board they are embedded in, then tapping the board back in place.

PULLING TOOLS AND TACTICS

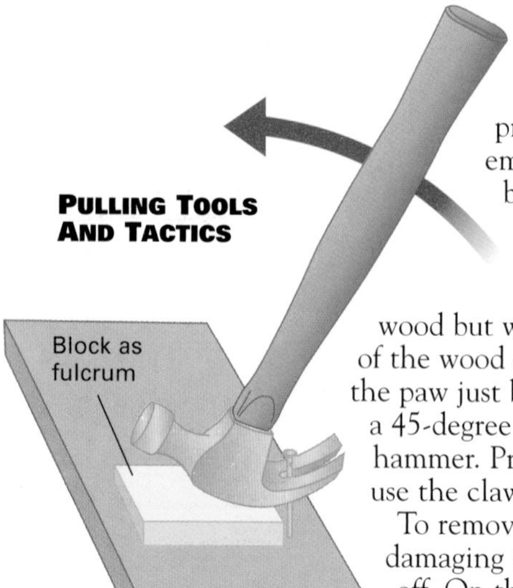

When all else fails, use a cat's-paw; this can remove nails deeply sunk in the wood but will take a big chunk out of the wood as well. Place the tip of the paw just behind the nail head at a 45-degree angle, and hit it with a hammer. Pry with the cat's-paw, then use the claws of a hammer.

To remove finishing nails without damaging the wood, first pry the board off. On the back side of the board, grab the nail with a pair of large channel-lock pliers. Squeeze tight, and pull the nail through by rolling the pliers downward.

Sometimes the best solution is not to remove the nail but to cut it. Use a reciprocating saw with a metal-cutting blade. The thin blade will fit into very small gaps, or make its own way.

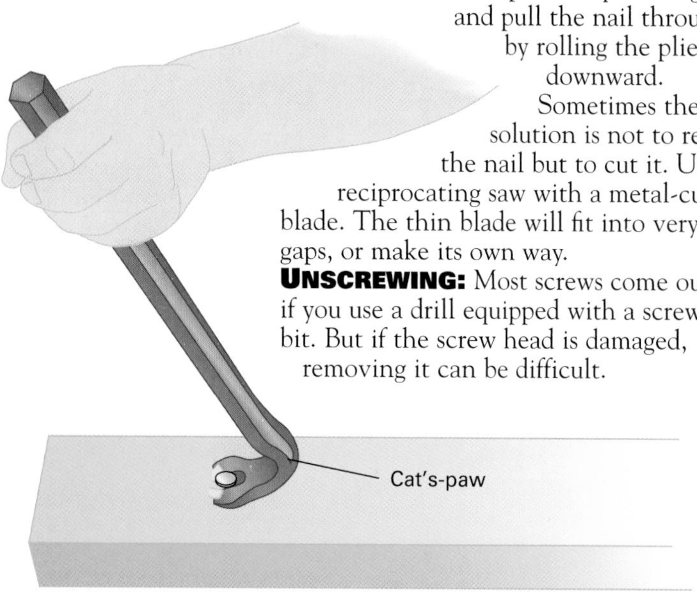

UNSCREWING: Most screws come out easily if you use a drill equipped with a screwdriver bit. But if the screw head is damaged, removing it can be difficult.

Remove old paint from screw heads. Use a screwdriver to chisel paint out of a slot-head screw; chip and scrape with an awl for a Phillips head.

Stripped Phillips-head screws can be very difficult to remove. Try drilling a small hole in the center of the head to allow the screwdriver to sink farther down. For a stripped slot-head screw, use a hacksaw to make the slot deeper. If these techniques fail, purchase a screw extractor from a hardware store or home center.

REMOVING BOARDS: Prying out boards usually causes at least a small dent, so start prying in the most inconspicuous place you can find.

A knife, a chisel, and a flat pry bar are your most useful tools for this job. If the joint between the board and the wall is painted, cut the paint line with a knife; otherwise, the paint will chip unattractively. Tap with a chisel to start prying, then switch to the flat pry bar. It usually works best to pry sideways.

If you're concerned that the board will split when you pry it, consider poking the finishing nails all the way through first. This works especially well on window and door casings where the molding is relatively thin. Pound the nail through with a thin-shanked nail set, and the board will come free.

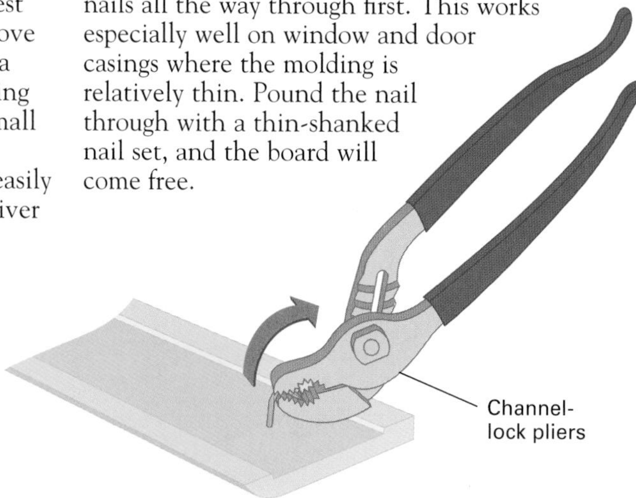

CUTTING INTO WALLS

Before starting major demolition, protect your home from debris and dust:

- Place fans in windows where the demolition will occur to blow dust outside.
- Seal doors with sheets of plastic and tape.
- Cover floors with cardboard or rosin paper; tape it securely and avoid any wrinkles that will rip with heavy foot traffic.
- Rent a trash bin if you will have a lot of garbage to haul.

Do not remove a load-bearing wall without providing alternative support for your house (*see page 74*). Remove all of the moldings before demolishing a wall.

WALLBOARD WALLS: Wallboard is easily broken—just bang it with a hammer. To remove it neatly, first mark and cut with a reciprocating saw. (You can use a circular saw, but it will produce much more dust.) Pry the edges with a flat pry bar, then use a hammer or your hands to pull off large pieces.

PLASTER WALLS: These are more difficult.

- Use a knife to cut a line around the area you want to remove.
- Although it will take time and effort, cut all the way through the plaster; this will protect the surrounding plaster from cracking.
- Use a hammer with medium force to break up the plaster to be removed. Pry off large chunks whenever possible.
- If there is metal lath (a sort of thick wire mesh), cut it with tin snips, and roll it up as you pry it away.
- Peek through the wood lath to check for electrical or plumbing lines.
- Pry the lath from the studs with a hammer or crowbar.

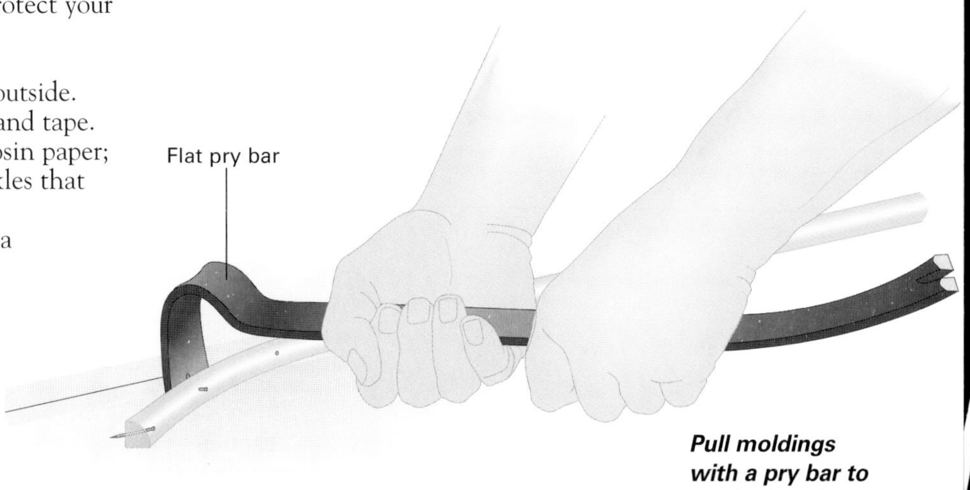

Pull moldings with a pry bar to reach the edges of drywall panels.

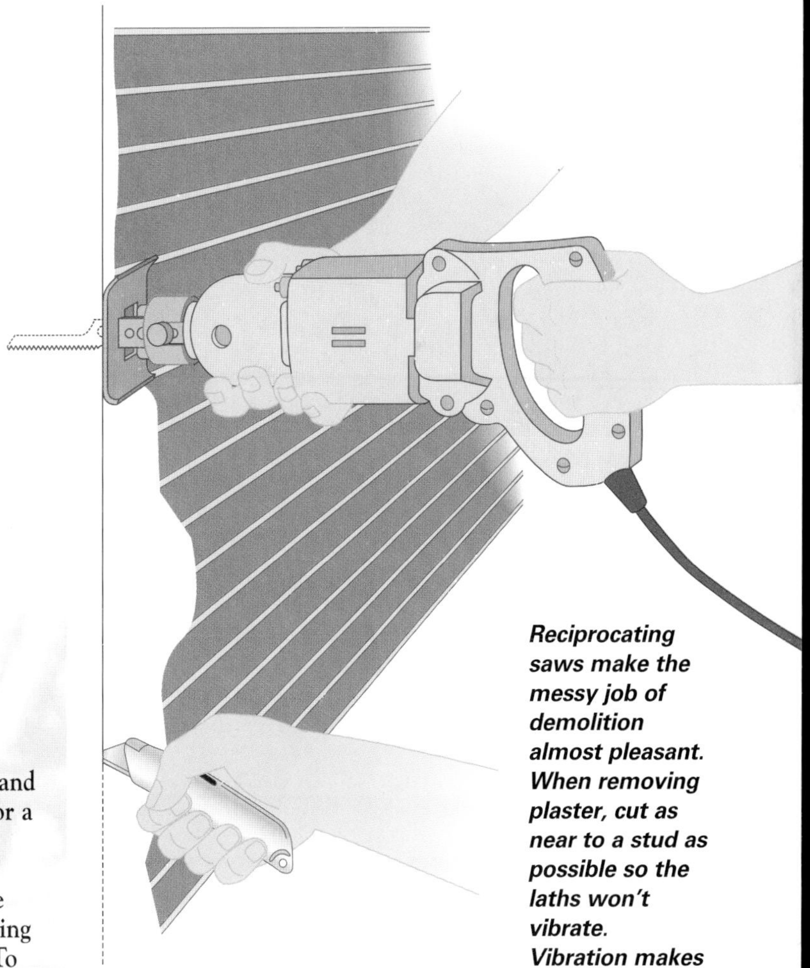

Reciprocating saws make the messy job of demolition almost pleasant. When removing plaster, cut as near to a stud as possible so the laths won't vibrate. Vibration makes cutting difficult and can crack the surrounding wall.

AVOIDING PLUMBING AND ELECTRICAL LINES

Behind the surface of your wall may lurk potential problems. Pipes and cables (especially copper pipes and nonmetallic cable) will not withstand a power saw or a well-swung hammer.

If a wall is extra thick and there are plumbing fixtures nearby, it is probably a plumbing wall; large drain pipes and supply pipes run through it. Removing such a wall will require extensive plumbing work. To avoid disaster, make your initial cuts shallow—just a half inch or so deeper than the thickness of the drywall or the lath and plaster. Probe a bit before proceeding with the demolition.

Houses settle, leading door frames astray, so planing a door ranks among the most common carpentry repairs.

Door Stop

The door may have trouble latching because it is warped, so it does not meet the door stop all along its length. If the door is obviously warped, replace it. For a minor problem, pry out the door stop, close the door, and reinstall the stop so it fits snugly with the door at all points. After you do this, the face of the door may not be flush with the edge of the jamb, but that is usually not very noticeable.

Sometimes a door can bind because it rubs against the door stop on the hinge side of the jamb. Try tapping the stop over slightly using a hammer and a block of wood. If such subtleties fail, then remove and reposition the stop.

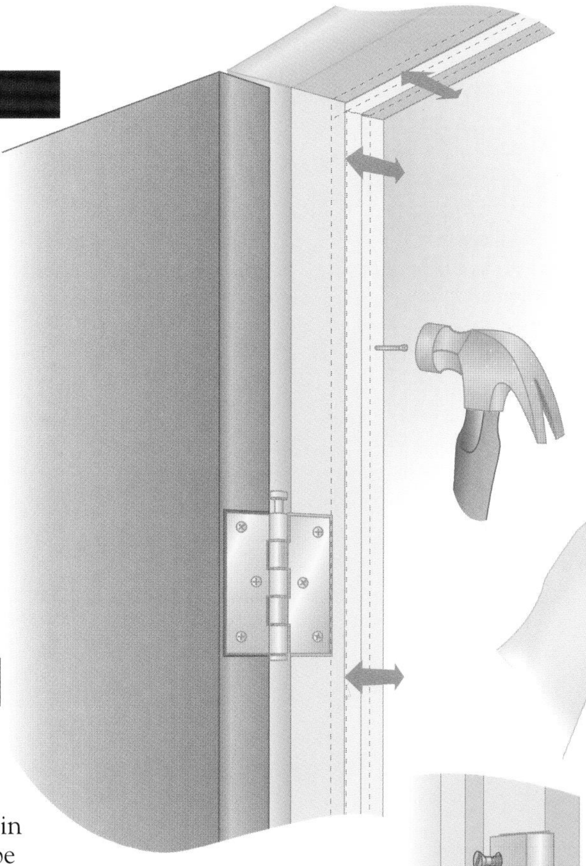

Move the stop to fix doors that don't latch or that rattle when they shut.

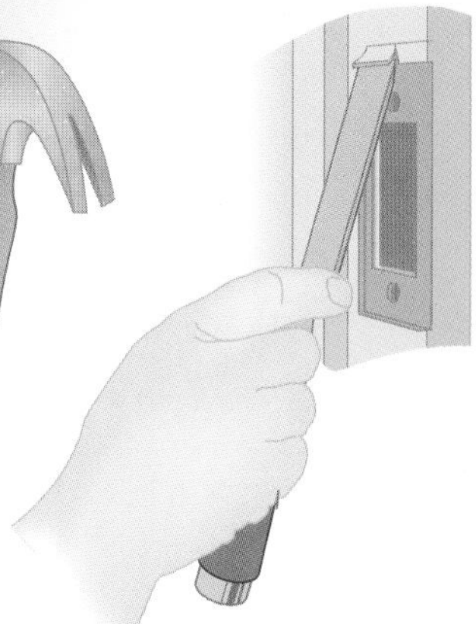

If the problem is minor, remove the strike and alter the mortise.

Door Moves by Itself

A door that moves by itself isn't haunted; the hinges are simply out of plumb. Hold a level—or a straight board with a level clamped to it—against the pin sides of both hinges. The hinges should be close to perfectly plumb.

If the hinges are out of plumb, unscrew one hinge and move it out. Drill pilot holes before refastening. Check the hinges for plumb. If they line up, fill the resulting mortise gap with wood putty.

The flat side of the jamb will rarely be out of plumb. This requires a more complicated fix: You'll have to remove the casing and adjust the jamb. You'll probably also need to adjust the jamb all the way around so the door will fit into the opening.

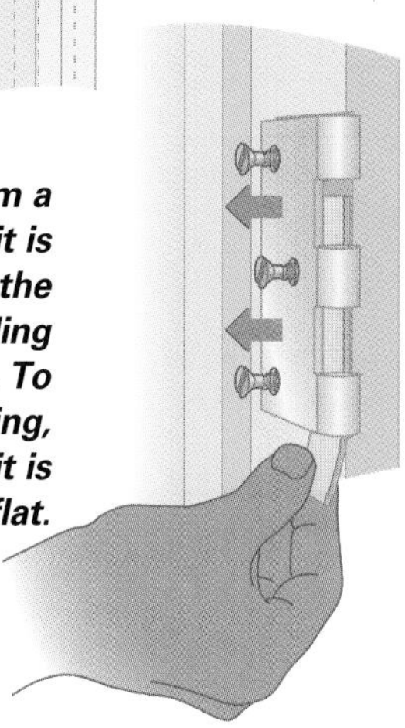

Move or shim a hinge so it is flush with the surrounding wood. To prevent binding, make sure it is flat.

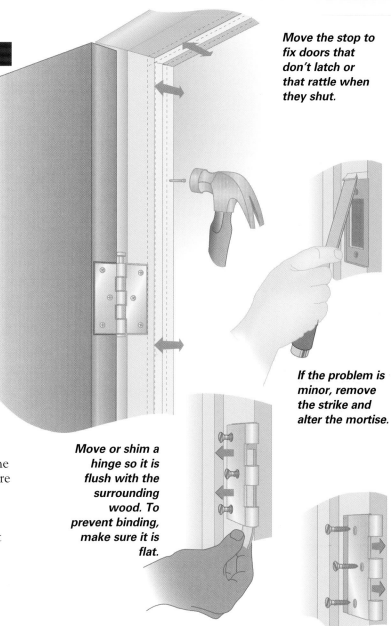

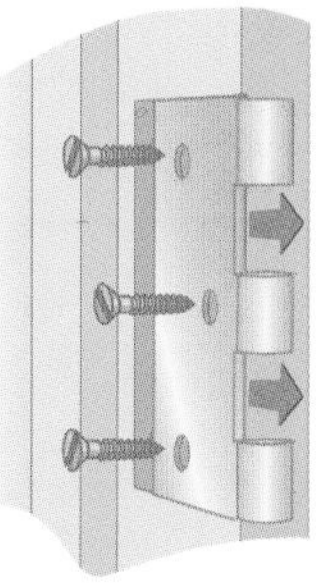

Door Symptoms and Cures

Symptom	Cure
Door binds or will not close.	Tighten hinges if they are loose. Or, find where the door is rubbing against the jamb or floor, and trim the door (*see pages 48–49*).
Door has trouble closing even though it is not binding.	Examine the hinges as you close the door. If one (or both) of the hinges flexes, you may need to shim it out so it is flush with the jamb or door edge. Or, remove caked-on paint.
Door sticks in humid weather.	If the sticking edge is unpainted, painting it may solve the problem. If not, test for binding in humid weather and plane the door.
Door closes but will not latch.	Examine the latch and strike plate to see if they align; if not, move the strike. If the gap between the latch and the strike plate is too large, shim out the strike plate.
Door rattles when it is closed.	Move the strike plate in, toward the stop, so the latch grabs tightly.

PLANING AND CUTTING A DOOR

Removing and shaping a door is not as difficult as the job may sound. However, take great care when marking and cutting because once wood is removed from the edge of a door, you can't fill it in again.

HOW TO DEAL WITH MISFITS

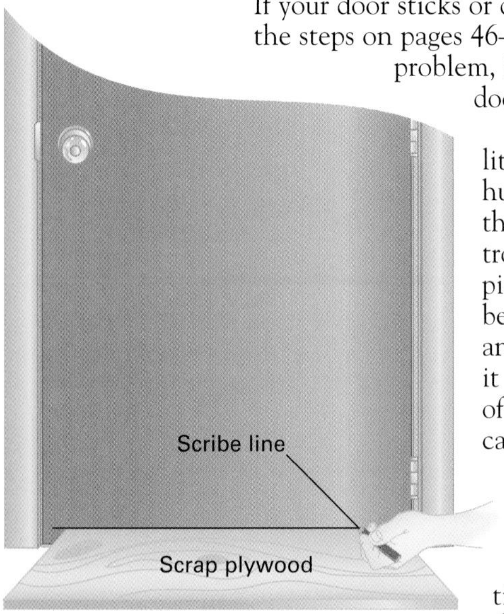

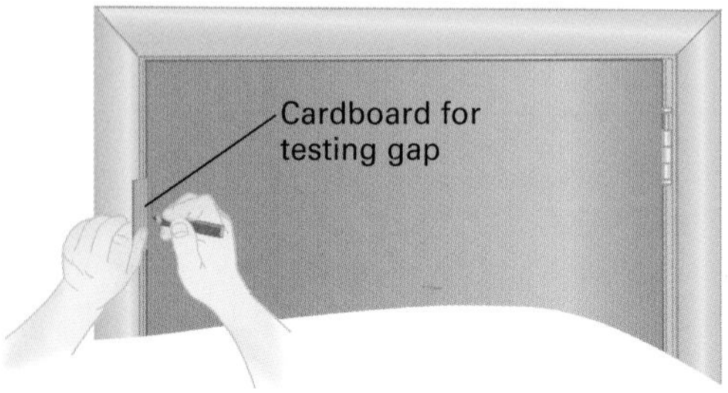

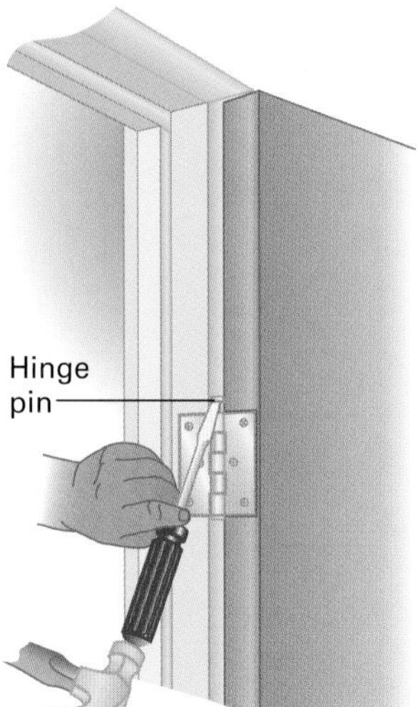

MARKING OR SCRIBING

If your door sticks or does not close, and the steps on pages 46–47 do not solve the problem, it's time to mark the door for cutting or planing.

If the door sticks only a little, or sticks only during humid weather, close it all the way and find the trouble spots. Insert a piece of thin cardboard between the door edge and the jamb, and slide it along the sides and top of the door. Wherever the cardboard sticks, draw a pencil line on the door so you will know where to plane.

If the door sticks tight or is difficult to close, shut it gently until it just starts to bind. (If you force the door shut, you will have inaccurate scribe lines.) From the inside of the door, scribe a line, using the door jamb as the guide. Hold the pencil flat against the jamb so it stays at the same angle while you slide it along. The resulting line will reveal the exact outline of the jamb on the door.

If the door binds at its bottom (as often happens when new carpeting is installed), first decide how much of a gap you want between the door and the floor or threshold. Interior doors usually have a gap of about 1/2 inch; an exterior door must be tighter, and it might need to fit snugly against a rubber gasket in the threshold. Scribe a line that matches the floor or threshold, using a scrap of 1/2-inch plywood on the floor as a guide, *top left*.

PLANING

Remove the door, supporting it at the bottom with shims so it is firm but not tight. Use a hammer and screwdriver to tap the top hinge pin loose; then tap the bottom pin loose. Remove the top pin, then the bottom pin. If the hinge is old and rusted and the pin won't come loose, remove the screws attaching the hinge to the door.

Moving a latch is a difficult job. So, if your scribe marks show that you need to remove 1/8 inch or more from the area around the latch, cut the hinge side instead; remortising the hinges will not be as difficult. Use a straightedge to transfer your scribe lines to the hinge side.

Position the door so it will be stable and easy to work on. To plane an edge, lean it against a table and brace the bottom. To plane a top or bottom, clamp it so it overhangs a table. If you need to remove a lot of material, buy or rent a power planer.

When planing across the grain, or when planing a door that has plywood veneer, clamp a straightedge and use a knife to cut a line that is 1/16 inch behind your scribe line. This should prevent any splintering on the face of the door.

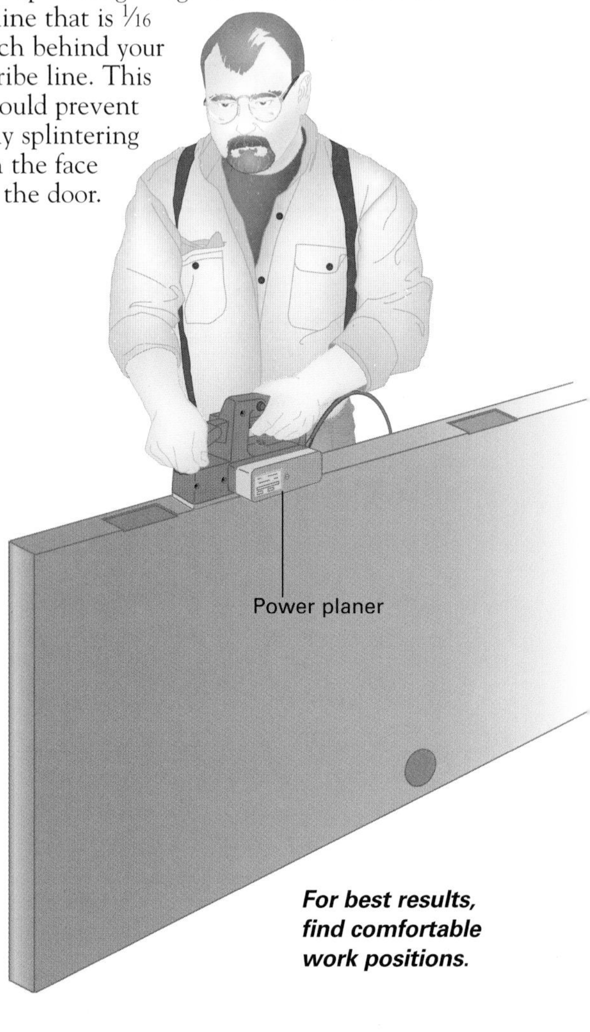

For best results, find comfortable work positions.

See pages 30–31 for planing techniques. If the edge of the door is slightly beveled, maintain that bevel as you plane. It often helps to straddle the door when planing a door edge. If you can see the wood grain, plane with the grain lines going upward ahead of you. If you can't see the grain, you'll have to experiment: If the plane is gouging, try moving in the opposite direction.

CUTTING A HOLLOW-CORE DOOR

A hollow-core door is reinforced with solid wood for only an inch or so around its perimeter. So, if you have to cut off more than an inch, you will have to fill in a hollow space.

Use a straightedge and knife to cut all the way through the veneer about 1/16 inch behind the cut line. Then, clamp on the straightedge as a guide for cutting the door with a circular saw. Save the cutoff.

Use a chisel to scrape and push away the cardboard reinforcement in the opening. Chisel away the veneer from the cutoff piece and pry off the little side pieces. Test to see that the board will fit in the opening. Squirt wood glue on the inside of the door and on the wood piece, tap into place, and clamp.

CUTTING A DOOR

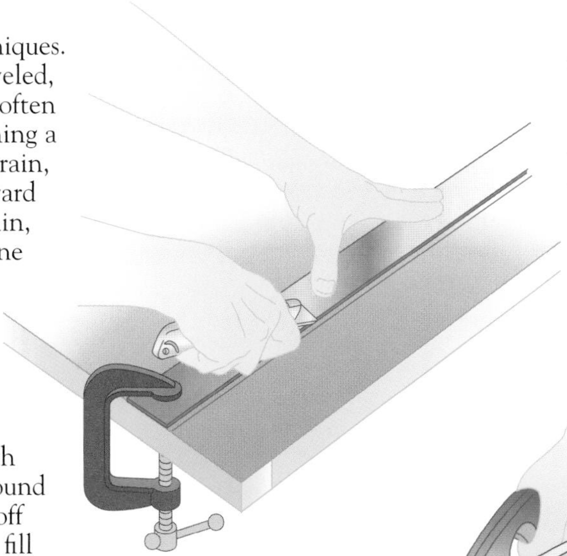

***1.** First, cut a knife line slightly back of the cut line so there will be no splinters. Check for embedded nails and remove them or drive them in with a nail set.*

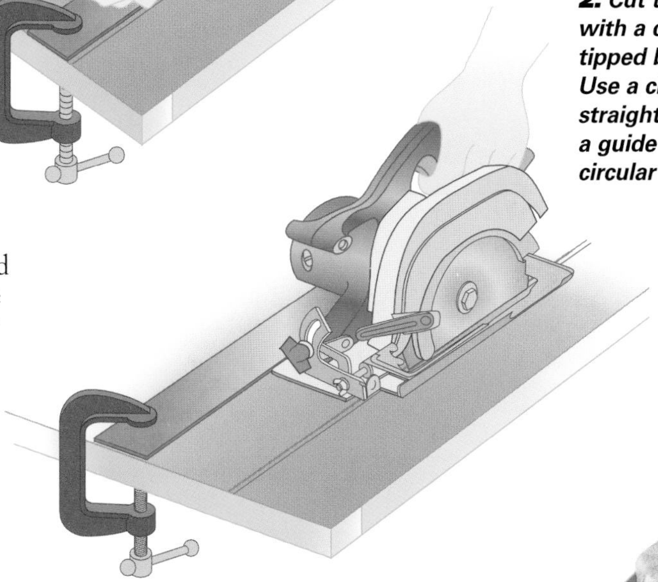

***2.** Cut the door with a carbide-tipped blade. Use a clamped straightedge as a guide for your circular saw.*

***3.** Use a chisel to trim away the veneer from the piece you cut off. Sand it smooth with sandpaper.*

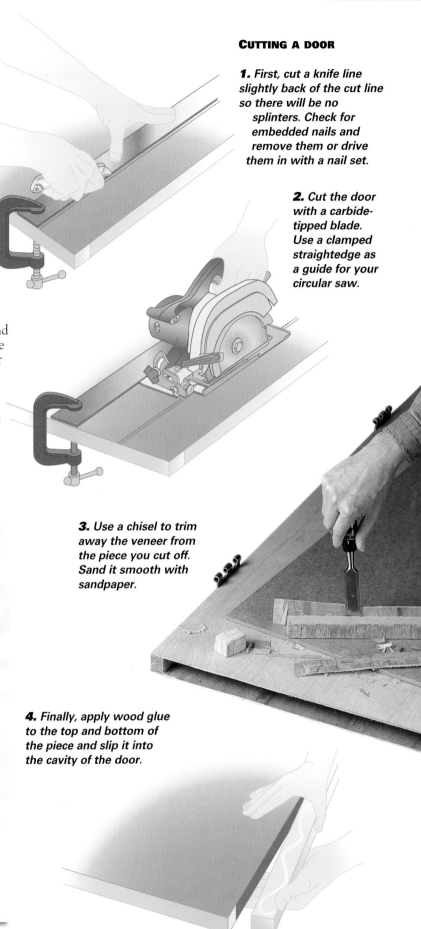

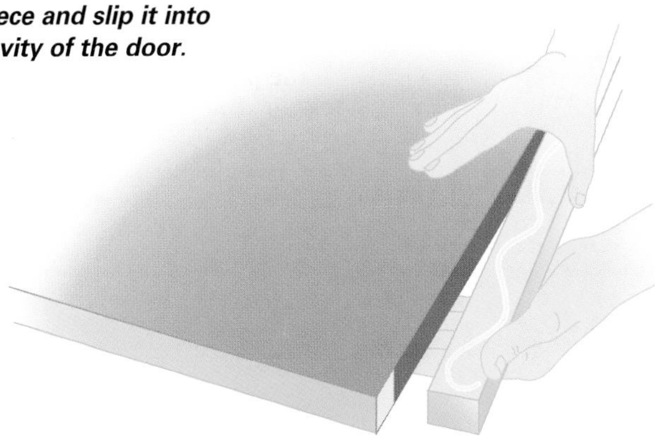

***4.** Finally, apply wood glue to the top and bottom of the piece and slip it into the cavity of the door.*

FIXING A FLUSH DOOR OR A PANEL DOOR

A *flush door* has a smooth face; a *panel door* is made of horizontal and vertical *rails*, with *panels* that fit into them.

If the laminate facing of a flush door is peeling off, fix it right away or the problem will get worse. Remove the door, squirt in carpenter's glue, and clamp overnight. Sand off any rough edges that could get caught and cause further peeling.

If a panel door has come apart, remove it and set it on sawhorses or a workbench. Use bar clamps or pipe clamps to squeeze the door back together; you may find that you have to scrape away stuck-on debris or paint. Once you know that it will go back together, use a flat bar to pry the pieces far enough apart so you can squirt glue in all the joints. Clamp firm for a day. If the door is badly damaged, it may help to drill angled pilot holes and drive screws at the top and bottom, to hold the vertical and horizontal rails together.

FLOORING

Properly maintained, wood subflooring and flooring will last for centuries. But if moisture or wood-boring insects enter the picture, a floor can fall apart in a hurry.

Floor repairs are not especially difficult, but working on your knees all day will be tiring.

Most floors are made of two layers of wood. The subfloor will be plywood or, in an older home, 1-by boards laid at an angle. On top of that is a finished tongue-and-groove floor or another layer of plywood, on which tile or carpeting is laid. To find out how thick each layer is, remove a piece of molding at the beginning of a stairway going down.

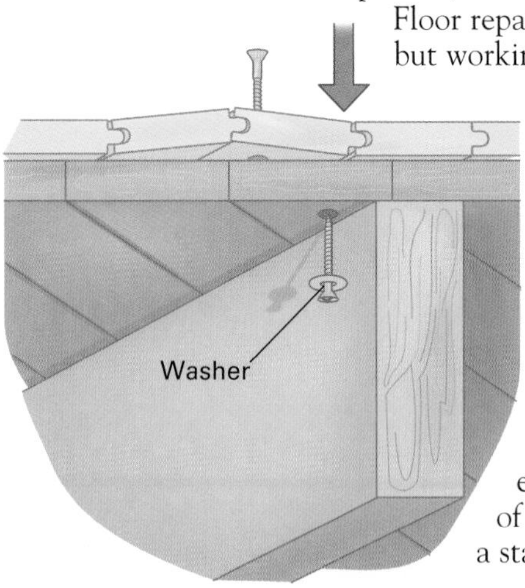

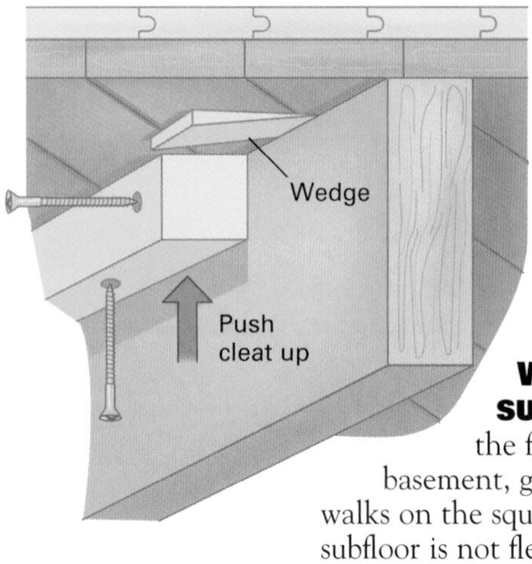

Use washers when driving screws through the subflooring (top). They will keep the screw head from sinking in, which could cause the screws to poke up through the flooring. When attaching a cleat, first insert a wedge into the gap, then fasten the cleat in place.

STOPPING SQUEAKS

Squeaks rarely indicate a structural problem, but they can certainly be annoying. Pinpoint the source of a squeak by having someone stroll by while you lie on the floor and watch closely; often, you will see a flex in the floor surface even if it is carpeted.

WHEN YOU CAN SEE THE SUBFLOOR: If the area under the floor is an unfinished basement, go down there while a helper walks on the squeak. Look and listen. If the subfloor is not flexing, drill pilot holes and drive screws up through the subfloor and into the flooring. Be sure the screw won't poke up through the flooring.

If that doesn't work, attach a 2×2 cleat to the side of the joist, and drive screws up through it to pull the floorboards back into line. If the subfloor flexes, drive shims between the joist and the subfloor.

If a joist is sagging or flexes, you may be able to firm it up by splinting on a length of 2×6 fastened with lag bolts. Or, install an adjustable steel post (often referred to as a "jack post") beneath the sag.

WHEN YOU CAN'T SEE THE SUBFLOOR: You can solve some squeaks by just driving a screw into the subfloor; other squeaks require that you find a joist and fasten a screw to eliminate the squeak. There is usually no need to pull up a carpet to fix a squeak. Drive trim-head screws directly through the carpeting; in most cases, they will disappear. (Drive a test screw in an inconspicuous spot to be sure.)

Tighten loose floorboards with screws driven through carpet.

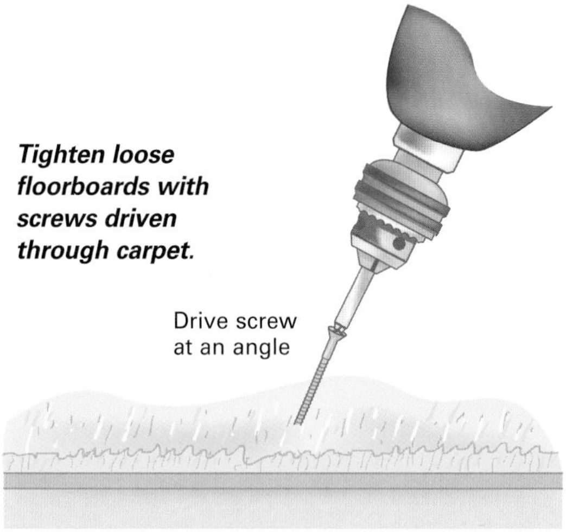

Tiled floors present a bigger problem. If the squeak is severe, you may have to remove a tile, drive screws to eliminate the squeak, and replace the tile.

If a hardwood floor squeaks and you can't get at it from underneath, drill pilot holes, drive trim-head screws, and fill the holes with wood putty to match the color of the floor. Or counterbore and plug (*see page* 35).

REPAIRING A FLOOR

If a large area is bouncy or sags, you need to reinforce the joists and perhaps install a beam. This is a major job, although it will be easier if the area underneath is an unfinished basement. Call in a pro.

REPLACING SUBFLOOR: If a section of your floor and subfloor is rotten or insect-damaged, cut it out and replace it. Remove any fixtures (often this happens around a

TO REPLACE A SECTION OF SUBFLOOR

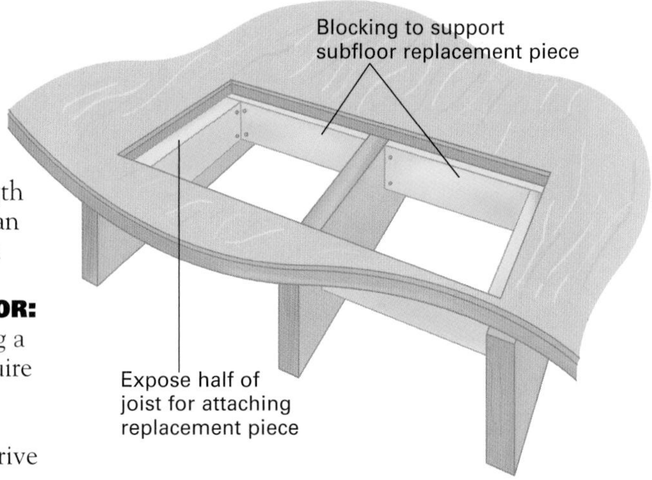

toilet) and carpeting or tile. Find out where the joists are, and use a framing square to mark a rectangular area that extends from the edge of one joist to the edge of another.

You may well cut through some nails, so put a carbide blade in the circular saw. Wear safety goggles. Set the blade to just 1/4 inch deeper than the thickness of the floor, and cut out the area.

Frame for the patch by providing a nailing surface all around the perimeter. You can put cleats along the sides of the joists on the ends and run blocking from joist to joist. Cut a plywood patch of matching thickness and attach it with screws.

PATCHING HARDWOOD: Tongue-and-groove flooring is hard to remove without damaging the surrounding area, so patching it can be time-consuming.

Remove whole boards, when possible, because it's difficult to cut a perfectly straight line in the middle of a floorboard. Use a 1-inch spade bit to drill a series of holes down the middle of the board, several inches apart. Then use a chisel to chop out a strip from the middle of the board. Once the middle is gone, pry and slide out the tongue side and the groove side.

To remove a section of a board, bore several 3/8- or 1/4-inch holes across the board (*as shown at right*). After you have chiseled out and removed the section, use a framing square and knife to score a square line close to the holes, and then chisel away the line. It will take some effort to end up with a clean cut that is square.

Some older hardwood floors don't rest on a solid subfloor but on sleepers—1×3 boards running perpendicular to the flooring every 12 inches or so. If you have this arrangement, support the ends of the boards by wedging in short pieces of 1-by lumber or 3/4-inch plywood. If the flooring board ends are not supported, they will flex and crack.

If you have a number of boards to replace, the easiest method is to cut out a rectangular section with a circular saw, and then fit in pieces that are all the same length. But that will be unattractive—an obvious patch. Instead, make the extra effort to remove boards in a staggered pattern so they weave together.

The universal rule: Boards that are either next to each other or separated by only one board must have their joint lines staggered at least 4 inches (*right*).

Facenail replacement pieces in place. Drill pilot holes and use 6d finishing nails. Often, you'll only need to nail along one edge; the adjacent tongue or groove will adequately hold the other edge.

TO REMOVE AND REPLACE DAMAGED FLOORBOARDS

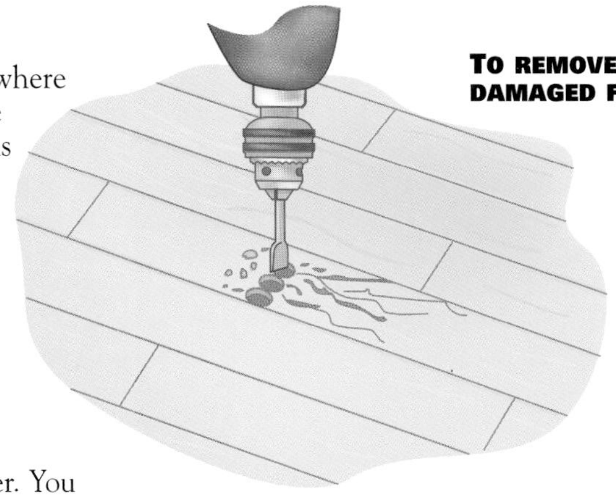

***1.** First, drill a series of holes on either side of the damage.*

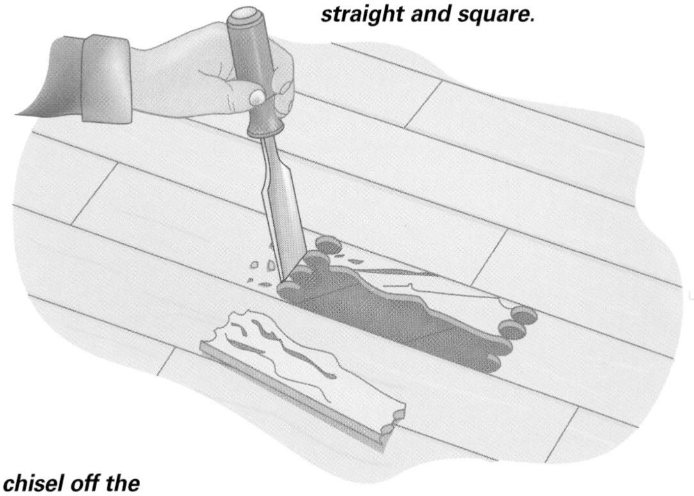

***2.** Chisel the edges of the hole until they are straight and square.*

***3.** Saw or chisel off the bottom edge of the groove from the patch. Slip the tongue side in first, then facenail the other side.*

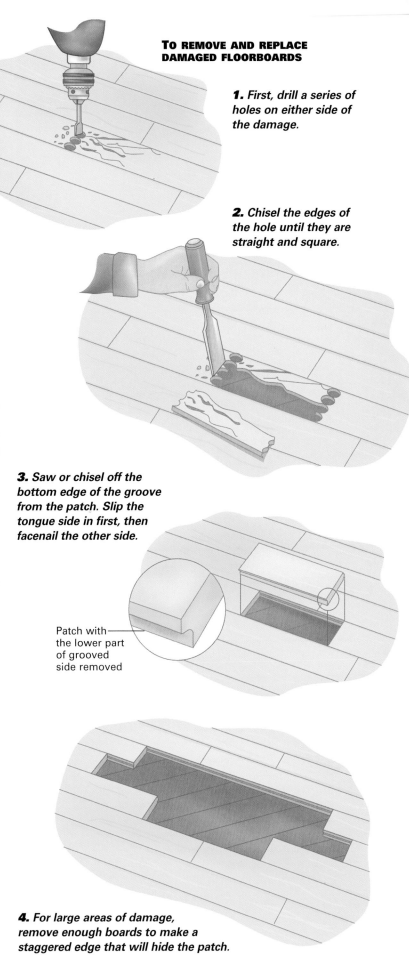

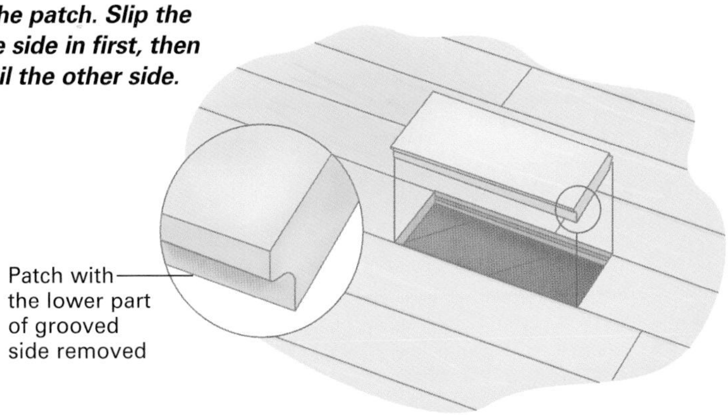

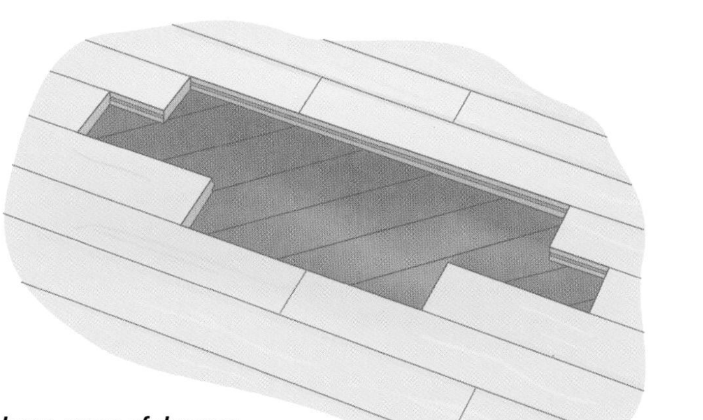

***4.** For large areas of damage, remove enough boards to make a staggered edge that will hide the patch.*

STAIRS

An interior staircase is more complicated than the stairs used on porches or decks. The treads may rest on open stringers, with tooth-like cutouts for the treads to rest on, or on closed stringers, which have grooves cut in them. Some stairways use both types of stringer. The rail post is often notched at the bottom to fit precisely into the bottom tread and riser. The balusters are milled and angle-cut for a tight fit at an odd angle. Repairing this furniture-like structure calls for more than driving in a few screws.

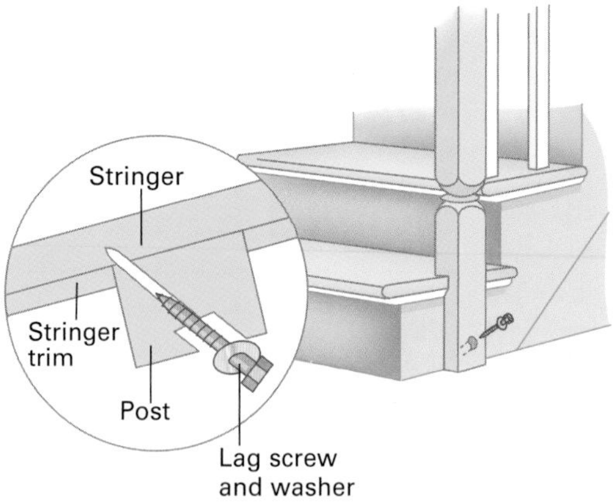

Measure and drill carefully when reinforcing a post bottom, to avoid splitting the post. Angle the screw downward or sideways (inset) for maximum holding power.

RAILING REPAIRS

Loose posts and balusters might crack or come out altogether, so solve the problem while it is a quick fix.

POSTS: Rail posts handle a lot of abuse, and they often come loose because they are anchored only at the bottom. Some posts are anchored to floor joists, but most are tied to the stringer and stair tread only. To repair a rail post, drill pilot holes and countersink or counterbore holes, then drive hefty screws into the stringer and tread. For added strength, use several screws at different angles. If you can, crawl under the stairway and drive a screw through the stringer and into the post.

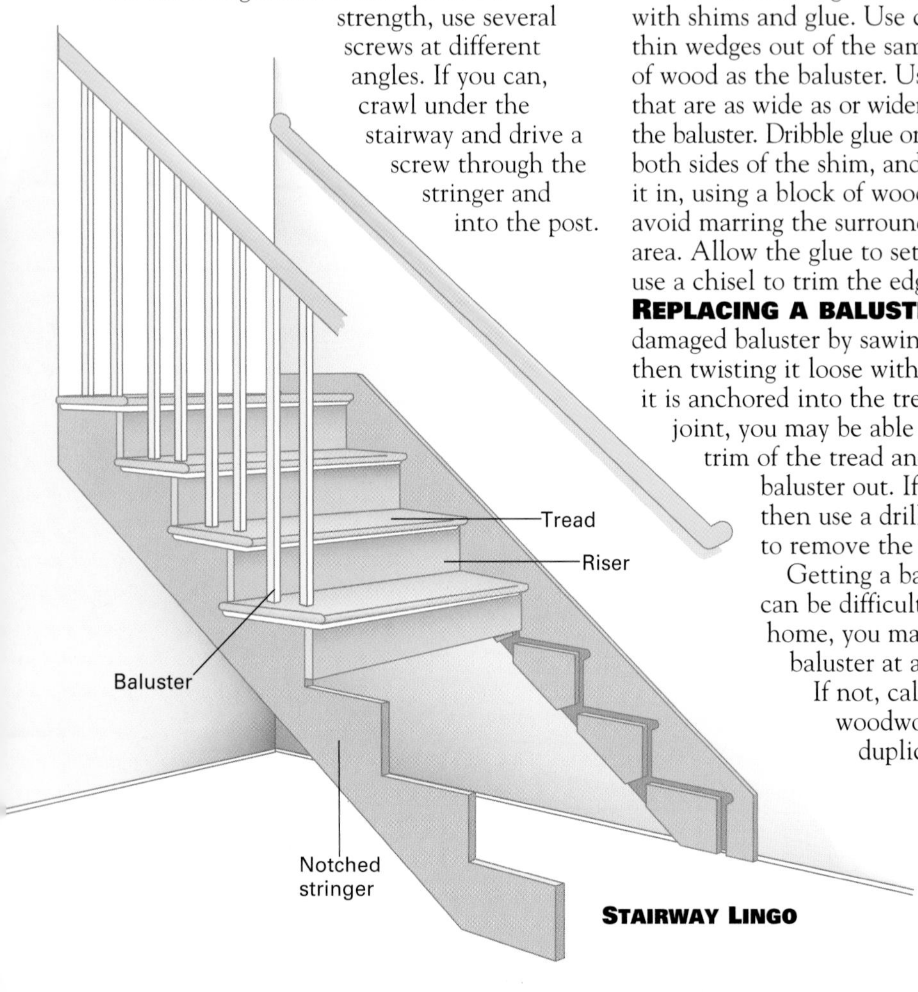

STAIRWAY LINGO

LOOSE BALUSTERS: If you can twist a baluster easily by hand, reinforce it. The most effective fix is to chisel a ¼-inch sliver in the base of the baluster, drill a pilot hole angled up into the rail or down into the tread, and then drive a trim-head screw to stabilize the baluster. Hide the work by gluing the sliver back in place. If you fill the hole with putty, it will be visible unless you paint over it.

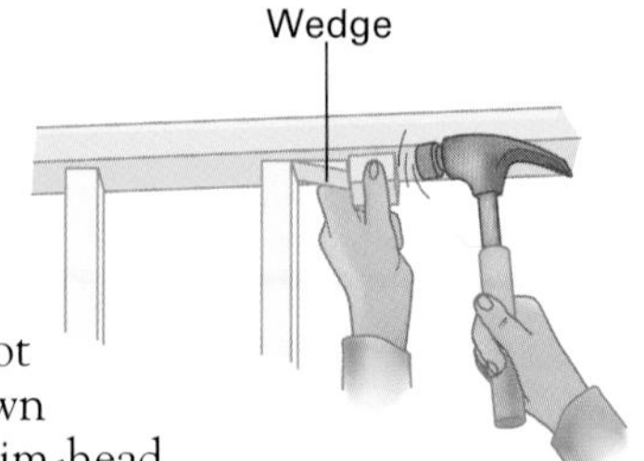

SHIMMING LOOSE BALLUSTERS

To avoid making a hole, tighten the rail with shims and glue. Use cedar shims, or cut thin wedges out of the same species of wood as the baluster. Use shims that are as wide as or wider than the baluster. Dribble glue onto both sides of the shim, and tap it in, using a block of wood to avoid marring the surrounding area. Allow the glue to set, then use a chisel to trim the edges flush.

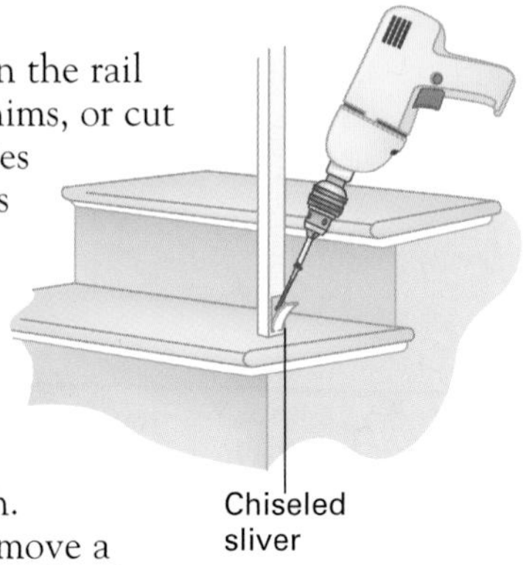

REPLACING A BALUSTER: Remove a damaged baluster by sawing it in half and then twisting it loose with a pipe wrench. If it is anchored into the tread with a dovetail joint, you may be able to pry out the end trim of the tread and then tap the baluster out. If not, saw it flush, then use a drill and a small chisel to remove the inset wood.

Getting a baluster to match can be difficult. If yours is a newer home, you may find a matching baluster at a good lumberyard. If not, call around to find a woodworker who can duplicate balusters.

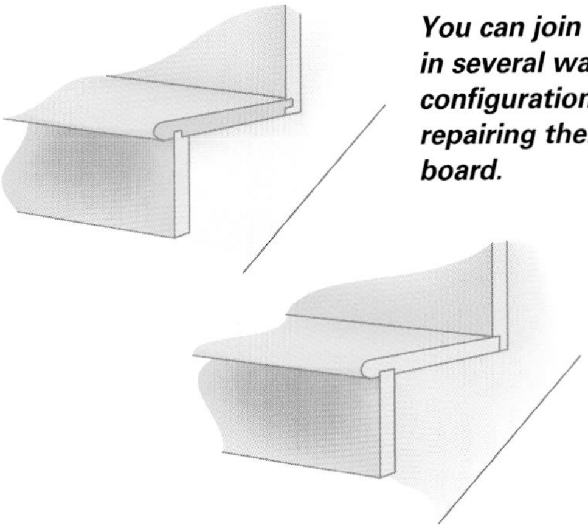

You can join treads and risers in several ways. Understand the configuration of your stairs before repairing them or you may split a board.

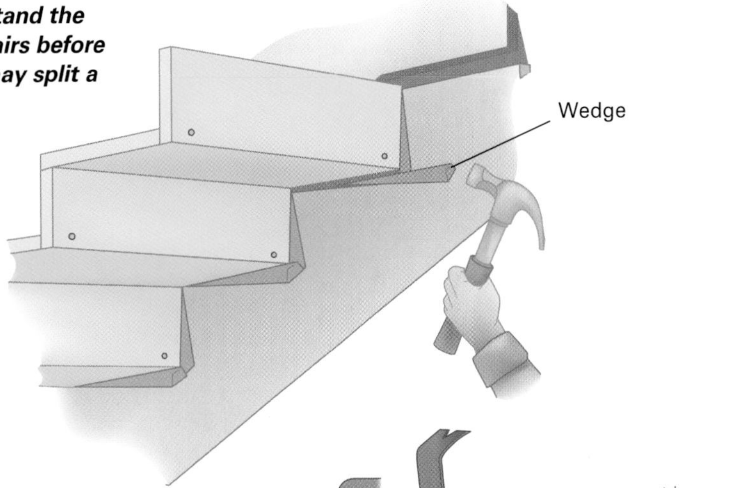

TREADS AND RISERS

Evaluate the health of your stairs by having someone walk on them while you watch closely. You may be surprised to find that some of the treads flex noticeably. If so, you should solve the problem right away.

SQUEAKS: If there is no major flexing but a step makes an annoying squeak, you can usually solve the problem quickly. If the squeak comes from the front of the tread, drill pilot holes and drive trim-head screws down through the tread and into the riser. If the rear of the tread squeaks, work from underneath the stairway and drive screws up through the tread and into the riser. To fix from above, tap glue-coated shims into the joint between the tread and riser, and trim them flush when the glue has set.

LOOSE TREADS: If the treads are very loose, a stringer may be damaged, or it may have moved outward, so it no longer supports the tread adequately. You have to get under the stairs to fix this. If the area beneath the stairs is covered with drywall or plaster, remove two or more treads and risers to get under. For extensive repairs, it may be less trouble in the long run to cut out the drywall so you can work from underneath.

A sagging or cracked stringer can be reinforced by attaching 2×4s running vertically up from the floor or by attaching a strip of ¾-inch plywood to the side of the stringer with lots of screws.

Treads on a closed stringer (where problems usually arise) are snugged into the groove with vertical and horizontal wedges. Sometimes just hammering the wedges back into place will do the job.

If the treads and risers are pulling out of the closed stringer, use pieces of ¾-inch plywood to provide new support. Drill pilot holes for all screws or you may crack the stringer.

To support sagging treads, install a carriage brace *(right)*. Construct the brace from 2×6 lumber and install it along the length of the stairway, in the middle.

REPLACING A TREAD OR RISER: To remove a tread or riser, work carefully to avoid splitting adjoining boards. Remove any molding pieces first. Use a flat pry bar *(right)* to pry in several directions. If you can get underneath, you may be able to tap the piece loose. You can often pry up the tread and hammer it back down in order to pop the nails up. If the pieces do not respond to prying, saw a riser in half lengthwise.

Treads are often an odd thickness—1¼ inches. Lumberyards carry wood specifically used for interior treads. The wood should be free of knots and be close-grained for maximum strength.

Use the old tread or riser as a template for cutting the new one. If the front edge of the tread is beveled, make sure the new one is also. Install the new pieces with trim-head screws.

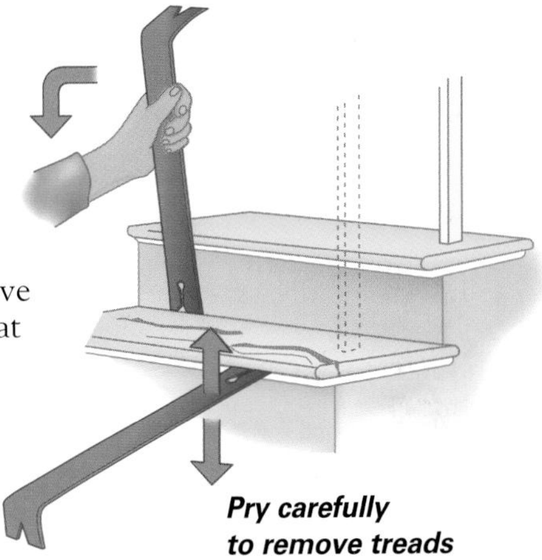

Pry carefully to remove treads or risers without damaging the adjacent boards.

Carriage braces reinforce sagging stair treads.

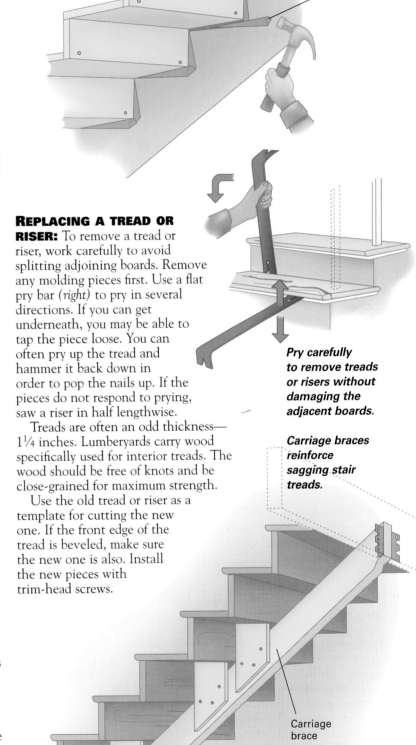

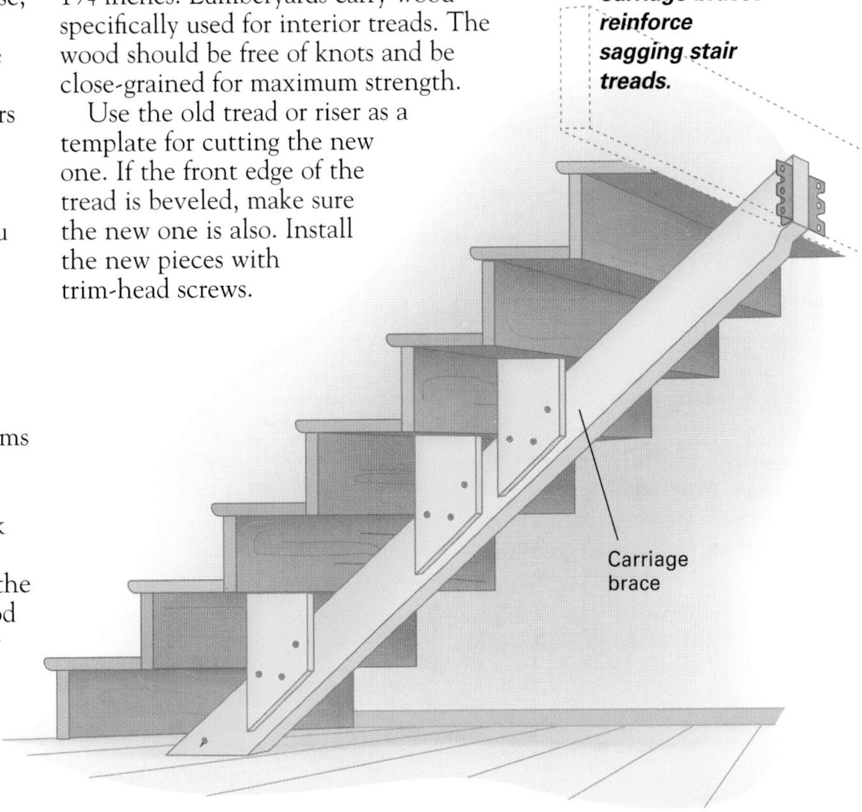

SASH WINDOWS

A double-hung window has two sashes that slide up and down. In many older homes, the top sash has been stuck by old paint or even nailed shut. If you free the top sash, you will be able to clean the outside of your windows from the indoors.

Keep your windows tight by filling any gaps in the glazing putty that seals the glass to the frame on the outside. If a sash is broken, some lumberyards will make replacement sashes. But consider replacing a window that is badly damaged; you will save money over time with lower utility bills.

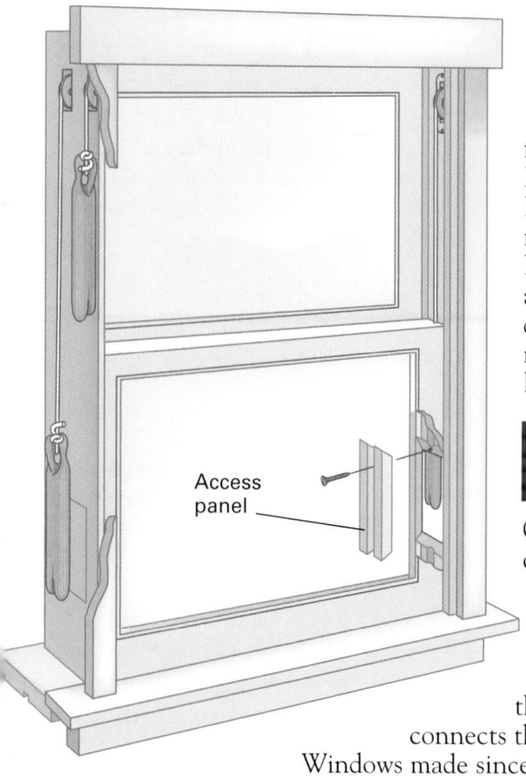

Smooth-working sash weights give older windows a lift.

REPLACING SASH CORDS

Older sash windows are counterweighted so they open easily and stay in place when raised. On each side, a cord or chain runs through a pulley and connects the sash to a weight. Windows made since the 1960s use friction or spring lifts instead of weights.

Cords usually last about 10 years, so replacing one is a common repair. If one cord is broken, replace both of them because the other is probably badly worn. Chain lasts longer than rope, but it makes more noise when you raise the window.

Pry off one of the stops. (Cut the paint line with a knife first so the paint won't chip.) Lift the sash slightly and pull it out. If you have an unbroken cord, pry the knotted end out of the groove, and insert a nail into the knot so it will not slip through the pulley.

Set the window to the side, and pry off the access panel. To get at it, you may have to remove stop molding or a strip of metal weather stripping. You may also want to remove the top sash at this point.

Check that the pulleys spin freely. If you can't free them up, buy replacements. Poke one end of a new cord or chain through the pulley, and thread it downward until you see it in the access panel. Tie it to the weight.

Set the sash on the sill. Pull the weight up until it is a couple of inches from the pulley, then cut the cord or chain to fit. Attach it to the sash by tying a knot that fits into the groove, and secure the knot with a short screw. Make sure that it glides freely, then reinstall the access panel, any weather stripping, and the stop.

To get to the sash weight and replace the cord, remove the stop and pull out the lower sash. After detaching the cord from the window, open the access panel, raise the weight, and set it on the sill.

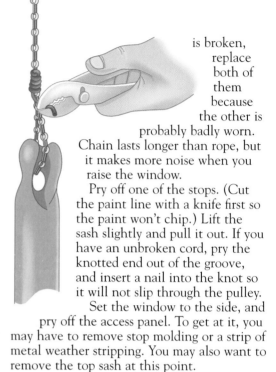

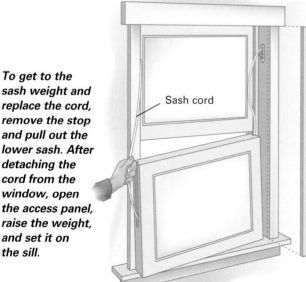

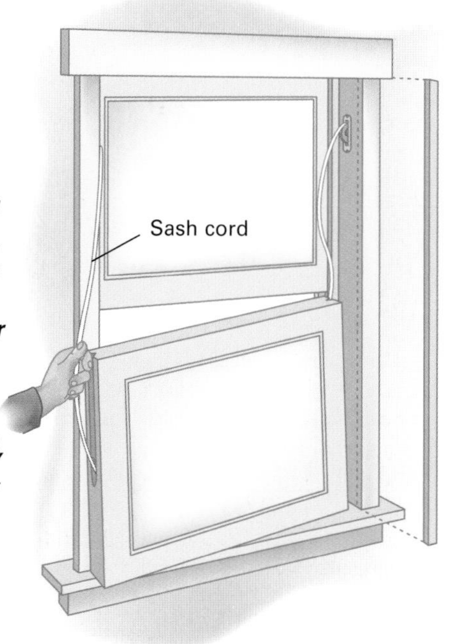

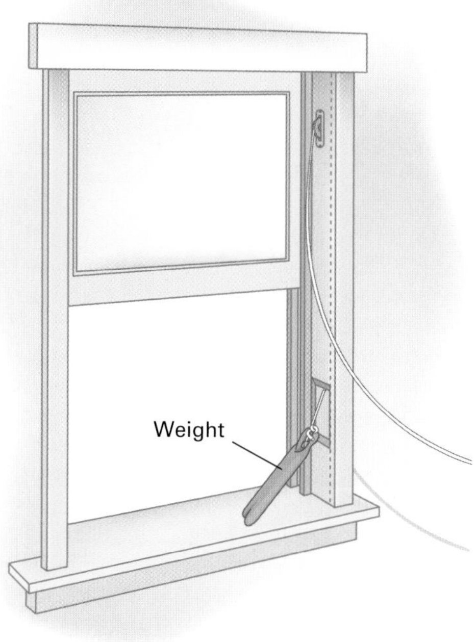

TENSION SPRING AND CASEMENT MECHANISM

For repair of windows not covered here, consult the manufacturer's directions.

TENSION SPRING: Some windows use a spring balance rather than weights to maintain sash tension. The springs become worn out after a couple of decades, so the sashes won't stay up. If the sash creeps up on its own, the spring is too tight.

With the sash still in place, unscrew the top screw carefully so it does not come out of the tube. Pull the tube out, and wind it clockwise to tighten or counterclockwise to loosen. If the spring is broken, pry out the stop, unscrew the tube's top screw, and pull the sash out far enough so you can unscrew the screws holding the spring to the bottom of the sash. Install a replacement unit.

CASEMENT WINDOWS: These open sideways with a crank. Removing four screws will enable you to slide the crank mechanism out for inspection. The gears may need cleaning and lubricating. If any part is broken, replace the mechanism.

ANOTHER TWIST ON OPENING WINDOWS

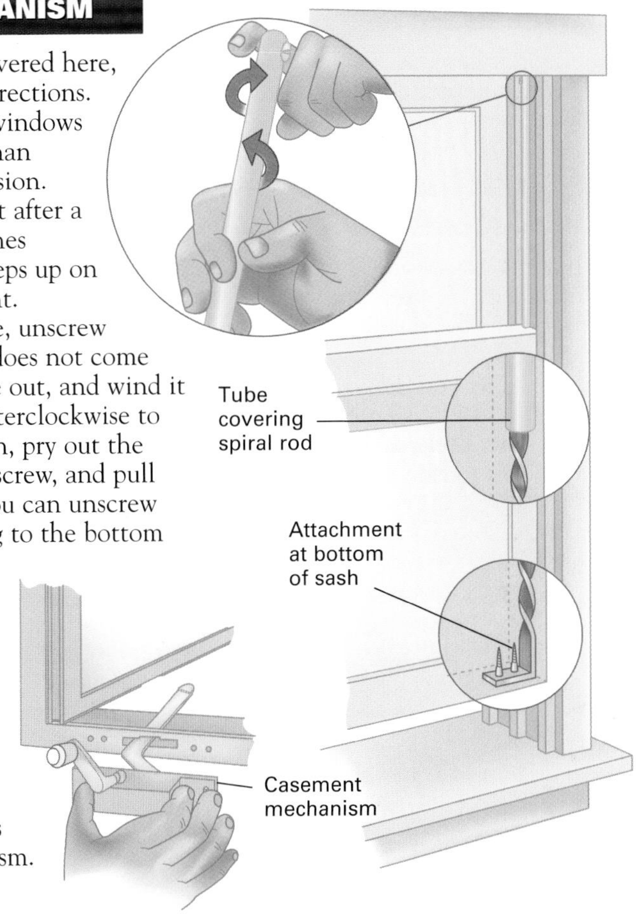

HELPING A WINDOW GLIDE SMOOTHLY

If a sash is stuck shut, cut the line between sash and jamb with a knife. Vacuum and wipe away any debris that is in the way. If the problem is built-up paint, sand it down. Rub the jambs with a candle to lubricate. If the sash is binding against the stop, scrape away any built-up paint, or nudge the stop over by tapping it with a hammer and a block of wood. If that doesn't work, remove the stop completely and reinstall it a bit farther from the sash. If the sash rattles, move the stop closer.

REPLACING A WINDOW SILL

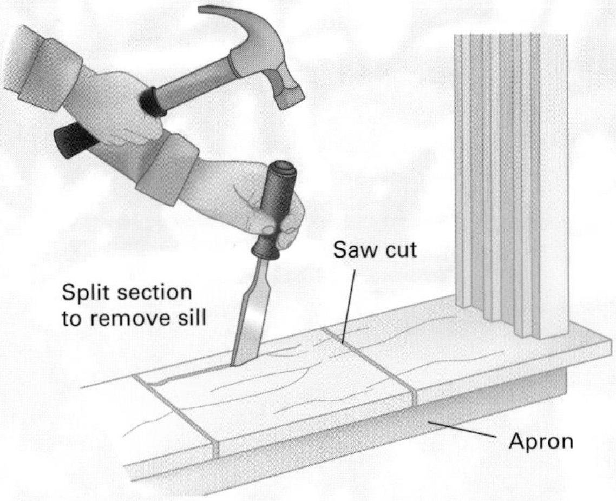

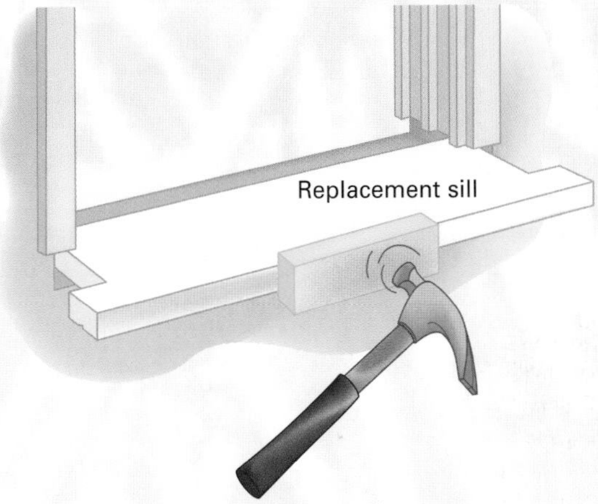

Fill in rotten areas on a window sill with epoxy filler (*see page* 56). If the sill is beyond repair, replacing it is not a big job. Pry it out carefully: Cut all the paint lines, and remove the apron at the same time. Use a reciprocating saw with a metal-cutting blade to cut through nails. Remove the sill by sawing through it in two places, then chiseling it out.

Save the wedges and shims that held the old sill in place. Lay the pieces of the old sill on top of the material for the new sill, and use them as a template. Copy the bevel cuts on one or both edges of the old sill. The new sill should slide in easily; if it doesn't, trim it a bit. Sand and prime the sill, and tap it into position with the wedges and shims. Drill pilot holes and drive deck screws through the bottom of the sill.

DAMAGED WOOD

Whenever you find rotten or cracked wood, try to determine the cause before repairing it so that the problem won't recur.

DIAGNOSING PROBLEMS

MILDEW: A black slimy surface indicates mildew, which rarely causes a structural problem. Clean the area with mildew remover or a bleach solution, and improve ventilation so the wood can dry out.

WOOD-EATING INSECTS: Thin channels drilled along grain lines indicate the presence of wood-eating insects, such as termites or carpenter ants. Because they like to eat in darkness, most of the damage is usually done by the time the damage is visible. Check for insect damage by rapping on lumber and listening for a hollow sound or by sticking an awl in suspected boards. Inspect any lumber near to or touching the ground, especially pieces that are attached to foundation walls.

Wood structures near the house provide entrée for these uninvited guests. For example, storing firewood in or up against the house is asking for trouble; store it away from the house. Insects need water to live in your home, and they thrive where roofing or siding damage keeps an area moist. However, bugs often live underground outside and come in to eat; in that case, they need no moisture from your home. Although you may be able to exterminate some types of insects yourself, it's not worth the risk. Call an exterminator while the damaged wood is exposed.

WET AND DRY ROT: Wet rot either is black and spongy or has dark brown strands. Dry rot is lighter in color but just as soft; it actually thrives in moist conditions.

Take steps to ensure that the wood can dry out, or see that it is completely covered with paint. Often, the solution is as simple as sweeping away collected leaves so that air and sunlight can get to the wood.

EPOXY FILLER FILLS A NEED FOR REINFORCEMENT

Epoxy wood filler, a type of epoxy resin that dries to a workable and sandable state similar to wood, is durable and long-lasting. You can even drill pilot holes and drive screws into it. Use it for exposed areas, such as window sills, that endure the full brunt of the weather, or for areas where you need to reattach fasteners.

***1.** If possible, do this work while the weather is warm and dry. Chisel and cut away most of the rotten wood. Allow the wood to dry out; this could take a week or two. Drill a series of ¼-inch holes to give the epoxy more surface to grab onto.*

***2.** Mix the two parts of the epoxy until you reach a consistent color. Press in the mixture with a putty knife, making sure it bonds to all the surfaces. Smooth the area. Don't try to make it perfect now; mound it up slightly so you can sand it down later. Use a scrap of wood to form an edge.*

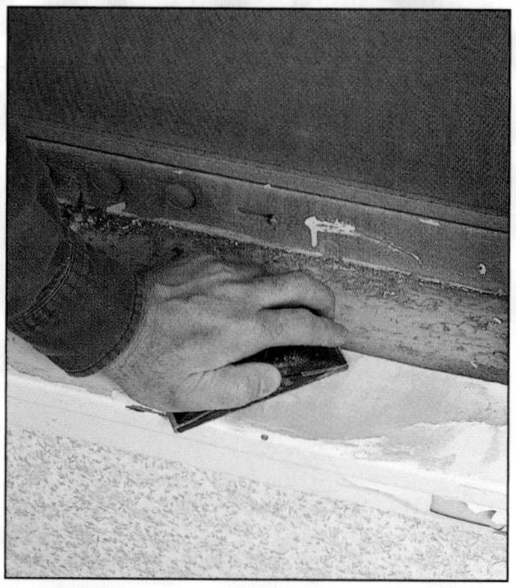

***3.** After the epoxy has dried and cured completely, use a sanding block to make the patch flush with the surrounding surface. Paint with a primer, then with the finish paint.*

Cracked paint allows water in and makes it hard for the moisture to evaporate—a dangerous combination. When replacing, use pressure-treated lumber.

FILLING HOLES

If an area is spongy, you may be able to solve the problem by pouring on a wood hardener or epoxy consolidant. You will probably need to fill holes as well. Vinyl spackling compound is easy to apply and easy to sand but it's not very strong; use it for vertical interior wood. Ready-mixed wood filler is strong enough for most wood holes but not for wood that will be stressed or exposed to standing water. Dry wood putty that you mix with water will be stronger but more difficult to sand. "Plastic" fillers become rock-hard but may not bond well with the surrounding wood. For exterior repairs, use only filler designed for outdoor use.

REPAIRING A SPLIT JAMB

If a section of a board is badly damaged, the solution is usually to remove and replace the whole board. But sometimes it is easier to patch it. A careful patch job becomes nearly invisible once it's painted.

***1.** Cut a patch larger than the damaged area. The corners do not have to be square. Hold the patch on the place where it will go, and scribe its outline on the damaged board with a knife to prevent splintering when it is cut.*

***2.** Cut out the scribed area. Use a circular saw, then a keyhole saw, a reciprocating saw, or a chisel to finish the corners.*

***3.** Begin the horizontal cuts with a keyhole saw and complete them with a chisel. Test the patch piece. It should fit snugly. If tapping with a hammer and block of wood does not push it flush with the surrounding area, remove the patch and trim it.*

***4.** You may need to shim the patch from behind until it is flush with the old surface. Fasten the patch by drilling pilot holes and driving finishing nails or trim-head screws. Fill the gaps with wood putty, sand smooth, then paint.*

DRAWERS AND CABINETS

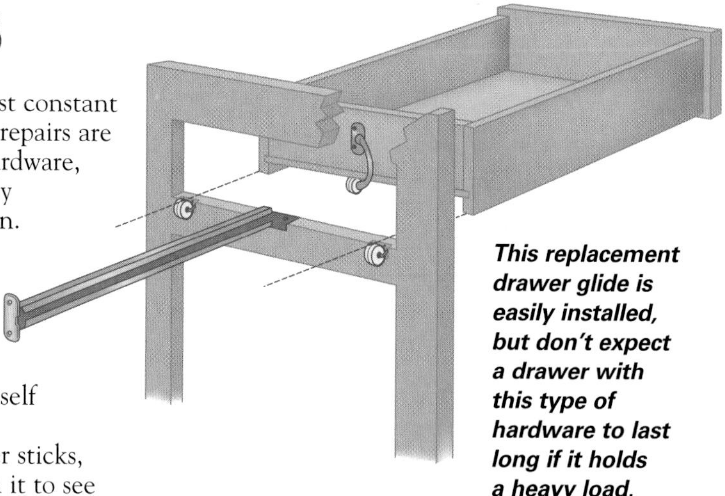

This replacement drawer glide is easily installed, but don't expect a drawer with this type of hardware to last long if it holds a heavy load.

Kitchen cabinets are in almost constant use, so don't be surprised if repairs are needed. Drawers, drawer hardware, and door hinges are the most likely components to need your attention.

DRAWER REPAIRS

Drawers and their hardware are closely allied. If the hardware is damaged, check that the drawer itself has not suffered, and vice versa.

STICKY OPERATION: If a drawer sticks, watch closely as you pull and push it to see where the rubbing is taking place; these trouble spots may show signs of wear. Sand or plane the drawer at those points.

If your drawer runs on a center glide and two side rollers, check to see if the rollers are supporting the bottom of the drawer. If not, you may need to attach them more firmly or even replace them. If side roller glides are sticking, remove the drawer. You may need to push down on the metal tabs at the front of the glides, or just lift up on the drawer once it is pulled out all the way. Clean out any debris, and lubricate the glides with graphite.

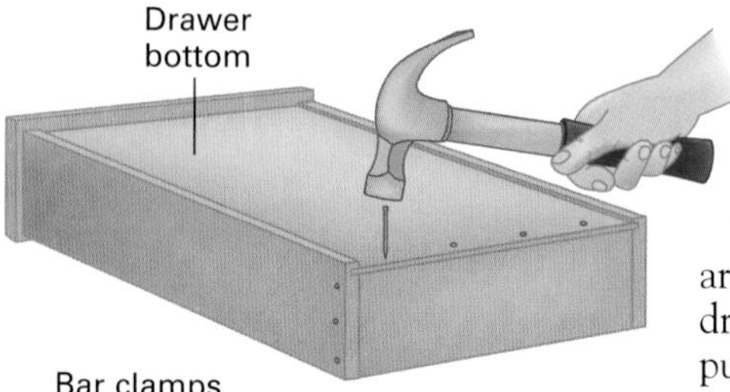

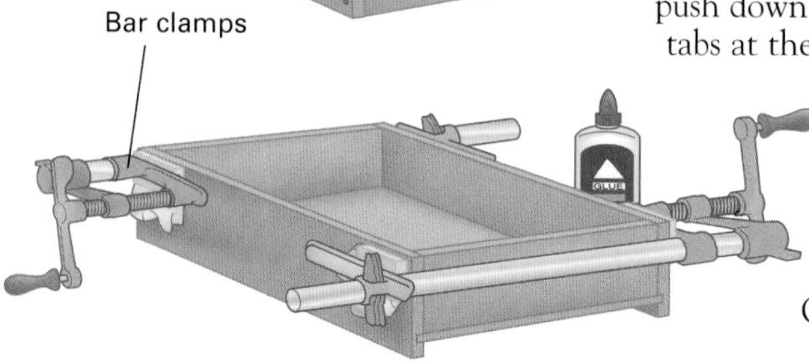

Use panel nails to cinch up a loose drawer bottom and bar clamps to help glue get a tight grip.

If a side of the drawer is cracked or worn below its groove (called the runner), cut the entire runner off in a straight line. Cut a thin piece of hardwood for the new runner; glue and clamp it.

COMING APART: Whenever you repair a drawer, check for square as you refasten it. The problem in a drawer that's coming apart is most often related to the drawer bottom. Usually, it fits into grooves in the side and front pieces. If the small nails holding the bottom and the sides to the back have come loose, pull them out, squirt glue into the joint, and drive in paneling nails, which have grooves for a tight fit. Make sure the bottom fits all the way into the grooves.

If the drawer has come loose at several points, tap the pieces apart with a hammer and wood block. Glue and clamp the whole drawer back together.

NEW GLIDES

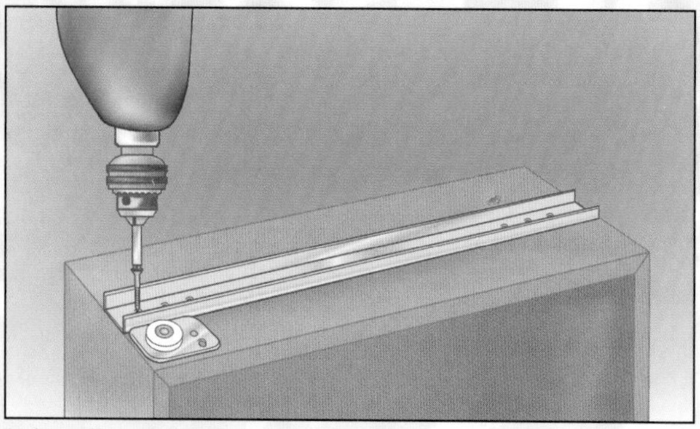

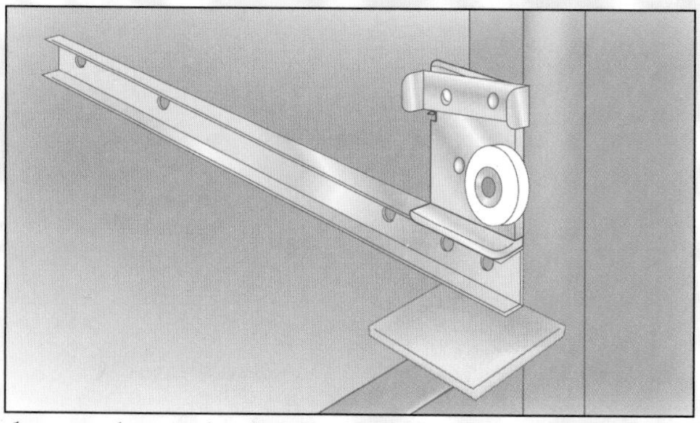

Side roller glides are the smoothest and most durable option for drawers. To provide solid support for the piece that attaches to the cabinet, you may need to install a nailer to the side of the cabinet. The piece that attaches to the drawer should butt up against the back of the drawer face and align with the bottom of the drawer. Make sure it is parallel with the bottom of the drawer, as well.

DOOR REPAIRS

If a door does not shut all the way, check the hinge first. Often the screws that hold the hinge have become loose. Remove any loose screws, tap slivers of shim into the pilot holes, and drive the screws back in.

■ If a hinge is binding, causing tension just as the door is about to close all the way, it may be mortised too far into the stile. Loosen the screws and insert cardboard shims behind each hinge until the binding stops.

■ Cabinet door catches wear out—roller springs get loose, and magnets lose their holding power. Once one or two of your catches break down, you should replace all the catches in the kitchen or bath. It's not complicated work, but it can be tedious to get those little pieces to align. Replace with exact copies of the old catches if possible so you can use the old screw holes.

■ If a catch is not working because it is out of alignment, the problem often is easily solved. Most catches have at least one component that can be moved ¼ inch or so by simply loosening a screw.

■ If your doors do not line up with each other, you can easily re-align them if you have Euro-style adjustable hinges. One adjustment screw tilts the door front to back; the other works side to side.

■ Aligning a door with a non-adjustable hinge is more difficult. Loosening the screws that go into the cabinet and shimming the hinge out may help move the door slightly sideways. Otherwise, you need to remove screws, fill the pilot holes tightly with slivers of wood, and redrill pilot holes slightly offset from the old ones.

KNOBS AND PULLS

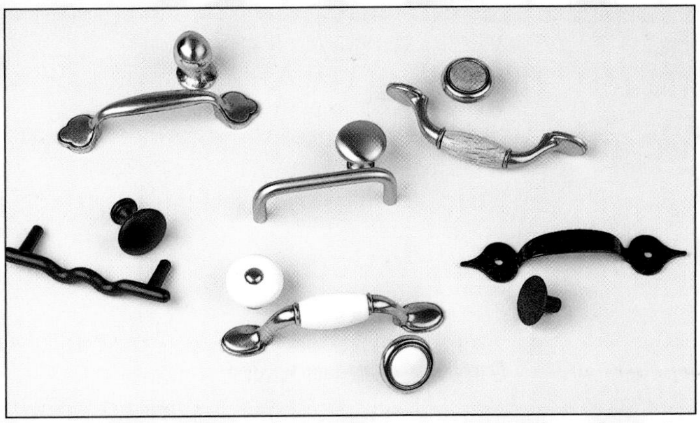

Relacing the knobs or pulls in your kitchen can make a dramatic difference in appearance. Buy new pulls that use screw holes the same distance apart as the old pulls. Replace a knob with a pull using the old screw hole and drilling one more. Avoid having to fill in a hole—unless you are painting—because wood filler won't blend in well enough.

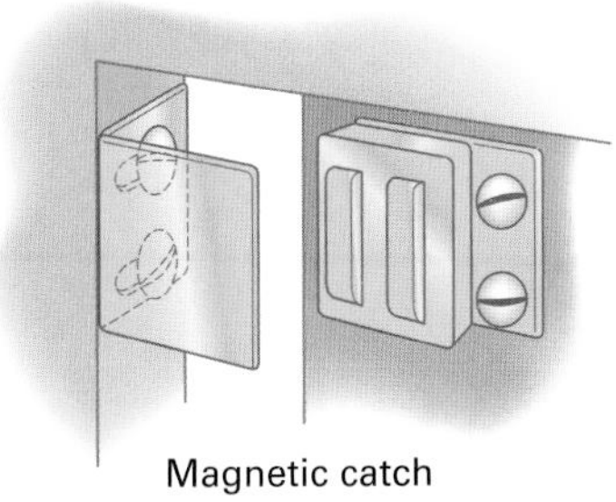

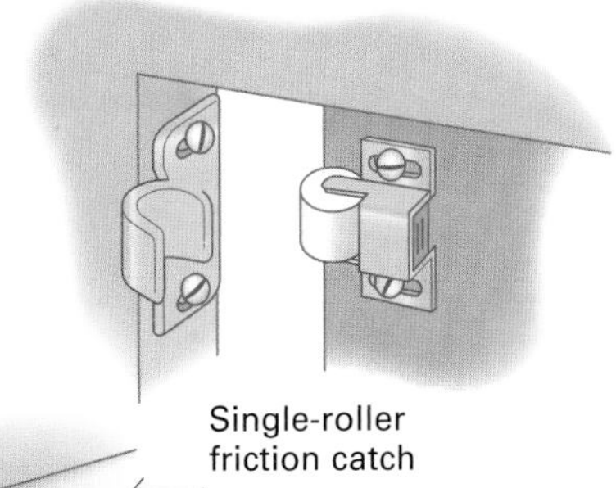

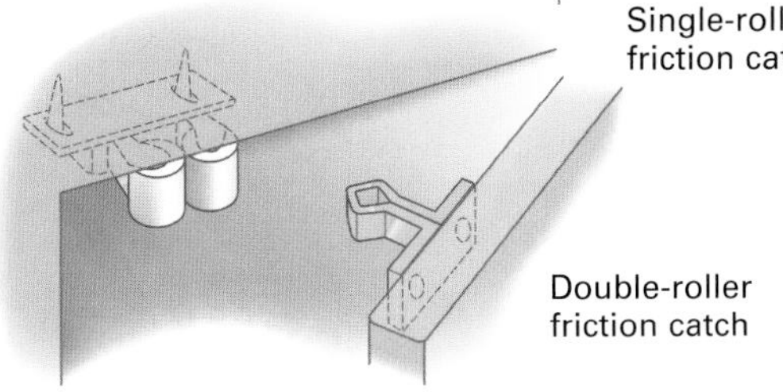

If a catch doesn't grab well, adjust the component on the cabinet outward. If a spring-action catch is misaligned, try bending the strike. You can adjust the door component of a single-roller catch so that it grabs more or less tightly.

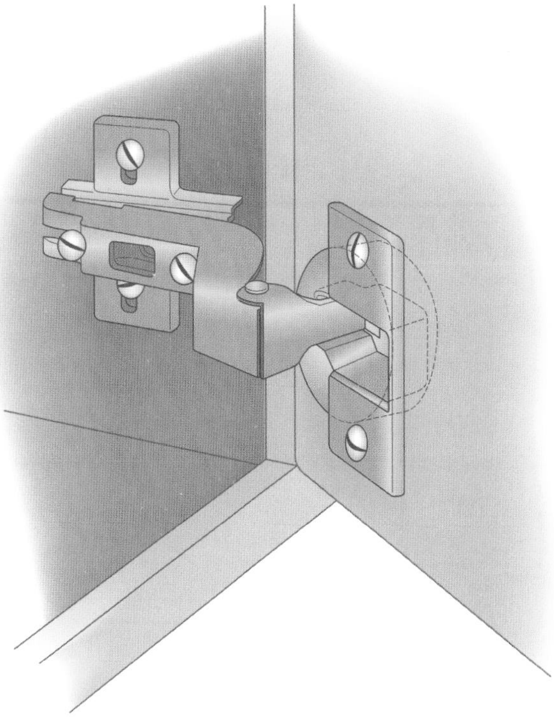

Micro-adjustments in door alignment are easy to make if your hinge is adaptable like this Euro-style model. While pricey, these long-lasting hinges ensure a precise fit.

PATCHING WALLS AND CEILINGS

Older homes usually have walls covered with lath and plaster, while most homes built since the 1960s use wallboard (*see pages 6–7*). Cracks in walls usually do not indicate a structural problem, unless they are very wide. (Sagging floors are a more reliable indicator of this.) If a crack grows noticeably in a year, call in a pro. See page 87 for taping and sanding techniques for all these repairs.

POPPED NAILS

If nail heads emerge from the wall, they may not have been driven in far enough. Test by pushing on the surrounding wall. If it pushes in, just pound in the nails.

Nails often pop out because they are not firmly attached to a stud. They may have just caught the edge of the stud, or perhaps they missed altogether. If they feel loose, pull them out with pliers and drive a new nail or screw into the stud.

WALLBOARD

Don't be surprised if kids' "rough-housing" someday dents or even pokes a hole through a wall. Wallboard will last many decades if not abused, but it is not strong.

PEELING TAPE: Wallboard joints are covered with paper or mesh tape and then mudded over with joint compound (*see page 87*). If paper tape is peeling off, cut it out with a knife (cut a bit more than is actually peeling). Press in mesh tape, and cover over with two or more layers of joint compound.

CRACK: The most common location for a crack is above a door, but it can occur wherever the structure shifts. Sand down or cut away any joint compound or paper that is protruding above the surface. Apply mesh tape over the crack, and cover with several coats of joint compound. Sand smooth.

SMALL HOLE: Use a framing square and knife to score a rectangular area around the hole; cut through the paper. Use a drywall saw or keyhole saw to cut out the rectangle, but do not go outside the scored line. If paper is ripped on the surrounding wall, cut it out.

Cut a piece of plywood about 6 inches longer than the width of the hole and no more than 4 inches narrower than the hole's height. Slip the piece in behind the hole and hold it firmly as you drive 1¼-inch screws through the wallboard and the plywood. Keep driving the screws until the plywood is snug against the back of the wallboard, but don't drive the screw heads so deep that they break the paper.

Patch damaged wallboard by first cutting a replacement piece. Then trace around the piece, cut the wall, and add a piece of plywood or scraps of 2×2 as nailers.

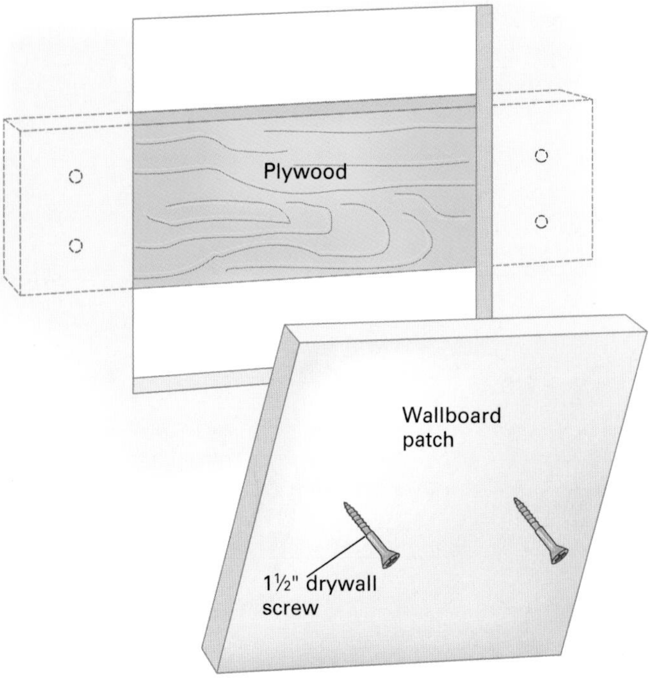

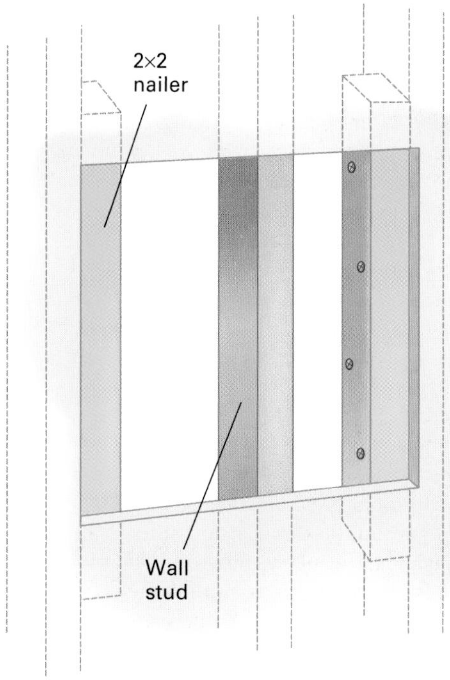

Cut a wallboard patch to fit, install it with $1\frac{1}{4}$-inch drywall screws, apply mesh tape to the joints, and then apply several coats of the joint compound.

LARGE HOLE: Cut out a larger area up to the studs on each side. Use a framing square and long straightedge to make a rectangular hole. Once you reach the sides, use the stud as a guide for your saw to cut straight vertical lines.

Cut two pieces of 2×4 or 2×2 that are several inches longer than the height of the hole. Slip them in and hold them tight against the back of the wallboard as you drive 3-inch drywall screws through these cleats and into the studs. Cut a patch, install with screws, apply mesh tape, and cover with several layers of joint compound.

PLASTER

Push against the wall surrounding a damaged area. If it feels spongy, remove the loose plaster. If a large portion of a wall or ceiling is cracked or weak, you should "skin over" with $\frac{1}{4}$-inch wallboard for walls and $\frac{1}{2}$-inch wallboard for ceilings. Remove moldings first, and install thin pieces of wood along the edges of jambs to compensate for the wall's extra thickness.

CRACK: Use a utility knife or the sharp point of an old-fashioned can opener (church key) to widen the crack. "Key" it so the back of the channel is wider than the front. Use a taping knife to fill the crack with joint compound, then apply mesh tape over the crack's length. Apply several layers of joint compound, feathering the edges out farther with each coat. Sand smooth.

HOLE: Cutting out a neat section of plaster with square corners is difficult because plaster is so hard and so securely stuck to the lath. Scoring a line with a knife may help, but probably won't. Use a hammer to chop out the inner portion of the damaged area. Remove only the plaster, not the lath. Then pry carefully along the perimeter so you don't crack the surrounding area. If the resulting hole is not rectangular, so be it. Measure the thickness of your plaster, and buy wallboard that is no thicker. Often, $\frac{3}{8}$-inch wallboard is the right thickness. Cut a patch to fit, but don't expect a tight fit. Fill gaps with joint compound. This will be easier if you mix perlited gypsum with dry-mix compound (*see box at left*). When that has dried, apply mesh tape to the perimeter, and follow with several coats of joint compound. Sand smooth.

PATCHING A CRACK

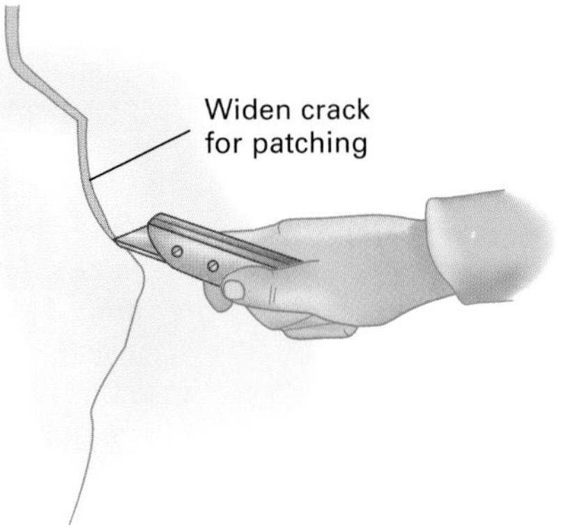

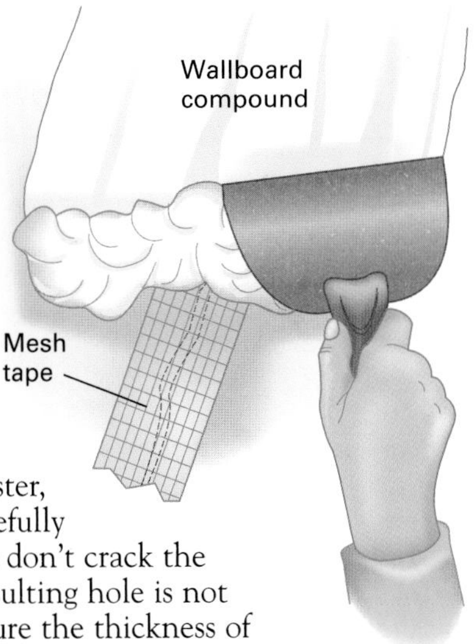

PATCHING A HOLE

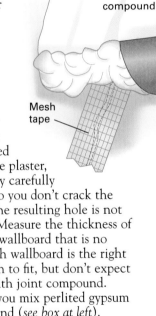

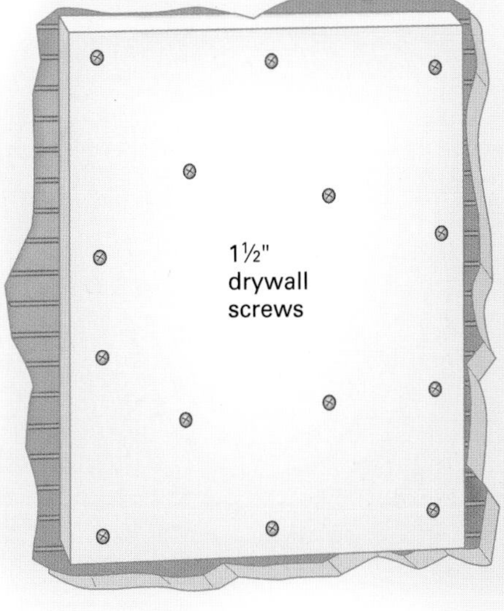

PATCHING MATERIALS

For small areas that do not need a lot of strength, vinyl spackling will do the job. It retains a bit of flexibility and is very easy to sand, but it is soft.

Ready-mixed joint compound in 1- and 5-gallon buckets is a bit harder but less flexible than spackling compound and is just as easy to use. The "lightweight" type is easy to sand but is soft. Dry-mix joint compound offers greater strength. You must mix it yourself and apply it promptly. There are usually three options, "90," "45," and "20." The numbers give a general idea of how many minutes before the material starts to harden.

Even the quick-hardening type will usually take most of a day before it is dry enough to sand. This material is difficult to sand. If you use dry-mix for the first coat and ready-mix for the top coats, you will have both strength and easy sanding.

To patch wide areas on a plaster wall, mix joint compound in equal amounts with perlited gypsum plaster, which comes in very large bags. The resulting mixture will be very resistant to sagging—a problem when filling in areas larger than $\frac{1}{2}$ inch wide.

Framing a new wall is a gratifying experience. If you plan carefully, taking into account door and window openings and providing nailing surfaces for the wallboard, you will be pleasantly surprised at how quickly the wall framing goes up.

Carpentry Projects

Once you've gained some basic skills, done a few repairs, and collected a workable set of tools, you may feel ready to tackle a building project or two. A successful home carpentry job will give you something to be proud of at a very reasonable price while you may add substantial value to your home.

Sometimes home projects get out of hand. Who needs added frustration and domestic discord? Well, it doesn't have to come to that. By assessing your limits and planning ahead, you can minimize disruption to your home and family.

Think carefully before taking the plunge. How much time can you realistically devote to the project? If you come home from work tired and weekends are usually full of activities, avoid large remodeling jobs. Be realistic: Make your best estimate of how long a project will take and then multiply by two or three.

And think about how the job will influence your home life. A basement project can go on for months without bothering the household, but a kitchen remodel will quickly get in everyone's way.

Prepare for a mess. Dust from demolition and construction is amazingly pervasive, working its way through the smallest cracks and into living areas. If you can seal the area off and use a separate doorway, you will lessen the effect.

Finally, be realistic about your abilities. Many homeowners start large jobs full of great expectations, only to get mired in months of struggling. The best way to test your mettle is to take on progressively larger jobs.

In This Chapter

Safety on the Job

Once your home becomes a work site, take the same precautions that safety officials would require if you were a union carpenter.

- Define the work area clearly, and take steps to keep small children away unless closely supervised by an adult.
- Keep the floor clear because people concentrating on work will not pay attention to what is underfoot.
- Take special care with nail-embedded lumber. Remove nails or throw away the pieces without delay.
- Prevent saw kickback by properly supporting boards to be cut (*see page* 19).
- Provide a worktable or set of sawhorses for convenience when cutting as well as for safety.
- Wear eye protection when using power tools or doing demolition. Wear a dust mask when sanding or using toxic liquids.
- Long sleeves can get caught in power saw blades unless they are tightly buttoned.
- Rolled-up sleeves are even more dangerous because they can quickly roll down, loose and unnoticed.
- Unplug saws and other power tools before changing blades or bits.
- Don't power saw with your fingers 3 inches or closer to the blade. Use push sticks or choose a longer board.
- Set up a system for plugging in power tools. Tangled cords and wet cables are dangerous.
- Stop work when you're tired or frustrated.

MOLDINGS

Most rooms have at least two types of molding: casing around doors and windows, and base molding where the wall meets the floor. Once you master the techniques for installing these two types, you'll have the skills necessary for installing other types. For crown molding at the ceiling, see page 66; for other molding options, see page 13.

Avoid overnailing. Use only as many nails as needed to hold the molding flat against the adjoining surface. Apply stain or a primer coat of paint before installing; then apply polyurethane finish or the topcoat of paint once the molding is installed.

CASING

CASING STYLES

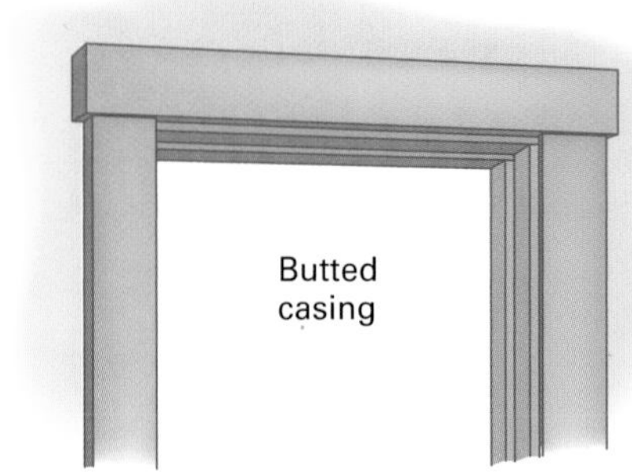

Choose a casing style. Mitered corners are the most common, but classic butted and blocked styles are easier to install.

PREPARE THE FIT: For casing to fit without noticeable gaps, the wall must be flat and the edge of the jamb must be flush with it. Sometimes the wall bulges near an upper corner because of built-up wallboard compound. Sand it down as much as possible. If the jamb protrudes from the plane of the wall, sand or plane it down. If it does not come out far enough, compress the wallboard near it by pounding with a block of wood, but take care not to dent the wall. Locate the studs.

SCRIBE AND CUT: Decide how much of the jamb edge you want revealed; ¼ inch is common. Mark the jamb edge with a compass set to ¼ inch. Run the compass along all three jamb edges, scribing a light line. Use this line as a guide for positioning the casing.

INSTALLING DOOR CASING

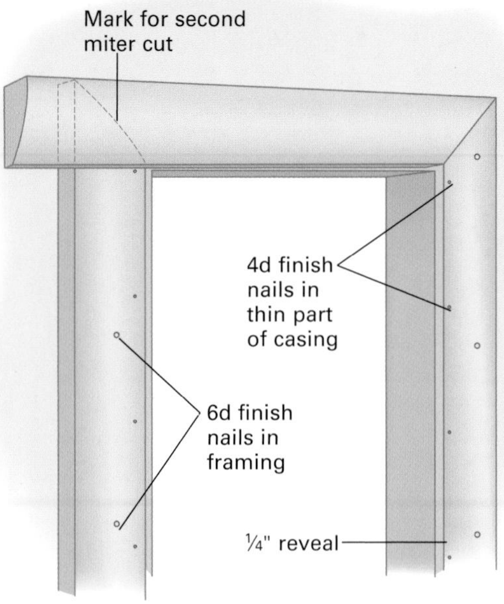

For each side piece, hold the board against the wall and jamb edge with one end resting on the floor. Use a sharp pencil or a knife to mark the point where the inside edge of the casing meets the scribe line on the top jamb.

Cut with a miter box and backsaw, or a power miter box. Be sure to cut to the right side of the mark, and hold the casing tight so it does not move while you cut.

THE TOP PIECE: Install the side pieces temporarily by tacking (partially driving) several nails in each so they are held flat against the wall.

If you are mitering the corners, cut one end of the top piece to 45 degrees. Hold the piece in place, and check to see that the miter matches up with the side piece miter. If they aren't, fudge the joints (*see box, opposite*). Mark the other end for its miter cut.

Cut the final miter, and set the top piece in place. You may need to adjust one of the side pieces to make both miter joints fit tightly. Lightly sand off any shredded wood fibers that protrude.

Drive 6d or 8d nails through the outer part of the casing into wall studs, and use 3d or 4d nails to attach to the jamb. If your molding is very thin on the inside edge, drill pilot holes to prevent splitting.

BASE MOLDING

Install casing first, then butt base molding to it. A more contemporary arrangement combines Colonial or ranch base molding with base shoe, which is like quarter-round except that the bottom edge is not as long as the edge that faces the wall. Older three-piece moldings add a decorative piece above the base, which is handy for hiding telephone and TV cables.

ATTACHING THE PIECES: Before installing base molding, drive test nails into the wall to find where the bottom plate and the studs are. When attaching the base shoe, do not drive nails down into a hardwood floor; the floor needs room to expand and contract with changing humidity.

BUTTED JOINTS: If a piece butts against a wall or casing at both ends, cut it a bit long, so you have to bend it slightly to fit it in. If a wall is too long for a single piece of molding, bevel-cut the ends of each butted piece for a more finished appearance than a simple butted joint will give. Where two pieces of molding join, cope-cut one of the pieces *(right)* as detailed on page 26.

OUTSIDE MITERS: Outside corners are rarely perfectly square, so cutting both pieces to 45 degrees may produce a joint with gaps. Use a scrap of baseboard to scribe the intersection lines on the floor *(right)*. Cut the far end of one piece, and hold it in place. Draw a line on the back of the piece using the wall corner as a guide; also make a mark on the front bottom, at the mark on the floor. Remove the piece, and then draw a line on the bottom edge connecting the two lines. This will tell whether a 45-degree bevel will make a tight joint or if you need to adjust your saw slightly.

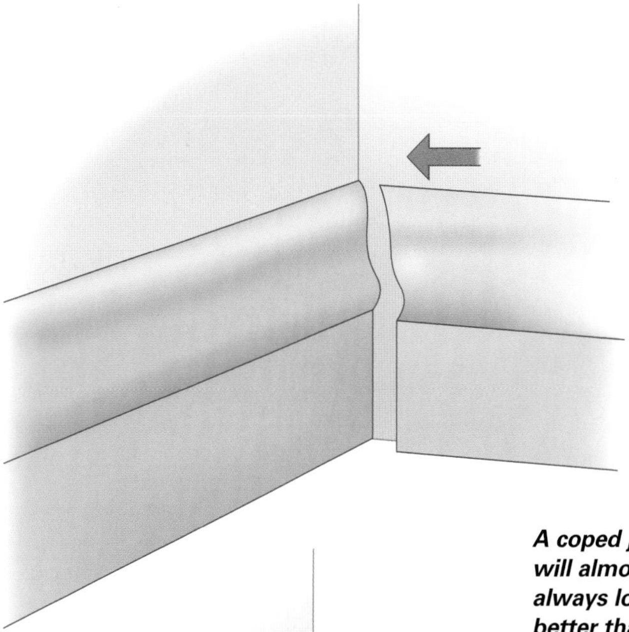

A coped joint will almost always look better than a joint made by bevel-cutting each piece at 45 degrees.

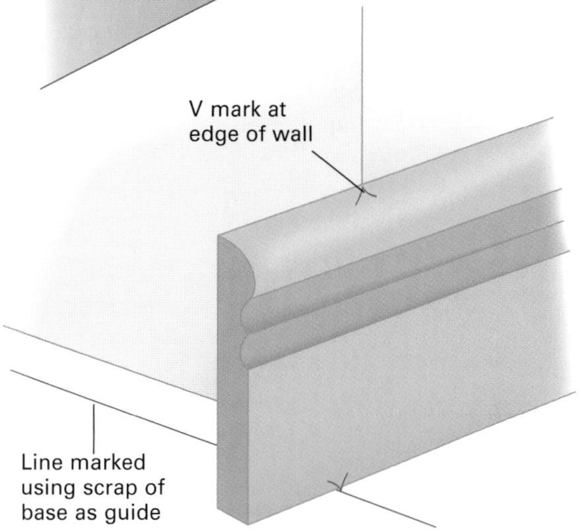

FUDGING JOINTS TO FIT TIGHTLY

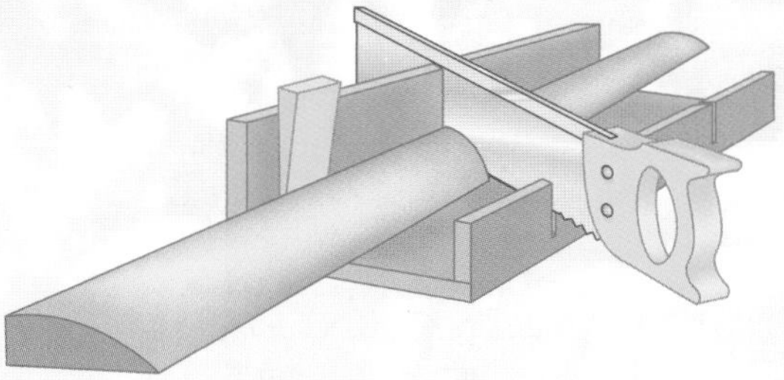

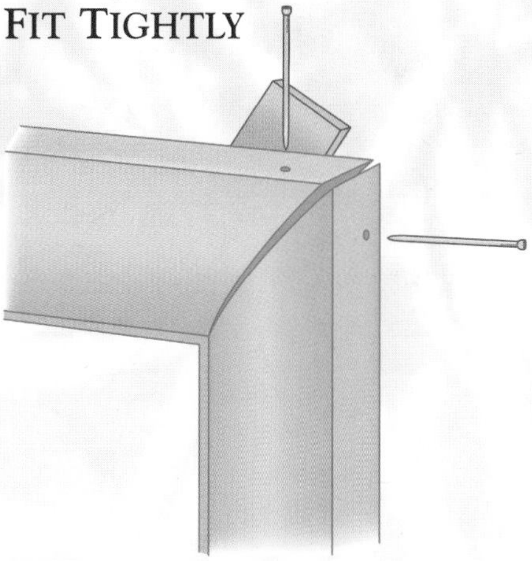

If a corner is not a true 90-degree angle, cut at least one of the pieces to an odd angle. To make a cut slightly greater or less than 45 degrees, insert a shim between the side of the miter box and the molding, then cut. You may have to experiment.

Often the wall and the jamb edge are not flush with each other. To compensate for this, shim out the two pieces at the corner to tighten the joint. Then drill pilot holes and drive finishing nails in both directions to hold the joint.

CROWN MOLDING

Once you've been initiated by installing standard moldings, you may be ready for one of the more demanding finish-carpentry tasks: installing crown molding. Crown molding is difficult to install because it is a wide molding, likely to show off your errors. Because you will place it inverted along the ceiling, you'll find it very hard to visualize its placement, so you can make the right cuts. To avoid having to buy extra pieces of this expensive material to replace your mistakes, think through each cut, measure twice, and allow plenty of time for this project. Plan the job so that you won't have to cope-cut both ends of any board.

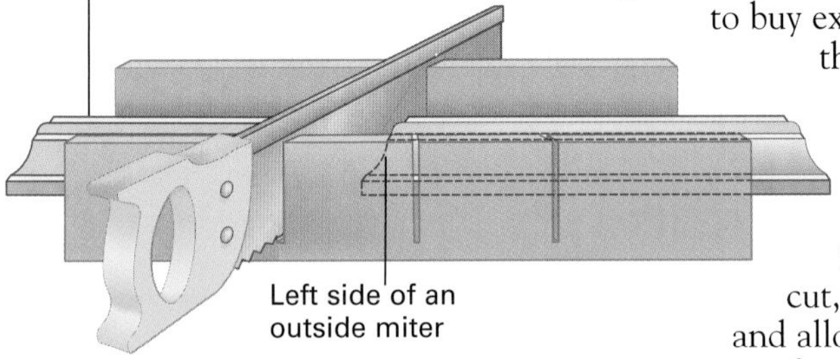

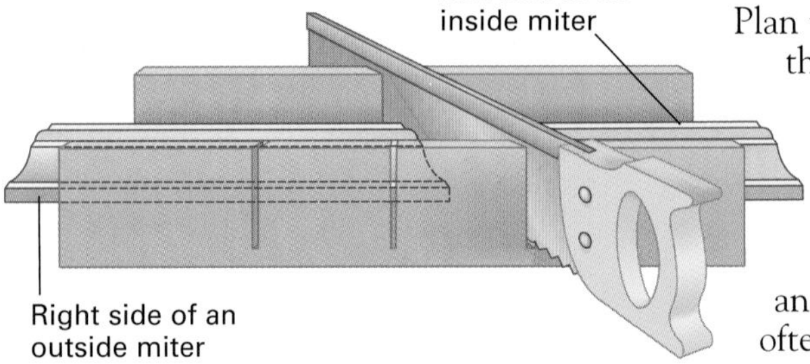

Cutting crown molding miters takes concentration; it is difficult to picture how the miters will fit overhead. As you cut the miters, make sure your work is properly positioned for the cut you want.

Because walls and ceilings are often out of square, test miter and coped joints by cutting scrap pieces first.

BUTTED PIECES AND OUTSIDE MITERS: Cut the first piece straight at each end, and tack it in place along the ceiling. If the room has an outside corner, install those two pieces first, with straight cuts at each end. You will probably need to experiment with scrap pieces before you find the precise angle for the miter cuts.

COPED JOINTS: To make a coped joint, miter-cut the next piece, then cut away the back side of the cut profile with a coping saw.

It takes some concentration to make the miter cut in the right direction. Place the molding upside-down in the miter box, as if the back of the box were the wall. Consult the illustrations to be sure. If possible, use a piece that is longer than needed so that if you make a mistake, you can try again.

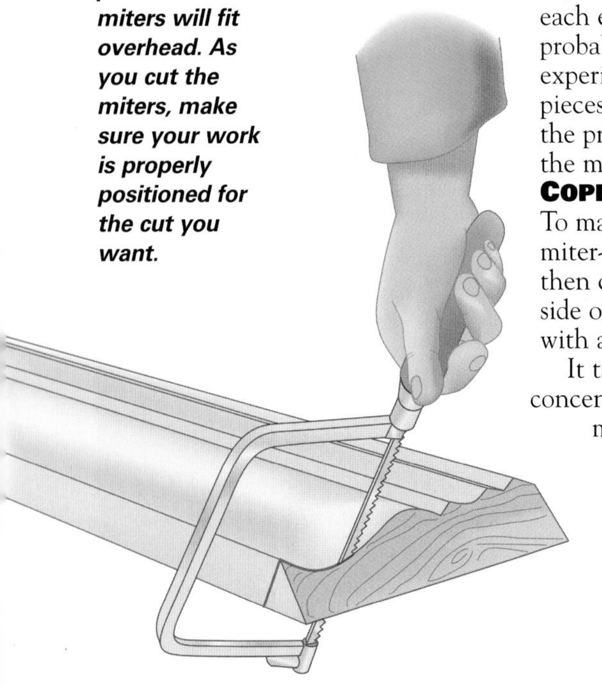

To cope with walls that aren't perfectly square at the corners, you just have to, well, cope. By back-cutting a mitered cut with a coping saw, you effectively notch the crown molding to fit over the butt-cut piece it meets. The result is a tight joint.

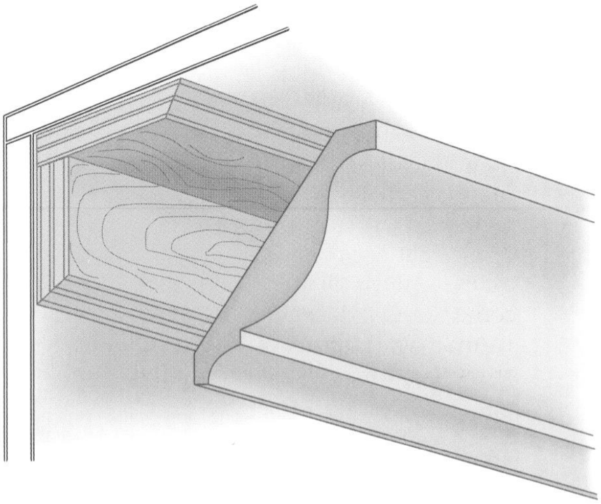

Part of the challenge of placing crown molding is positioning evenly so that the upper and lower edges are flat against the wall. In addition, framing members are often hard to reach or are too widely spaced. This backer of bevel-cut plywood solves both problems.

Don't be surprised if you have to make minor adjustments in your cuts. Take your time; working above your head can be tiring.

Usually, crown molding can be simply nailed into ceiling joists and wall studs. But if the wall or ceiling has waves, or if it is difficult to reach framing members, install bevel-cut strips of plywood for use as backing, as shown *above*.

WHICH SIDE IS UP?: Crown molding often has a profile that makes it difficult to tell the top from the bottom. The general rule is that the more complicated portion—the side with more lines—goes on the bottom, and the side with a simple curve goes up against the ceiling (*see illustration above*).

However, putting it the "right" way is not as important as being consistent. If you prefer the way it looks when it is upside down, then that's right-side-up for you.

INSTALLING CABINETS

A home center or cabinet outlet will help you design a kitchen and choose an ensemble of base cabinets, wall cabinets, and filler pieces that use every available inch of space. They can print out drawings of what your kitchen will look like from several perspectives. Standard base cabinets are 24 inches deep and 34½ inches high; wall cabinets are 12 inches deep and 12–42 inches tall. In addition to basic cabinets, most kitchens need a sink base, a corner base, a drawer base, a 12-inch or 15-inch wall cabinet above the range hood or refrigerator, and a corner wall cabinet.

PREPARATION

A *soffit* brings the wall outward above the wall cabinets, almost flush with the cabinet's frame. Soffits eliminate storage above the cabinets, but many people prefer not to have to clean up there anyway. Build a soffit with 2×2 or 2×4 framing so its finished edge will be 12½ inches out from the wall. Make sure its bottom edge is perfectly level. Cover it with finished wallboard before installing cabinets.

Remove the old cabinets and any obstructions. Use a level and a straight board to find the highest spot on your floor, and start your measurements there. Draw plumb and level lines showing the position of every base and wall cabinet.

The top of the countertop will be 36 inches from the floor. Put the bottom of the wall cabinets 54 inches from the floor.

Draw outlines on the floor, as well, to get an idea of traffic patterns in the room. You may even decide to move things around a few inches.

Decide on the locations of electrical receptacles and switches. Be sure to have enough circuits so you won't blow fuses when several appliances are running. Wire for fluorescent under-cabinet lights, or put in low-voltage halogen light fixtures after the cabinets are installed. You may need to cut a vent hole leading to the outside for your range hood duct.

Hire an electrician and plumber unless you feel up to the task of roughing in. If you have a lot of rough-in lines to run, you will probably eliminate problems later by removing the wallboard or plaster from at least some of the walls. Patch or replace wallboard after the rough plumbing and electrical wires are installed, and apply at least a primer coat of paint. There is no need to smooth or paint areas that you will cover by cabinets. Redraw your cabinet layout lines.

If you liked your old kitchen layout, you can just remove the cabinets and replace them with new ones of the same size. However, you will probably want to move some things around. Plumbing is difficult to move, but it's worth the trouble if it improves your kitchen.

It's easier to install a new floor before installing the cabinets; cover the floor with construction (rosin) paper so you won't damage it during construction.

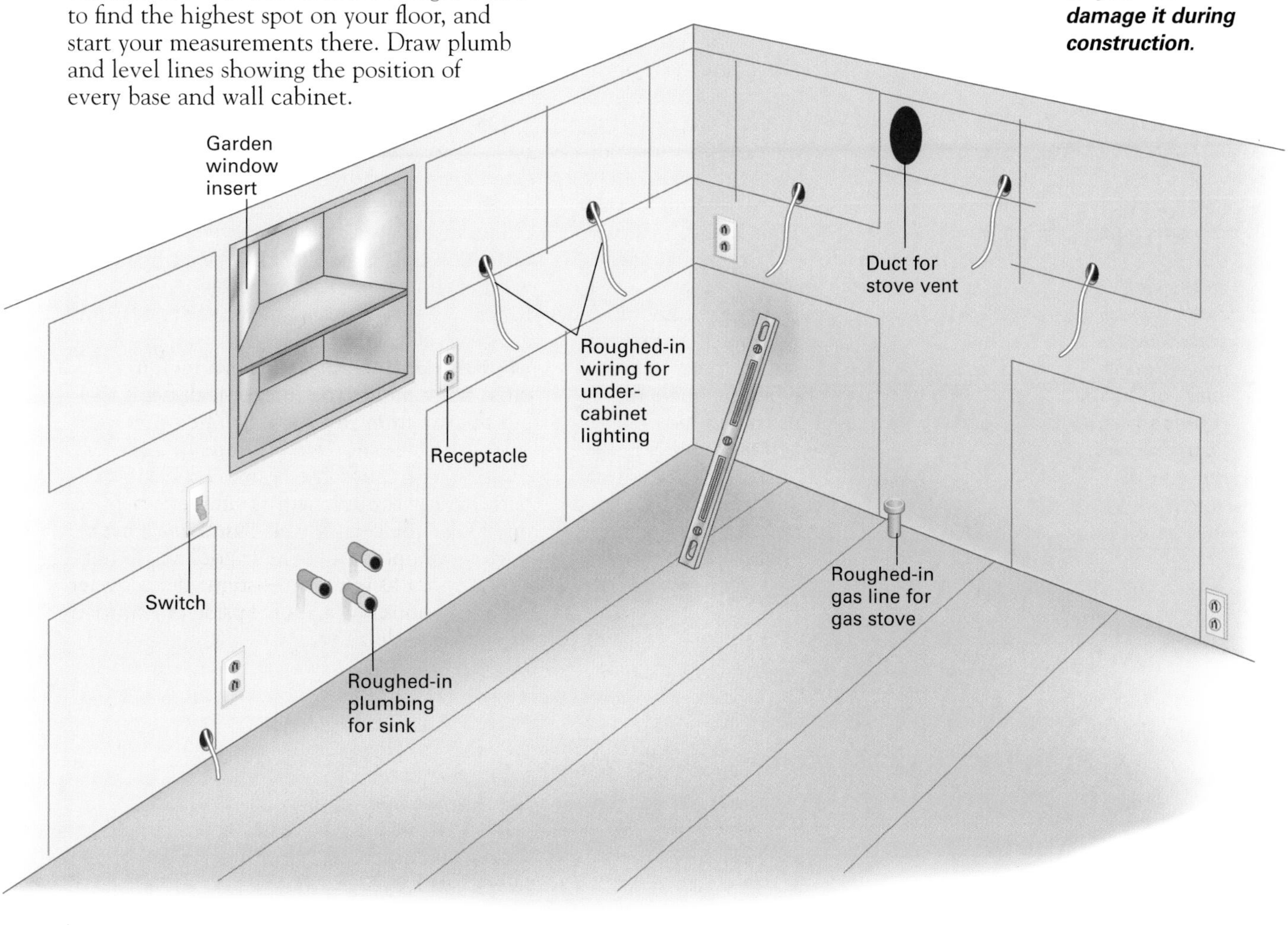

INSTALLING CABINETS

continued

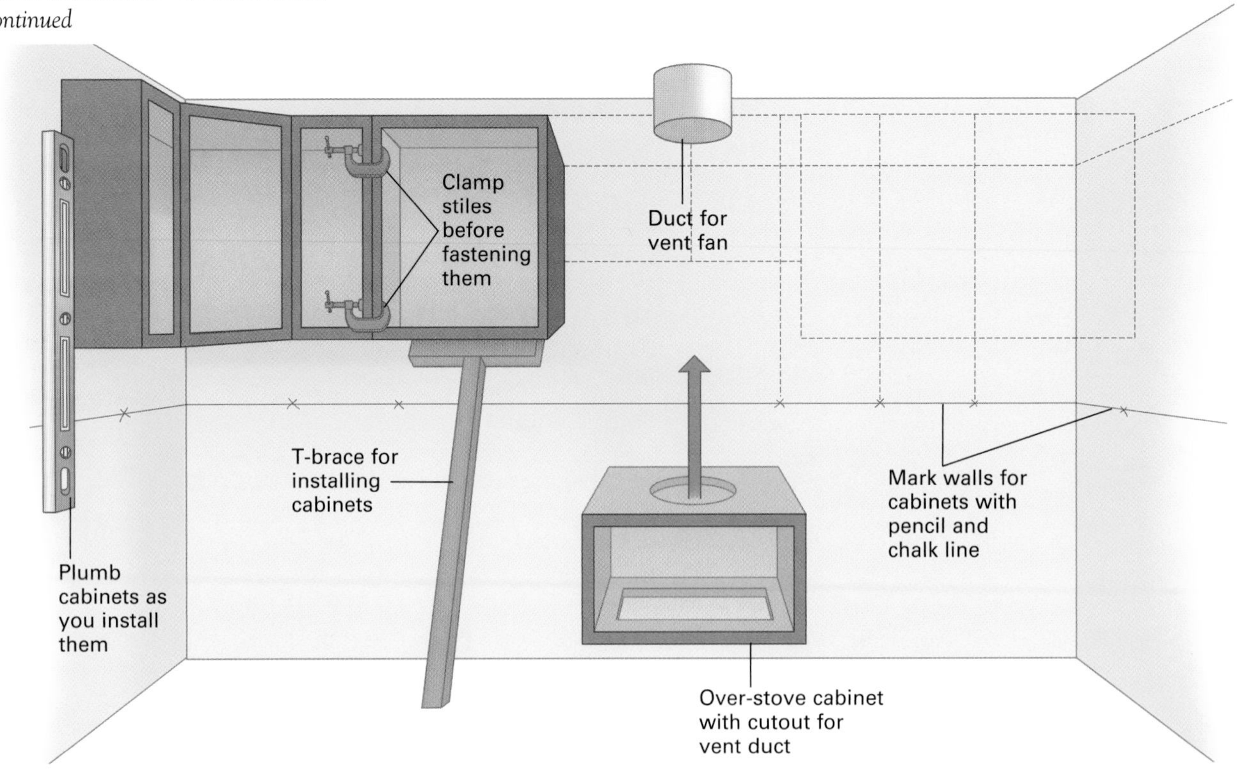

Lay out your cabinets carefully. Check them for plumb and level as you brace and clamp them before fastening.

Keep base cabinets level; otherwise, the countertop may be hard to install. Use shims and spacers to compensate for imperfections in the walls.

WALL CABINETS

If your plan calls for cabinets to turn a corner, install the corner cabinet first. Otherwise, begin with the one that goes against a wall where you will not install a filler piece.

Some frameless cabinets are attached to the wall with a metal support rail; fasten it to the wall and hang the cabinets on it. Most cabinets attach to the wall simply by driving screws through them and into studs.

INSPECTION: Examine all of the cabinets for defects. After they've been installed, you may not be allowed to return them.

Mark the location of studs with erasable lines that will be visible above and below the cabinets. Use screws with finished-looking heads that will not sink into the cabinets; manufacturers often supply these. Drive screws in places where they will not be clearly visible.

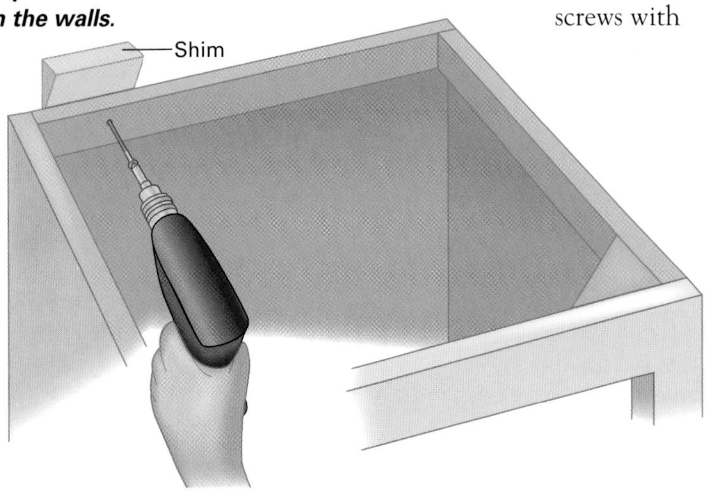

Remove the shelves, if possible; this will make the cabinets lighter and easier to handle. Start several screws, driving them in just enough to stay put. Be sure they hit the center of the studs.

SQUARE START: With a helper, lift the cabinet into place, and drive two screws. Make sure the cabinet is perfectly plumb and level; any slight error here will be magnified as you install the other cabinets. You may need to loosen the screws and tap shims behind the cabinet to achieve plumb.

To attach the next cabinet, lift it into place, support it with a brace, and clamp it perfectly flush with the first cabinet. Drill pilot holes through the side, and drive two or three screws to join the cabinets together. Don't drill all the way through both frame pieces. Use screws that are not long enough to poke through. Drive screws through the back of the cabinet to attach it to the wall.

SPACER: If the last cabinet is close to a wall, you will need a spacer, a stile-like piece finished like the cabinets. Clamp the last cabinet in place and measure for the spacer. Measure in four places because the wall might wave a bit. Take the cabinet down, attach the spacer to it by drilling pilot holes and driving screws, and then install the cabinet.

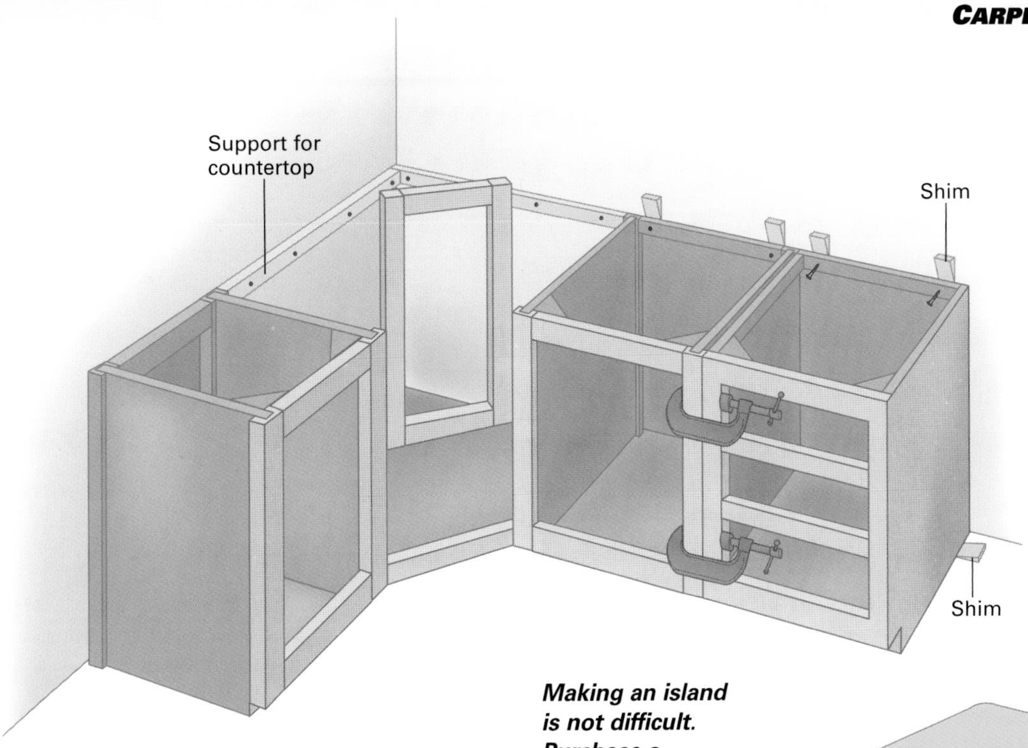

Money was saved in this example by using wall cleats and a base made of 2×4s and plywood for the corner cabinet. Only the door and its frame had to be bought. A more expensive corner cabinet could include a lazy Susan.

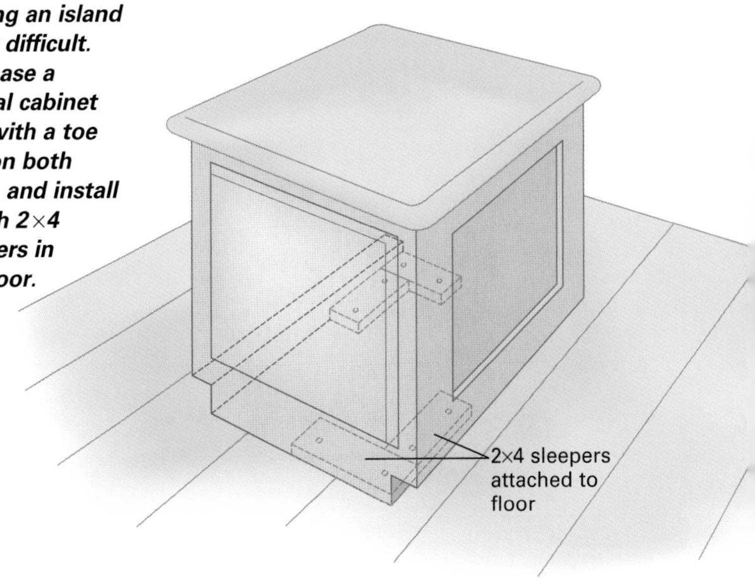

Making an island is not difficult. Purchase a special cabinet unit with a toe kick on both sides, and install it with 2×4 sleepers in the floor.

BASE CABINETS

Start with a cabinet at the floor's highest point. If it is not in a corner or up against a wall where you will not put a filler piece, shim it and attach it to other base cabinets until you reach the wall, and then attach all the cabinets to the wall at once.

Check base cabinets for level in both directions. Use shims at the wall and floor where needed; don't depend on screws to hold any part of a base cabinet off the floor. Recheck for level after attaching because screws can pull a cabinet out of level.

Clamp and then screw base cabinets together as you did with the wall cabinets. To join base cabinets together at the back or in the middle, you may need to insert a spacer.

ACCESS: At the sink base, you will need to cut holes for plumbing and possibly for an electrical receptacle (for the garbage disposal). Measure to the center of each round hole, and drill with a hole saw that is slightly larger than the pipe needed. Although these will not be clearly visible, do this carefully so you can cover the holes neatly with pipe flanges, to keep mice out.

APPLIANCES: Draw a level line on the wall where the range will be installed between base cabinets, and follow it closely so the countertops will be aligned on both sides.

Finish with a filler piece as you did with the wall cabinets. If a dishwasher will be at the end of a run, install a panel made by the cabinet manufacturer. Anchor the panel firmly to the wall with angle brackets; it will be attached at the top to the countertop. If you have unsightly gaps where cabinets meet the floor, install vinyl cove base molding.

COUNTERTOPS

Because walls usually have some waves in them and often are out of square, it is usually worth the extra money to pay a countertop company to install the countertop of your choice. They will make a cardboard template and then return with a top that fits snugly.

If your walls are not out of square and are fairly straight, you can save money by buying a laminated postform countertop (with a curved front edge and back splash) from a home center. Color selection will be limited. Buy a single top to cover the whole area; making your own splice is very difficult.

If the countertop does not meet all along the wall, set it in place, and use a pencil to scribe a line where the top of the back-splash meets the wall. Use a belt sander to remove material along the scribe line.

You can laminate your own square-edged countertop with particleboard, contact cement, and plastic laminate. However, it's very easy to make irreparable mistakes, and it might not save you money.

SHELVES

Building shelves is a good first carpentry project. Even the simplest systems call for several basic concepts and skills: keeping things level and plumb, using the correct-size lumber, measuring and cutting for tight fits, finding and attaching to studs, and fastening securely.

ADJUSTABLE UNITS

If you will be loading the shelves with books or other heavy items, don't use shelf spans that are too long to support the weight. Shelves made of 1×8 should be no longer than 24 inches between brackets; 1×10 or 1×12 shelf spans can be up to 32 inches long; 3/4-inch plywood can span 36 inches. You can increase usable spans by attaching 1×2s along the edges.

To make a basic shelf system, build a rectangular box. Cut the top and bottom pieces 1/4 inch longer than the width of the unit, and attach so that their ends overhang the side pieces by 1/8 inch. Attach a back made of 1/4-inch plywood; use two factory-cut sides of the plywood to square the unit as you fasten it.

If the unit uses 1-by lumber and is more than 4 feet tall, attach one fixed shelf somewhere near the middle to keep the sides from bowing out. Check the fixed shelf for square, and drive trim-head screws through the side pieces and into the shelf.

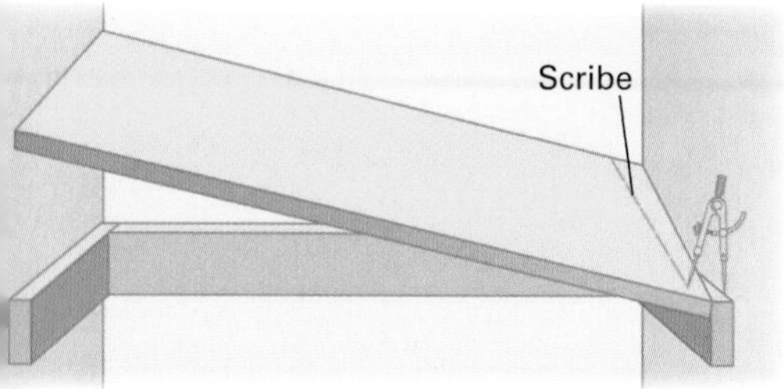

To fit a shelf in a space that is not square, cut the board 1 inch longer than needed, tip it into position, and scribe a cut line.

HOLES AND CLIPS OR DOWELS: Drill a series of parallel holes, 3/16 inch in diameter and 1/2 inch deep, down each side piece. Use a piece of perforated hardboard (pegboard), to ensure the holes are evenly spaced. Cut 1-inch lengths of 1/16-inch dowel as supports, and fit them into the holes. Or purchase metal clips made for the purpose.

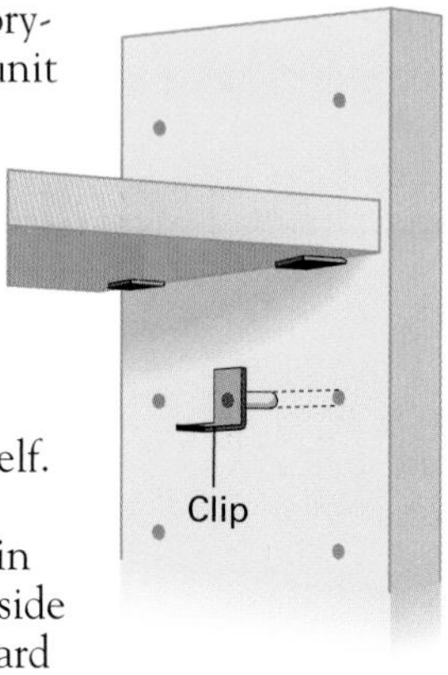

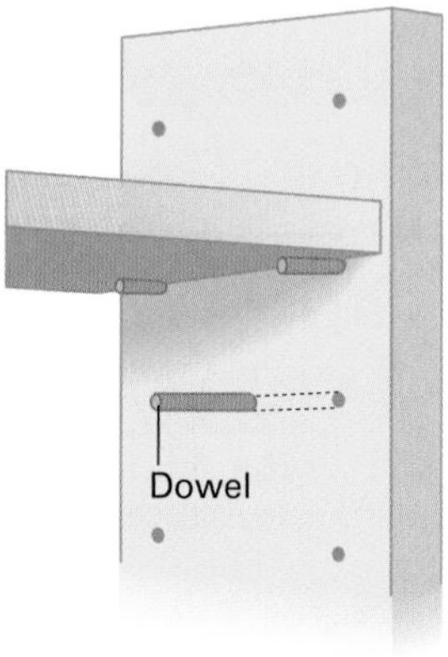

STANDARDS AND BRACKETS: These are commonly available and are easy to install. Simply fasten them to the surface with screws. Make sure all four standards are level so the slots all line up with each other. For a more finished look, cut grooves in the board for the standards to fit in. Special clips will snap into the slots.

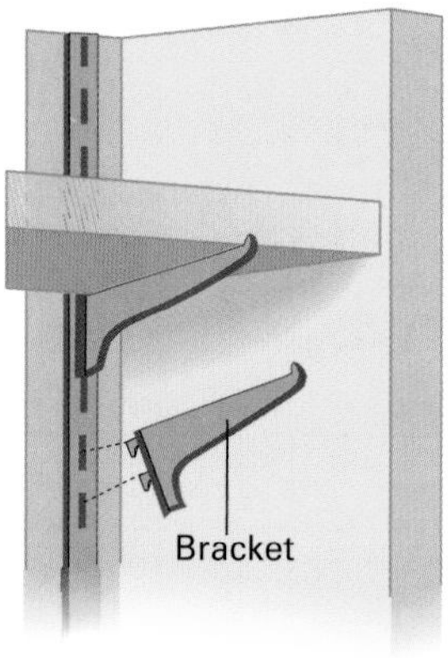

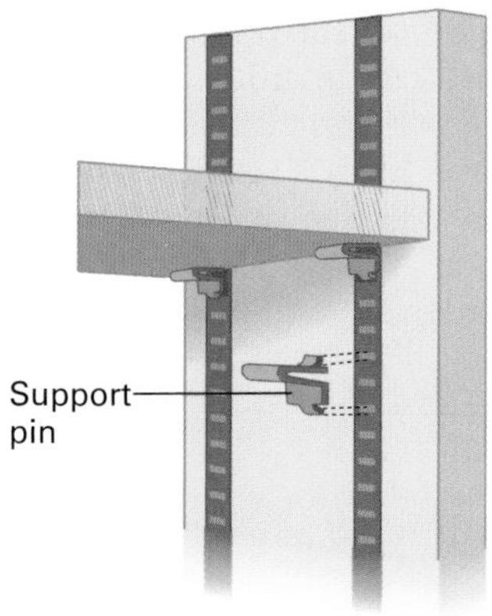

STANDARDS AND BRACKETS

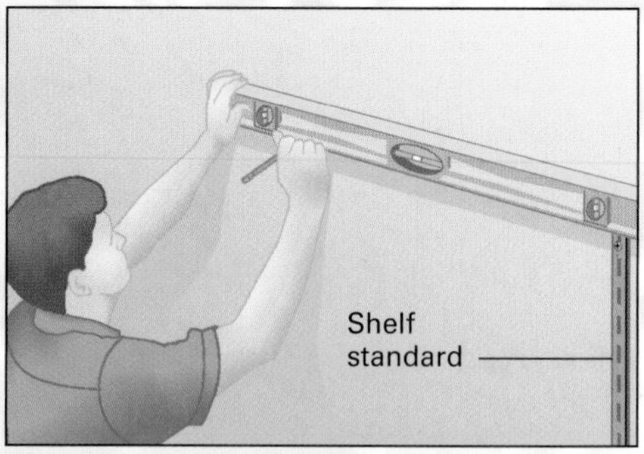

Use standards and brackets to attach shelves directly to walls. Attach the first standard so it is plumb, arrows pointing up, by driving screws into a stud. Use a level to mark for the height of the other standard, and attach it in the same way. If you need more than two standards, install the outer ones first, then use a straightedge to establish the heights of the inner ones. Choose brackets that are the right size for your shelving's width.

FIXED SHELVING

This is a very straightforward project, but it requires precise cuts and dadoes. Gaps of even 1/16 inch will look sloppy. Use boards that are very straight.

DADOES AND RABBETS: Cut the side pieces to length, and lay them side by side, with their ends perfectly aligned. Use a framing square to mark for dadoes in the middle and rabbets on the ends, all 3/4 inch wide. Cut the dadoes 3/8 inch deep, using a table saw or radial arm saw with a dado assembly (*see pages 24–25*).

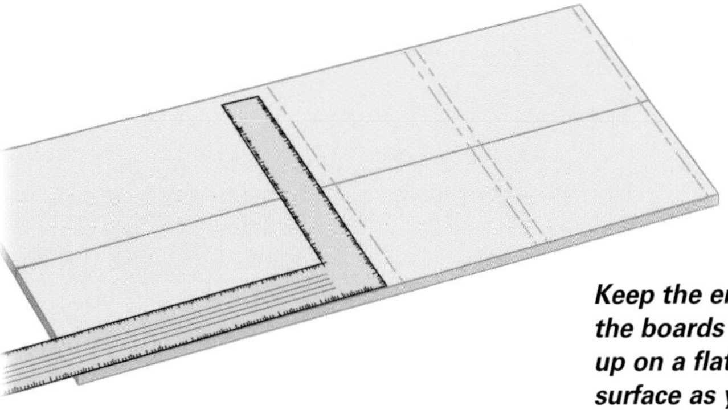

Keep the ends of the boards lined up on a flat work surface as you mark for dadoes.

You also can cut dadoes with a circular saw and a speed square. Practice on a scrap piece until you are familiar with the technique. Use a saw blade that makes clean cuts. Set the blade so it cuts 3/8 inch deep; check the depth by cutting a scrap. First, cut to the inside of each line; make these cuts precise. You may find it helps to first score the cut lines with a knife. Then make two or three cuts along the inside of the dado; these do not have to be precise. Clean out the middle with a chisel. Pry the pieces, then scrape the bottom of the dado with the chisel held bevel-side up. It's important to really clean it out; remove a little more than needed, to be sure.

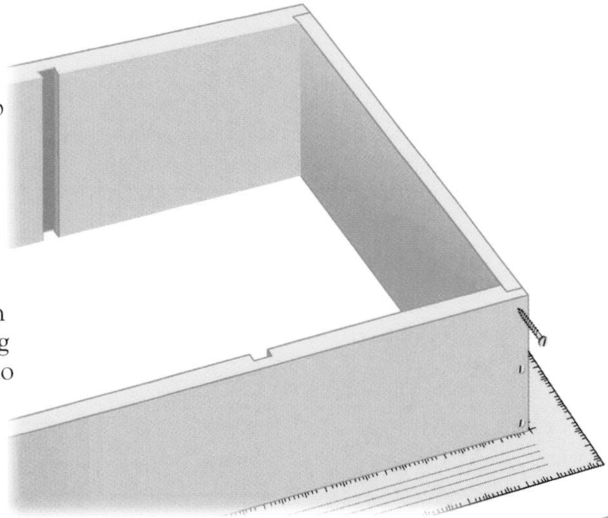

You may prefer to use finishing nails, which make a smaller hole. Adding wood glue will make a strong joint.

ASSEMBLE THE BOX: Cut the top and bottom pieces 3/4 inch shorter than the width of the unit. Set all four pieces on a worktable, and use a framing square to align them. Apply glue at each corner, drill two or three pilot holes, and drive trim-head screws. Check for square frequently as you assemble the box.

ADD SHELVES: Cut shelves to the same length as the top and bottom pieces. These pieces will fit snugly. Dry-fit them to make sure that they do not cause the side to bulge out; you may have to cut them slightly shorter, or chisel out the dadoes more thoroughly. Apply glue, then tap the shelves in with a hammer and a block of wood.

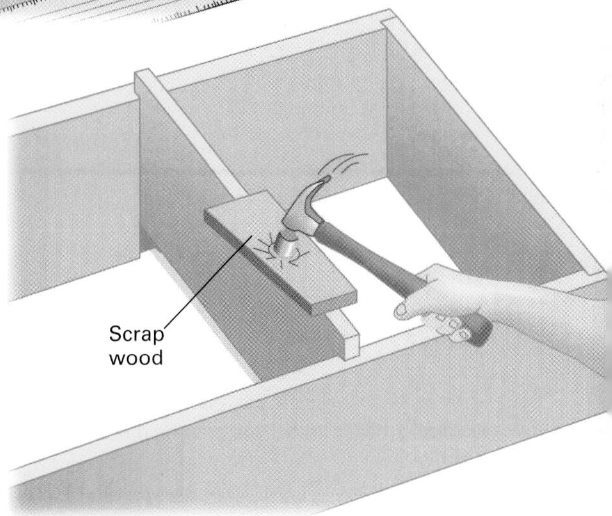

Tap the boards carefully, using a scrap as a pounding block so you will not create splinters as the shelves slide through tight dadoes.

ATTACH THE BACK: Cut a piece of 1/4-inch plywood 1/4 inch shorter all around the unit. Set the plywood on the back of the unit with a 1/8-inch gap all around. Fasten the back with small nails or 1 1/4-inch screws all around the perimeter. Drive one or two nails or screws into each shelf as well.

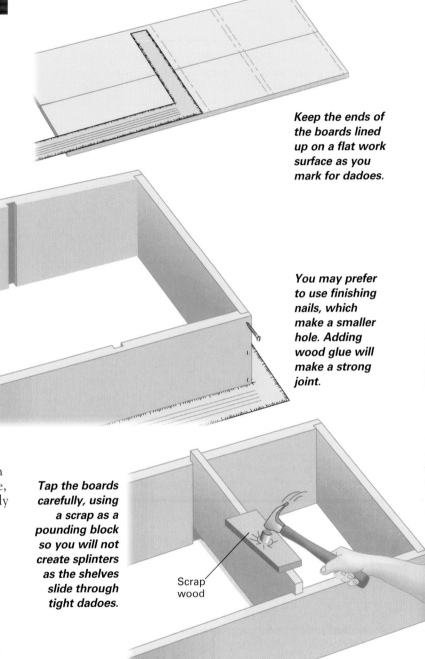

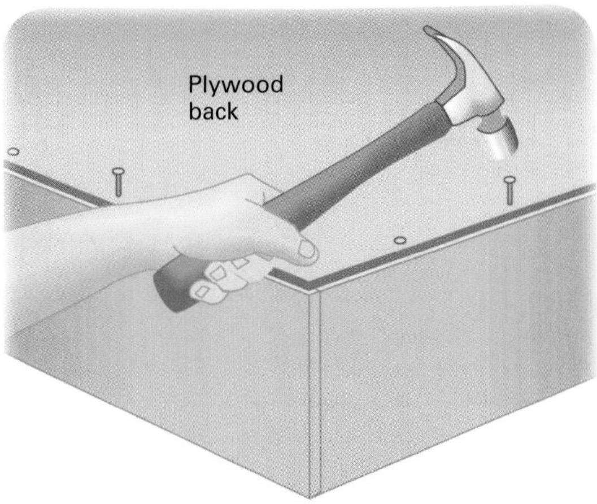

A plywood back ensures that the assembly will stay square and strong.

BUILDING A WALL

If you want to remove a wall and replace it with one in a different location, first find out whether the original wall is load bearing. Exterior walls, walls directly under an upstairs wall, and most walls that are perpendicular to the joists are load bearing; removing even part of them could damage your house's structure. Don't gamble on this; check with a pro to be sure.

LAYING OUT

Find out the *rough openings*—the size of opening in which they are designed to fit for doors and windows. For a door, this is usually 2 inches wider and taller than the size of the door itself. See the manufacturer's specs for windows; most catalogs will indicate rough opening dimensions.

LOCATE AND CUT PLATES: Use a framing square and chalk line to mark for both sides of the wall. Most walls use 2×4s, so the framing is $3\frac{1}{2}$ inches thick. Cut the top and bottom plates for the walls from long, straight boards. If you are building on a slab or a place that might get wet, use a pressure-treated board for the bottom plate. If the wall is too long for the plate to be one continuous piece, make the splice over the center of a stud, some multiple of 16 inches, minus $\frac{3}{4}$ inch, from the corner.

LAY OUT ON THE PLATES: Lay the plates next to each other so you can lay out on both pieces at once. Toenail the ends together with 8d nails so they will stay correctly aligned while you draw lines on them. Use a speed square to mark all of the lines.

Lay out door and window openings first. Mark the centerline, and draw a C through the line. Measure back half of the rough opening width on each side of the centerline; these lines show the inside of the trimmer (or jack) studs. On the outside of each line, draw a T to show the location of the trimmer stud, then make another line $1\frac{1}{2}$ inches over, and draw an X to indicate a floor-to-ceiling stud (sometimes called a "king" stud).

Now lay out for studs that are spaced 16 inches *on center*. (Wallboard and other sheet goods are sized in multiples of 16 inches wide and long, and they need to meet in the center of a stud.) Hook your tape measure to one end, and mark small Vs every 16 inches, minus $\frac{3}{4}$ inch ($15\frac{1}{4}$ inches, $31\frac{1}{4}$, $47\frac{1}{4}$, and so on). Mark through the Vs, using a speed square as a guide, and make an X for every full stud and a C for cripple studs—the short studs above and below openings.

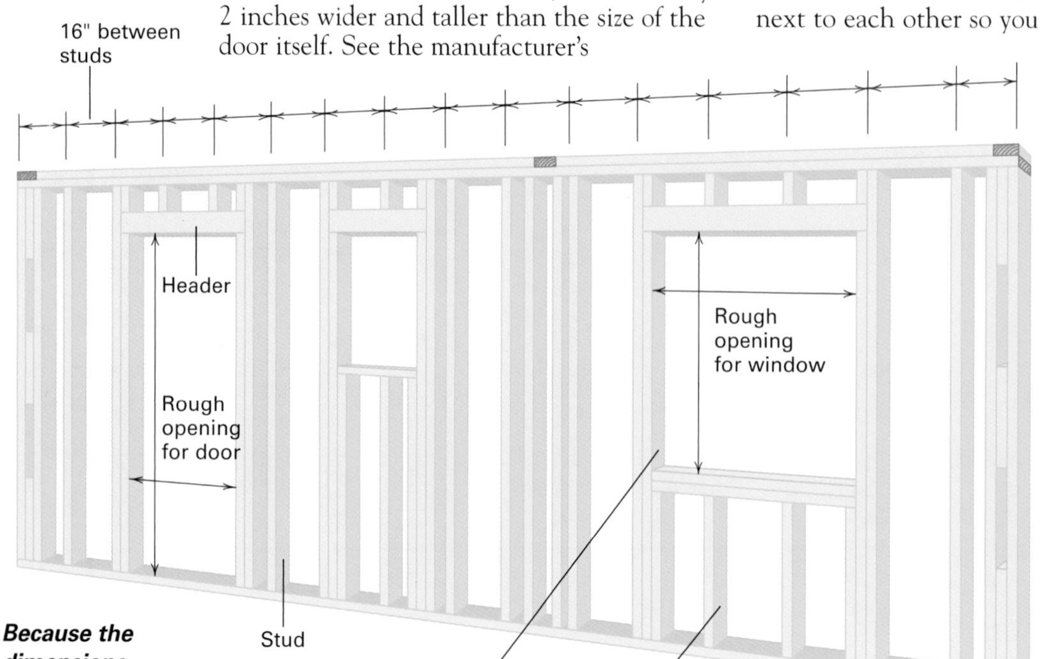

Because the dimensions of sheet goods are multiples of 16 inches, framing is laid out to match. That requires a 2×4 nailer every 16 inches. Frame doors and windows, allowing for jambs and shim space.

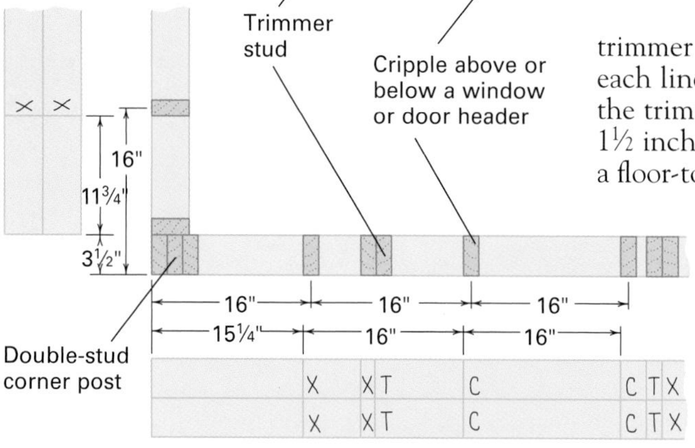

Two studs with blocking between them will provide nailing surface for the wallboard where these two new walls meet. Fasten the wallboard to the wall with the smallest nailing surface first.

Visualize the wall, and make sure that there will be nailing surface for the ends of wallboard sheets. Where one new wall meets another new wall, you will need to add extra studs, perhaps with blocks to space them away from adjoining studs.

BUILDING AND INSTALLING

If the new wall is parallel to the ceiling joists, you will probably have nothing solid to nail the top plate to. Install 2×4 blocking every 2 feet or so. If the ceiling is unfinished, you will have to cut the wallboard first.

CUTTING THE PARTS: To avoid confusion, make a cut list showing the names, lengths, and quantities of all framing members. Measure from the ceiling to the floor in several places. Take the shortest measurement and subtract 3¼ inches to get the length of the full studs. (This takes into account the thicknesses of the plates and gives you a ¼-inch cushion to allow for imperfections in the wall or ceiling.)

Trimmer studs run from the plate to the top of the rough openings (for a door, usually 80½ inches). Headers are the width of the rough openings, plus 3 inches. Make headers by sandwiching a piece of ½-inch plywood between two 2×4s. Windowsills are the width of the rough opening. Make double sills for windows more than 4 feet wide. Don't cut the cripple studs yet.

ASSEMBLING AND RAISING: Lay the pieces out on a flat, swept floor. If possible, set one plate against a wall so the pieces won't jostle as you work. Make sure the studs are on the side of the line marked with an X. Align crowns to one side; use straight boards for window and door openings. Keep all edges flush as you work. Drive two 16d sinkers through the plate and into the studs.

Attach the full studs, then the trimmer studs, attaching them together. Then install the headers. Cut and install the cripples.

With a helper, raise the wall into place. Check it for plumb, and snug the wall with shims at the floor or the ceiling. Attach the top and bottom plates. Use 2-inch masonry nails on a basement floor, or drill holes and drive masonry screws. At a door opening, cut the bottom plate on each side.

Once you've tipped a framed wall into place, if the wall is tight, use a hammer and a block of wood to move the top or bottom plate.

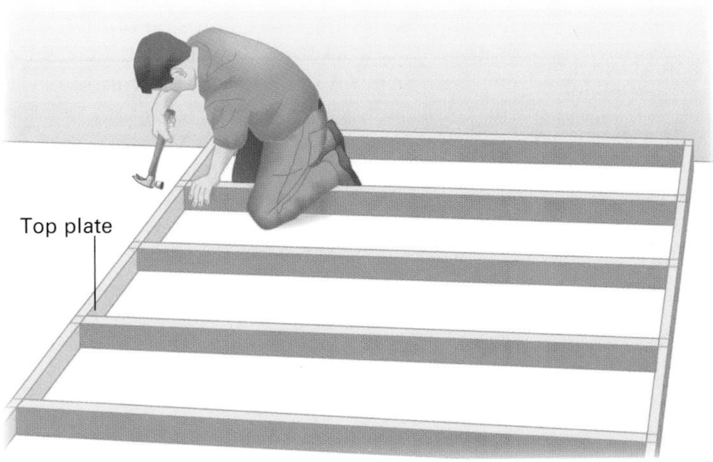

Keep the top of the stud flush with the top of the plate as you drive nails. With practice, you can do this standing up; use your foot to keep the edges flush.

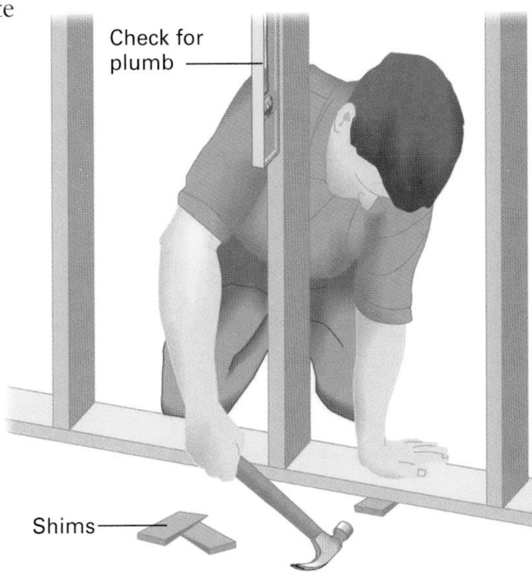

Drive shims into both sides so the plate will not tilt. Shim at either the floor or the ceiling. Cut the shims flush with the edges of the plate, using a chisel.

CUTTING AN OPENING

Assess your skills before taking on this job. If you have doubts, the best option may be to hire a carpenter on a time and material basis and work as an assistant. This is messy work, especially if the old wall is plastered. Cover your floors to protect every square inch. One effective method is to put down rosin paper (construction paper) with masking tape, then throw a canvas or plastic drop cloth on top to collect the big chunks.

If the wall is load bearing *(see page 72)*, the project will require substantial temporary support, even if you are only taking out two studs. If you plan to open up most of the wall, you may want to remove all of the plaster or wallboard. The method shown here minimizes wall patching.

Brace the ceiling when enlarging a window opening to make room for sliding doors. Pros use the same techniques when cutting an opening in an interior load-bearing wall. You should also support the joists beneath these temporary braces.

CUTTING THE OPENING

If you will be installing a window or door, determine the required rough opening. Use a level to draw the rough opening on your wall.

Make sure you don't cut through electrical or plumbing lines that may be lurking in the wall. Make your cuts shallow—just deep enough to cut through the wallboard or plaster. Once you have cut out a large enough section, feel or peer through with a flashlight to check for obstructions. Moving plumbing can be a big job; electrical lines may not be as difficult. Before proceeding, be sure you know how and where to move the lines.

For wallboard, simply cut with a drywall saw or reciprocating saw. For plaster, first score the cutout line with a knife, then saw carefully with a reciprocating saw. If the wall vibrates as you cut, the surrounding plaster will crack and loosen from the lath. Once you've cut out one side of the wall, tap nails through the other side as reference marks for cutting from that side.

Chalk a line showing the top of the header (see the chart on page 75 for determining size). With a reciprocating saw, slice through the studs where the header will be. Hold the blade level as you work. To remove the studs, first cut them in half with a circular saw. If there are nails between the top of the rough opening and the slices, cut them with a reciprocating saw.

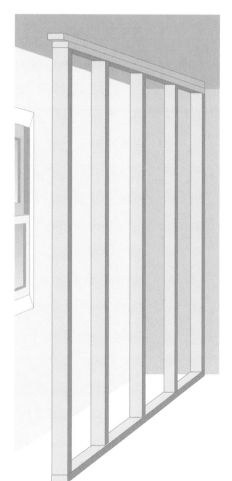

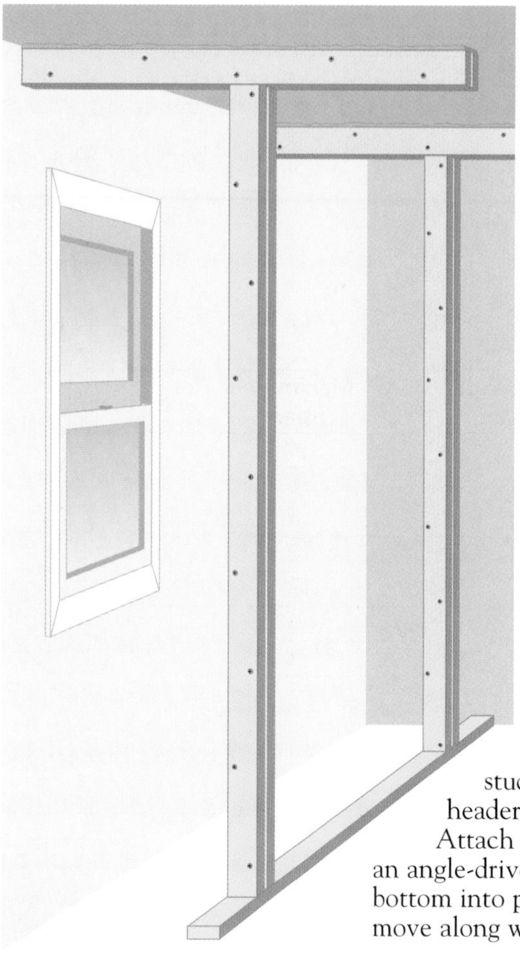

SLIP IN FRAMING

Scrape out the opening where the new framing will go, and test to see that you can slip in 2-by lumber at all points. Use straight boards for the framing; twisted or bowed pieces will be more difficult to fit. For standard framing methods, see pages 72–73.

Attach a trimmer stud to a king stud, slip them into place, and attach above and below with angle-driven screws.

Make the header out of 2-by material with $\frac{3}{8}$-inch plywood sandwiched between. With a helper, set one end of the header on top of the trimmer stud and raise the other end into position. Use a 2×4 slightly longer than the trimmer studs to brace the header temporarily. Attach the other trimmer stud to its king stud and slip it into place so the header rests on top of the trimmer stud.

Attach the header to the king stud with an angle-driven screw before you tap the bottom into position; otherwise, the top may move along with the bottom.

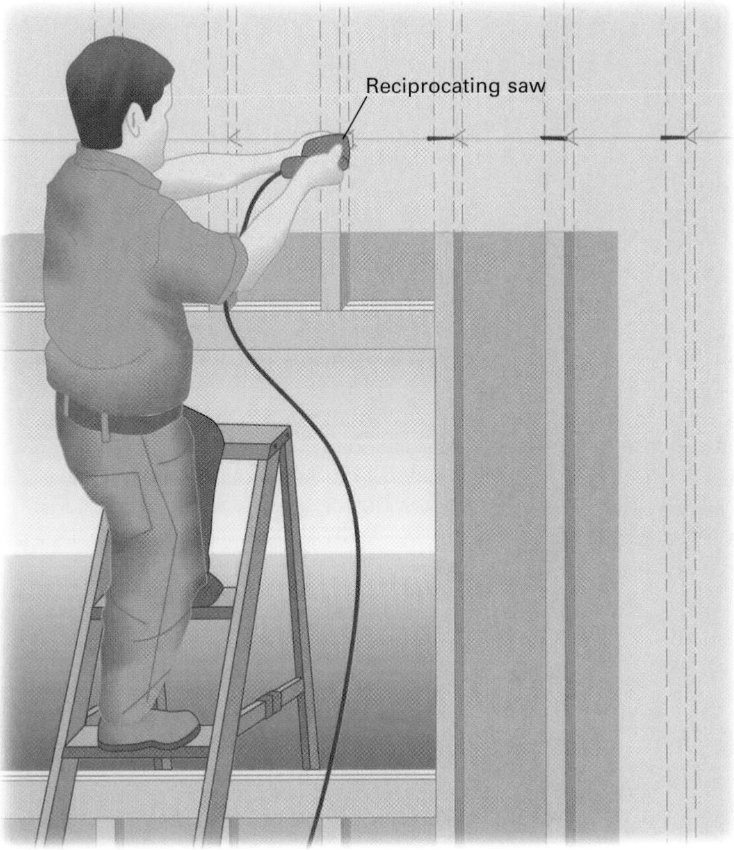

By slicing studs behind the drywall or plaster (rather than removing the drywall to make room for installing the header) you will make it easier to patch the wall later. With luck, you may not have to patch the wall at all.

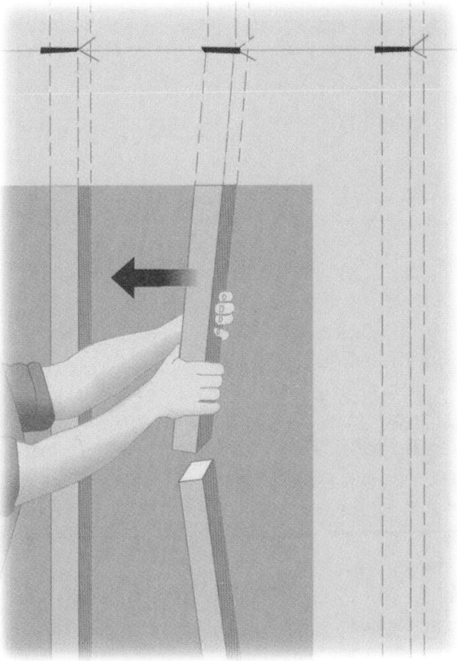

Once you've cut the tops of the studs, slice them midway and remove them. Clean out old nails and plaster to make way for the new header.

HEADER OR BEAM SIZES

If a header or beam is part of a load-bearing wall, it must have as much strength as the rest of the wall. Local codes vary, but these guidelines are accepted by most. The sizes refer to headers or beams made by sandwiching a piece of plywood between two 2-by lumber pieces.

Location	Size of Header Material	Maximum Span
Single Story or Top Story	2×4s	4'
	2×6s	6'
	2×8s	8'
	2×10s	10'
	2×12s	12'
Lower Floor, with Floor Above	2×4s	3'
	2×6s	4'
	2×8s	7'
	2×10s	8'
	2×12s	9'

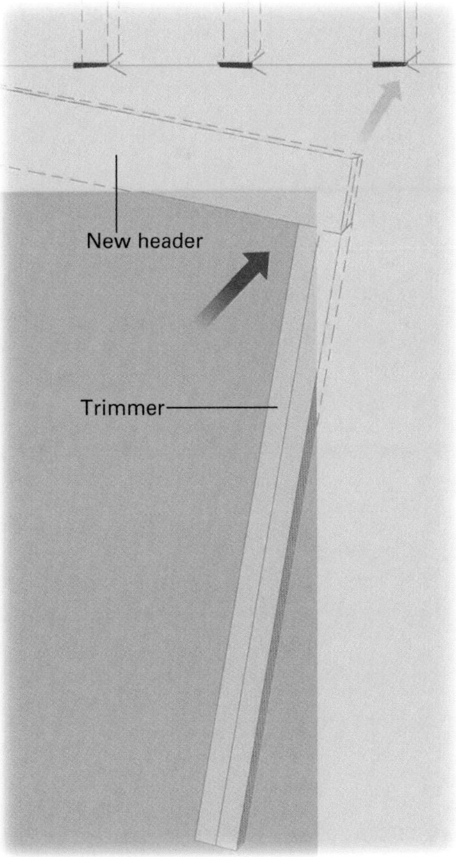

Drill angled pilot holes and drive 2- or 3-inch all-purpose screws to attach the new framing. The screws can draw pieces together, in addition to fastening.

ADDING A BEAM

Older homes often have small rooms. The best way to get the more open feel that people appreciate today is to remove a wall or two. If the wall is load bearing (*see page 72*), you will need to build a beam that is as strong as the old wall was.

If you have a tongue-and-groove floor, you will need to patch it (*see pages 50–51*); weaving the boards in and refinishing could be a bigger job than installing the beam.

PREPARING: Install a temporary beam (*see page 75*) and remove the old wall. At either side of the old wall, cut the wallboard or plaster back to the nearest stud on either side. Cut a channel in the ceiling so the joists rest directly on the beam.

MAKING THE BEAM: Consult with local building codes for span requirements. The chart on page 75 gives spans for beams you build yourself. Or, purchase a manufactured beam, which will be stronger. Some types use laminated pieces of plywood. A glue-lam beam uses stacked boards and is attractive enough to stain. Notch the ends of the beam so they will fit around the top plates of the adjoining walls.

INSTALLING: Make two support posts by nailing two 2×4s together. Measure for length by taking the distance between the top and bottom plates and subtracting the part of the beam that will be under the top plate. Subtract another ¼ inch to give yourself a little room. Set the support posts within easy reach. With a helper or two, raise the beam into position and place the posts under it at each end. Attach the beam and posts with angle-driven screws.

BRACING POSTS: Cut and attach 2×4 nailers to both sides of each post and header. Attach horizontal blocking pieces to add stability.

COVERING THE BEAM: Once the beam is in place, you can improve its appearance by cladding it with 1-by pieces. Butt-join the pieces and let the side pieces overhang ¼ inch; making a perfect joint the entire length of the beam is difficult.

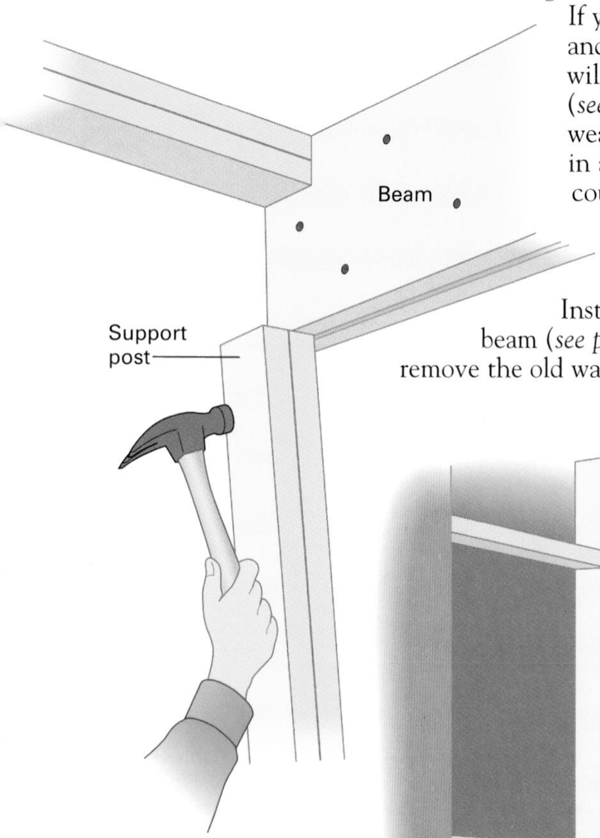

Make the notch slightly larger than it needs to be, to make installing easier. You can tap shims into any gaps after the beam is installed.

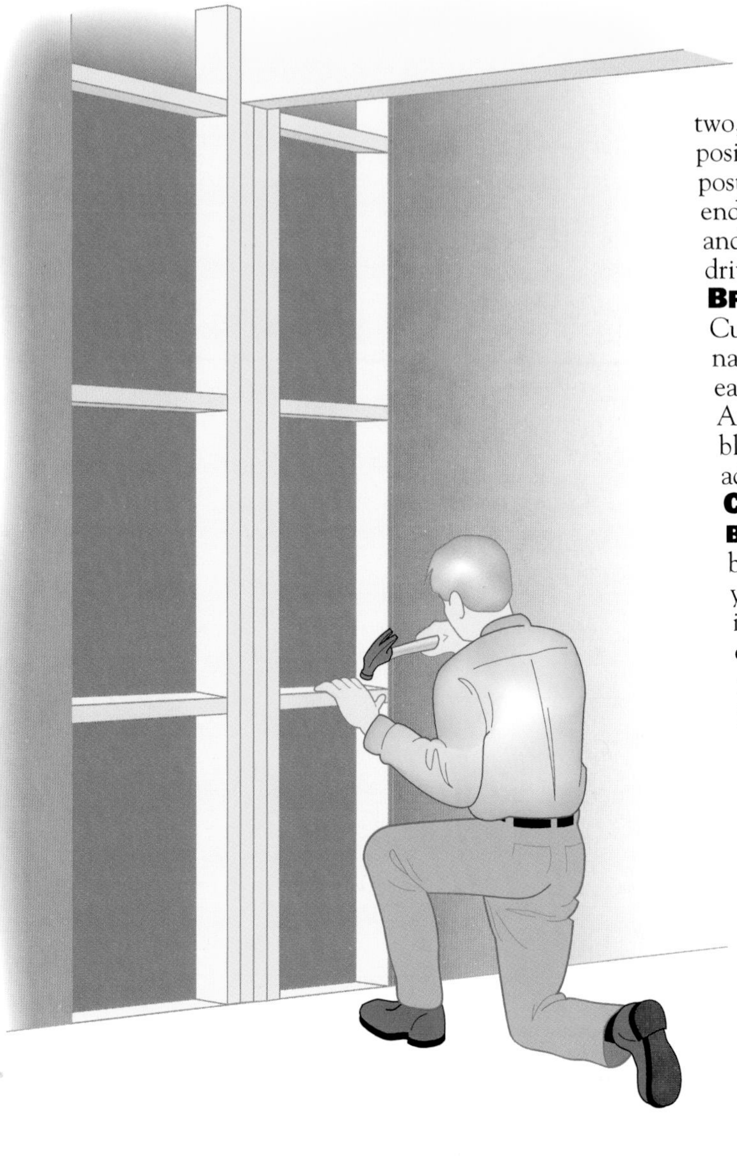

Once the nailer and blocks are in place, you are ready to cover the area with wallboard.

INSTALLING AN INTERIOR PREHUNG DOOR

Replacing a door in an existing jamb will mean scribing it to fit, cutting it, mortising it, and drilling new holes for the handle and lock. Save yourself time and aggravation by buying a prehung door, which comes with the jamb and trim all precisely cut and matched.

CHOOSE A DOOR: Measure both the width and height of your rough opening; some older homes have 7-foot-tall doors. Also measure the thickness of the wall or the old jamb. If it is wider than 4⁹⁄₁₆ inches, you will have to attach strips of wood to the edge of one jamb to make it wider. Make sure that the casing is wide enough to cover the gaps between door and jamb on the sides and at the top.

ATTACH THE HINGE SIDE: Position the door in the opening so that the edges of the hinge jamb are flush with the wall. You may need to shim it to get it plumb. There should be a set of shims every foot where the hinge jamb is not tight up against the stud. Always insert shims from both sides so the jamb will not get twisted.

Use a framing square to check the other two jamb pieces for square; you may need to raise the hinge side up slightly. Drive 8d finishing nails through the hinge jamb and into the stud.

ATTACH THE OTHER JAMBS: Close the door and make sure the gap between the door and the top jamb piece is a consistent ⅛ inch. You may need to raise up the latch jamb; support it with small pieces of wood so it won't move while you're working.

Insert pairs of shims every foot all along the latch jamb. (You will need to open and close the door repeatedly.) Check that the front edge of the jamb is flush with the adjoining wall. Drive 8d finishing nails through the latch jamb and the shims. You don't need to nail the top jamb piece.

ADD THE CASING: Use a handsaw to cut off the shims flush with or below the wall surface. Be careful not to damage the jamb while cutting.

The casing will be preassembled or at least precut. See page 64 for installation tips.

Check the gap between jamb and door before and after nailing the jamb. If nailing has moved the jamb over, pry it outward by tapping in shims, then drive new nails.

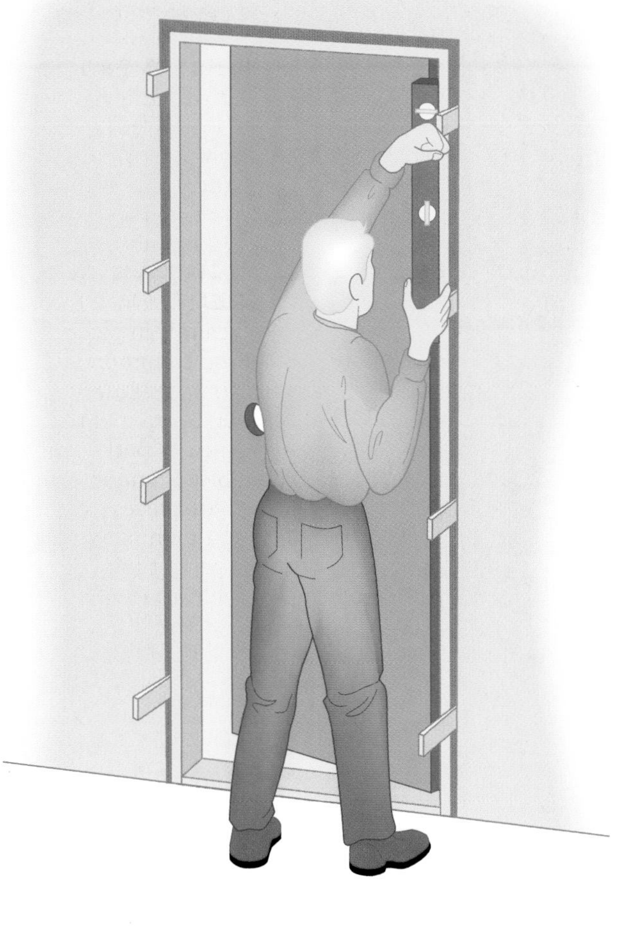

The hinge jamb holds the door in place, so it must be anchored securely. When possible, nail it up tight against the stud; use shims only where necessary.

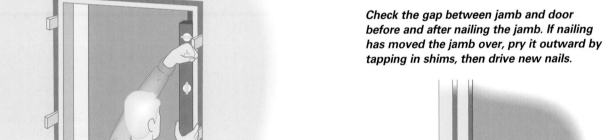

INSTALLING AN EXTERIOR PREHUNG DOOR

If you are simply replacing an existing exterior door, a new prehung unit might fit right into the space. (Make sure the casing will be the right width.) The instructions on this page describe how to install a prehung door in a new space that you have cut out.

SET THE DOOR IN PLACE: Most exterior doors have a wood threshold attached. Replacing it with a threshold that has a rubber gasket provides greater weather protection. Before installing, make sure your new threshold will fit under the door.

These doors are heavy, so work with a helper. Slide the door out of its box. Cut any plastic strips holding it together, but do not remove the block of wood holding the door closed.

With the brick mold attached, lift the door into place so the brick mold is up against the house siding. Have a helper hold the door on the outside while you work on the inside. Check for plumb. If you need to make any adjustments, place a shim under one of the jambs.

MARK AND CUT THE SIDING: Once the door is where you want it, use a pencil to mark the siding for cutting; the siding will butt against the brick mold for a tight seal against weather. If your siding is vinyl or aluminum, you may need to cut back more to make room for special trim moldings.

Remove the door, and cut the siding. Set your circular saw's blade depth so it just cuts through the siding. For beveled siding, tack a piece of 1×4 to the side of the cut to provide a stable surface for the saw's base plate.

WEATHER-STRIP AND INSTALL THE DOOR: Cut strips of roofing felt (tar paper), and wrap all exposed wood with it. Slip it a few inches behind the siding, and attach it to the framing with staples or roofing nails. At the top of the opening, install a piece of drip-edge flashing. (If it did not come with your prehung door, ask the supplier for one that will fit.) The drip edge goes between the siding and the felt, and it will hang over the brick mold.

Set the door in place, and fasten the jambs with shims and 8d galvanized casing nails (*see page 77*). Caulk the joint between the brick mold and the siding.

Prehung doors with precut hinge and lockset mortises make door installation simpler. Plumb and mark around the unit (right) to cut back the siding so the brick mold will fit against it.

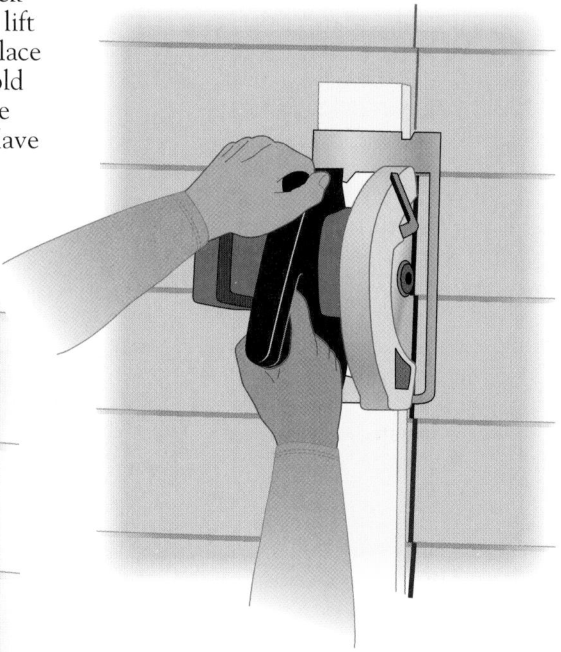

A tacked-on piece of 1-by lumber makes it much easier to cut beveled siding in a straight line. Use a chisel or a saber saw to finish the cuts at the corners.

INSTALLING A LOCKSET

Installing a security deadbolt on an older door is similar to installing a door handle on a new door. Installing the latch should be the last step in installing a door. But first make sure the door fits well and swings freely *(see pages 46–49)*.

DRILL THE DOOR HOLES: Fold the cardboard template that came with the lockset and place it on the door at the desired height. Mark the center points of holes on the face and edge of the door by poking through the cardboard with a nail.

Use a hole saw to drill out the hole on the face of the door. To avoid splintering the door, drill until the pilot bit starts to poke through, then drill from the other side. Use a spade bit or Forstner bit to bore a hole in the door's edge. Brace the door so it does not move from side to side, and make sure you keep the drill bit level and parallel to the surface of the door. Some locksets require that this hole continue into the rear of the larger hole through the face of the door.

INSTALL THE BOLT AND LOCKSET: Insert the bolt into the edge hole and hold it in position while you use a pencil or knife to mark for a mortise. Cut the outline of the mortise with a knife, then chisel out the area between. Be careful not to chisel too deeply; keep testing until the latch plate is flush with the surrounding wood.

Drill pilot holes and drive screws to attach the bolt plate. Insert the lockset parts on both sides, and drive the bolts to tighten them. Make sure the bolt or latch slides freely when turned from either side. If not, loosen the bolts a bit. If that doesn't work, remove the pieces and clean any debris from the holes.

INSTALL THE STRIKE PLATE: Start to close the door, and make a mark on the jamb's edge showing the height for the center of the bolt or latch. Make a mark on the jamb that is one-half the thickness of the door from the stop. Where the two marks meet, drill a hole with a 1-inch bit.

Place the strike plate on the jamb. Hold it in place as you trace around it with a pencil and knife. Cut the perimeter with a knife, and mortise it out until the strike plate sits flush. Drill pilot holes and drive screws to attach the strike plate. If the door does not latch, or if it rattles when latched, move the strike plate in or out.

***1.** Straight, clean holes make installation easy and make the latch and deadbolt operate smoothly. Use a hole-cutting saw for the lockset; drill most of the way through one side and then finish the cut from the opposite side of the door.*

***2.** Use the template provided by the lockset manufacturer to drill a hole for the bolt mechanism. Insert the bolt and mark around the bolt plate to cut a mortise. Fasten the bolt in place and insert the lockset parts from the front and back.*

***3.** To find the correct location of the strike plate, install it without mortising first. If the door does not latch, move it away from the stop. If it latches but rattles, move it toward the stop.*

REMOVING A WINDOW

There are two excellent reasons to replace a window. Newer windows are better sealed, so they will save you plenty in utility costs. Even if they are well sealed, old sash windows have large cavities (for the weights) that cannot be filled with insulation. And, many old windows are just too small. Opening up for a larger window will make a room sunnier and friendlier.

WOOD SASH WINDOWS

Place masking tape on the window panes so they won't shatter if you break them.

REMOVE MOLDINGS AND CUT CORDS: Review the parts of a sash window on pages 54–55. From the inside, pry off the casing, the apron, and the stool. Use a flat pry bar to minimize damage.

Once the molding is removed, you can measure your rough opening. Ordering a window to fit inside your opening will save you time but will cost extra if it is not a standard size.

If your old window uses weights, removing the weights will make the window considerably lighter. Hold a weight while you cut off its cord with a knife, or cut a chain with tin snips. You can remove a small window with the weights still in place, but it will be a bit awkward to carry.

If the window is large, you may want to pry off the stops and remove the sashes.

CUT THE NAILS: Use a reciprocating saw with a metal-cutting blade to cut the nails that hold the jamb to the studs. Peer in with a flashlight to make sure you have cut them all. At this point, the only thing holding the window in place is the outside molding, which is probably nailed to the siding.

REMOVAL: If the window is on the first floor, it will probably be easier to work from the outside. With two ladders and a helper, pry off the outside molding and tip out the window.

If the window looms high overhead, working from the inside may be your best bet. With the sashes removed, have a helper hold onto the frame while you lean out and pry off the moldings. Once the moldings are removed, you can pull the window inside.

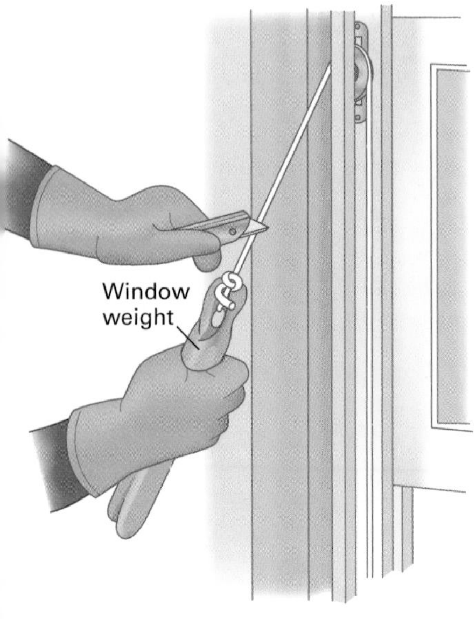

If your old sash windows have weights, cut them off; removing the old window will be much easier.

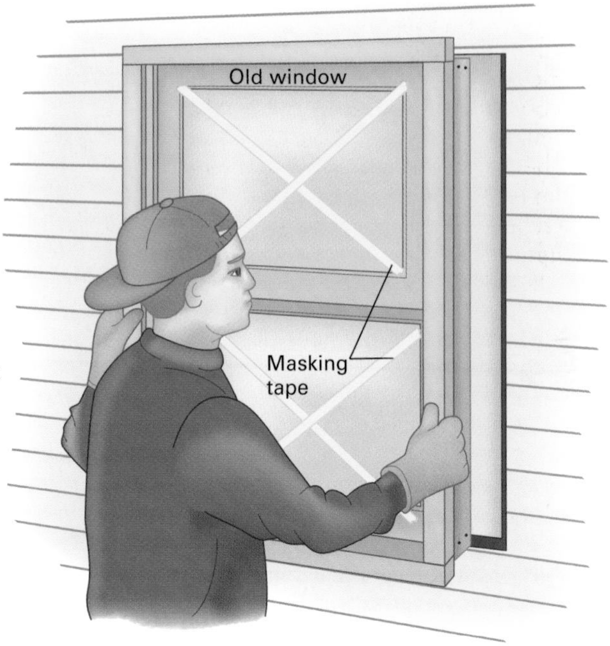

Working from the outside, pry the brick mold away from the house and lift out the window. For large windows, work with a helper. If the two of you are working on ladders, carry the window down in tandem, taking each step at the same time.

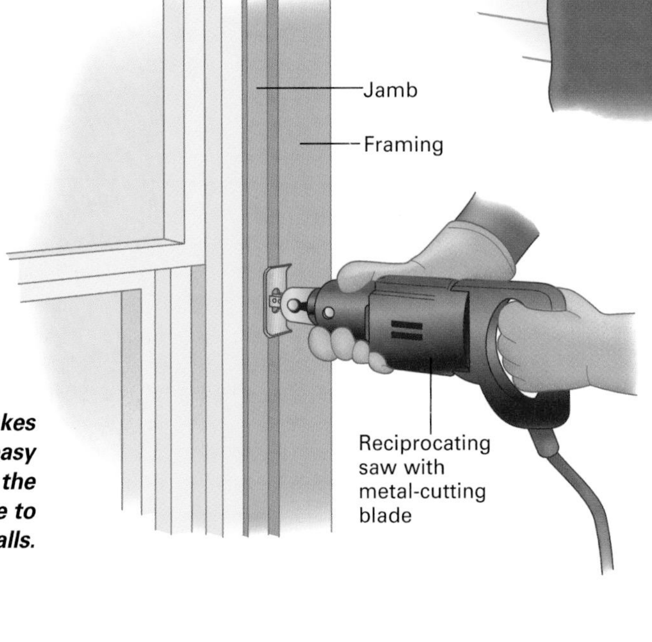

Cutting the nails makes window removal easy and minimizes the possibility of damage to the surrounding walls.

METAL OR VINYL WINDOWS

These are usually attached to the house with nails driven through a flange on the window; the outside molding is attached to the window with just caulk. If the window is large, remove the sashes first.

CUT THE SIDING: The siding is usually installed on top of the window's flange; you have to cut it back before removing the window.

Remove the molding carefully; you may want to reuse the pieces. Most flanges are $1\frac{1}{2}$ inches wide, so you should chalk lines $1\frac{3}{4}$ inches from the window's edge. Set the blade of a circular saw so it will barely cut through the siding. If you have beveled siding, use a tacked piece of 1×4 as a flat surface *(see page 78)*. Cut with a circular saw, then finish the corners with a chisel.

PRY IT LOOSE: Use a pry bar and hammer to pry behind the flange under each nail. Once a nail is popped up, remove it with the claws of your hammer. When all the nails are removed, the window will tip out.

OR, PRY BACK THE SIDING: This is more difficult, but it is worth the trouble if you are installing the same type and size of window. Carefully pry up each piece of siding surrounding the window and pull it back carefully. Remove the nails on the window's flange, and slip out the window.

1. If you cut carefully, you may be able to avoid piecing in siding when you install the new window; wider molding may cover the gap.

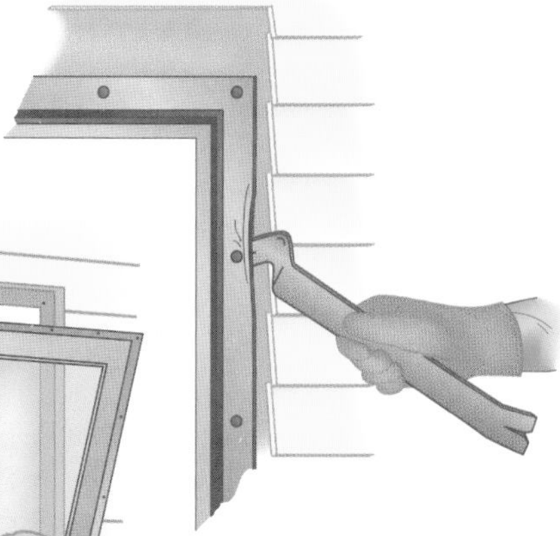

2. Working carefully around the window, use a pry bar to loosen the fasteners.

3. Once a window is released, get a firm grip on it and tip it out.

COVER IT UP

If you cannot install your replacement window the same day you took out the old one, don't take chances by leaving the opening uncovered. Even a light rain can damage wallboard, and a large opening is an invitation to thieves and curious children.

Plywood is the standard cover, nailed or screwed on the outside. However, any burglar with a screwdriver or pry bar will be able to remove that quickly. For greater security, also fasten a 2×2 nailer to the framing on the inside, and drive screws through it into the plywood.

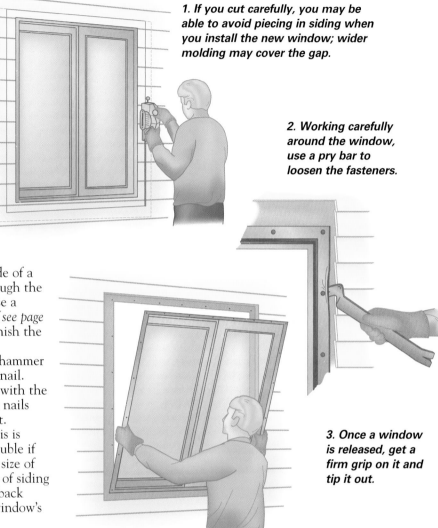

Pry carefully to avoid splintering wood siding or crimping aluminum or vinyl siding. You may need to pry the siding a couple of feet away from the window on either side.

INSTALLING A WINDOW

You'll save money in the long run if you spend a little more for a window with excellent insulating properties. Double-layer glass with low-E film reflects heat inward and is up to five times as energy efficient as a single pane. Wood is a good insulator but needs regular maintenance. Vinyl insulates well and requires little care but is unattractive to many people. All-metal windows are usually poor insulators.

PREPARE THE OPENING

Remove all trim pieces from the opening so that the framing is exposed on all four sides. If you want to change the size of the opening, refer to page 72 for the correct framing configuration.

You can often save money by ordering a standard-size window. You may be able to turn an odd-size opening into a standard size by simply removing or adding a jack stud or bottom plate. However, think about how the window will be trimmed on the outside; piecing in some types of siding can be difficult.

Test fit the window by setting it in the opening. Make sure you have room to make it plumb and level.

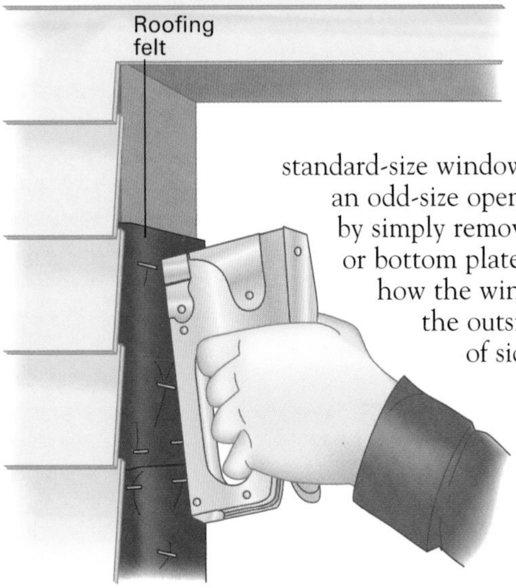

To prepare the opening, tuck in foot-wide strips of roofing felt. Wrap them around the framing and staple them.

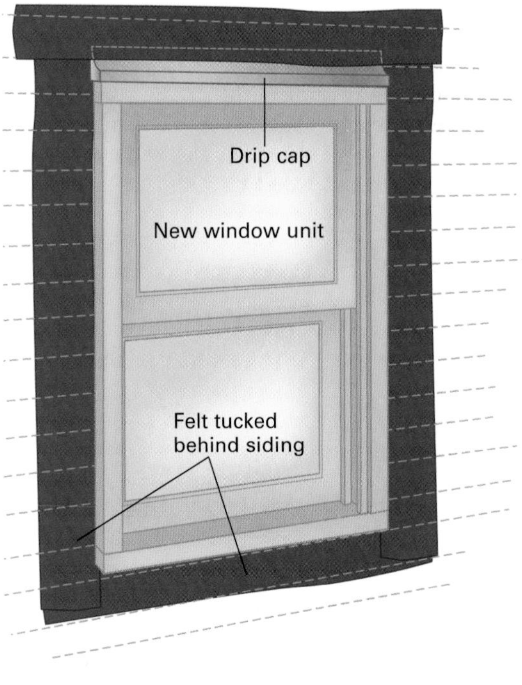

The drip cap and felt sheds water down and away from the house. That's why the uppermost piece of felt overlaps the drip cap and the pieces of felt at the side of the window, which overlap the bottom most piece.

WINDOW WITH BRICK MOLD

If your window has the exterior molding (brick mold) attached, the siding should be cut back so the molding can fit inside it. Set the window in place, level and plumb, mark the exterior wall for cutting, and cut the siding with a circular saw and a chisel (*see page 78*).

Cut lengths of 15-pound roofing felt about a foot wide. Starting at the bottom and working up, slip the pieces behind the siding, wrap them around the framing pieces, and staple them in place (*left*).

You may have to use a pry bar to carefully remove some nails from the siding. Pry the siding from behind to force the nail heads out slightly; then, using a piece of shim to protect the siding, use the pry bar to pull the nails out from the front.

If your window does not have a drip edge attached to the top piece of molding, purchase a piece of metal or vinyl drip-edge flashing; it should be slightly longer than the window's width. Slip it under the siding. Then slip a piece of roofing felt between it and the siding.

Apply caulk to the inside of the window casing and set the window in place. Adjust the drip cap if necessary so that it hangs over the top molding.

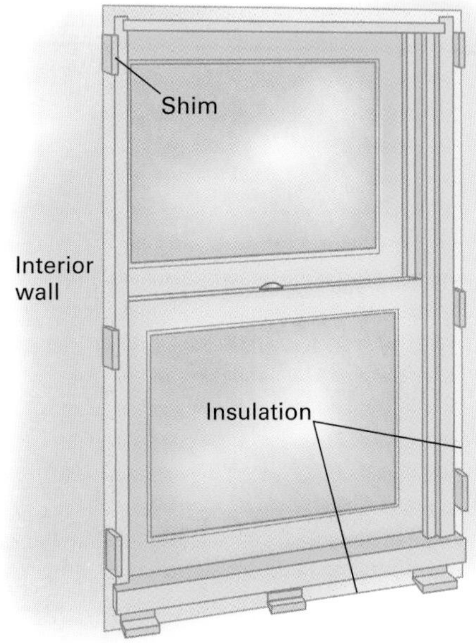

Stuff cavities around the window jamb completely but loosely with fiberglass insulation; it's the fluffiness that lends insulating value. Wear gloves and a dust mask because the fine particles can cause itching.

Shim from the inside so the unit is perfectly level and plumb. Tap—don't pound—shims in place so they do not bend the window frame. Drill a pilot hole and drive 8d finishing nails or trim-head screws through the jamb or the molding, depending on the type of window. Insert two nails or screws in each side of the window and test to make sure the window opens smoothly. If all is well, finish fastening and trim the shims flush with the framing. Stuff all the cavities with fiberglass insulation. From the outside, caulk the joint between the molding and the siding.

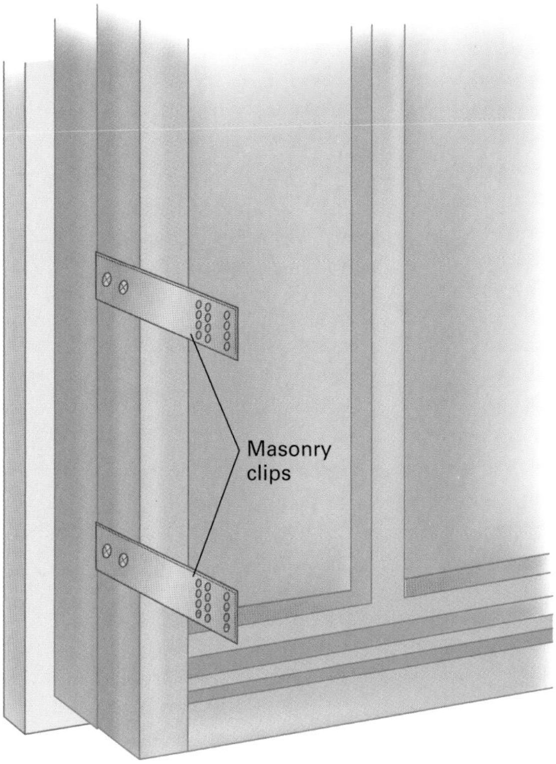

If your house has a masonry surface, attach the brick mold with the masonry clips that are attached to the window. Then attach the framing with screws.

WINDOW WITH A FLANGE

Most metal and some vinyl windows attach to the framing with a flange; no brick mold is attached. The window itself is easier to install, but trimming it takes longer.

The opening must be large enough for the flange, unless you want to slip the window behind siding that has been bent back (*see page 81*). Either way, there must be enough nailing surface for the flange. Wrap the opening with roofing felt.

Make sure the drain holes are on the bottom edge. Set the window in place, and have your helper go inside to adjust the window's position. Once the window is level, plumb. When centered in the opening (the inside trim will look odd if it is not centered), drive nails or screws through the flange and into the framing about every 6 inches.

Starting at the bottom of the window and working up, slip pieces of felt under the siding and over the flange. (This will be a second layer of paper.) Finish with a single piece at the top.

To install molding on the outside, first place narrow spacer pieces—slightly less thick than the siding—over the flange so the molding will lie flat. To trim the inside, first rip cut jamb pieces so their front edges are flush with the finished wall surface; then install a sill, apron, and casing.

GARDEN WINDOW

A greenhouse-style window adds color and interest to a room. Consider adding one above the kitchen sink: It provides an ideal environment for plants and flowers and can dress an otherwise dull view out the kitchen window.

Installing the window itself is not difficult, but trimming it out will probably take some time. Some types fit inside the frame. Others are snugged up against a weather-stripping gasket on the outside of the house. Measure your existing window—either the glass size or from jamb to jamb—and a window dealer will be able to tell you which size will fit with the least amount of trouble. The gasket-mounted type may allow you to keep your existing sill and inside casing, saving plenty of work.

INSTALLING WALLBOARD

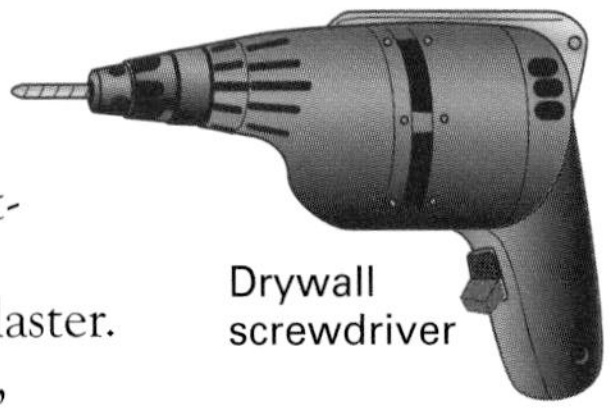
Drywall
screwdriver

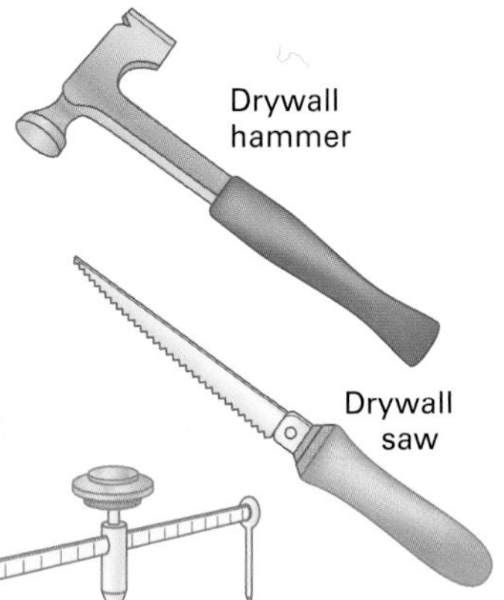
Drywall
hammer
Drywall
saw

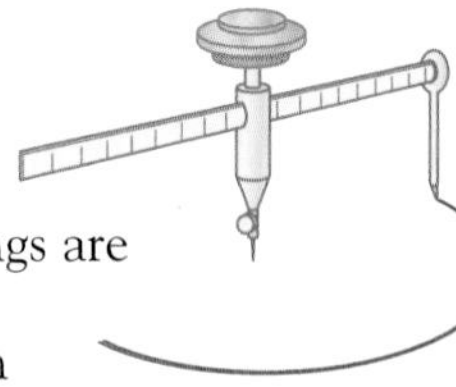
Circle
cutter

Thank goodness for wallboard, which makes it possible for a do-it-yourselfer to finish walls without spending a year or so learning how to plaster. But it's still dusty, difficult, sweaty work, involving heavy lifting in awkward positions.

PLANNING THE JOB

Though hanging the sheets is heavy work, taping takes much more time. Gaps are difficult to tape, so take the extra time to cut accurately and to position the sheets tightly together.

Hang the ceiling sheets first, then the wall sheets. A rented wallboard jack (or hoist), will make the work easier and the seams tighter. It raises sheets, allowing you to position them carefully.

Using 10-foot or even 12-foot sheets is worth the extra trouble if you can avoid butt joints, which are the most difficult joints to tape *(see page 87)*. Use ½-inch wallboard for the ceiling. Consider using ⅝-inch sheets for the walls. It's harder to lift so you may need jamb extensions, but the wall will be significantly more solid.

NEW CONSTRUCTION: Inspect the framing to make sure you will have nailing surfaces for the ends of all your sheets. You may need to add nailers at inside corners. If only half a stud's thickness is available for nailing in a corner, plan to install against that stud first; if you nail to the adjoining wall first, you will lose ½ inch of your nailing surface.

OVER OLD WALLS: If your plaster walls and ceilings are cracked and spongy, you can "skin over" them with ½-inch wallboard on the ceiling and ¼-inch wallboard on the walls. (If you use ¼-inch wallboard on the ceiling, it may eventually sag.) To skin over walls, you will need to remove all moldings; butting the wallboard up to molding is difficult and produces a sloppy appearance. Before you replace the moldings, cut baseboard pieces and provide jamb extensions for the casing.

Another option is to remove only the moldings and plaster, leaving the lath in place. Depending on the thickness of the plaster, install ⅜-inch or ½-inch wallboard. Removing plaster is messy and difficult, but the finished wall will be very strong and you won't have to modify moldings.

When skinning over or attaching to lath, sheet ends do not have to meet on centers of studs or joist edges; attach them to the lath with screws (not nails), and apply adhesive.

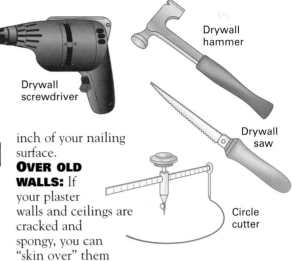

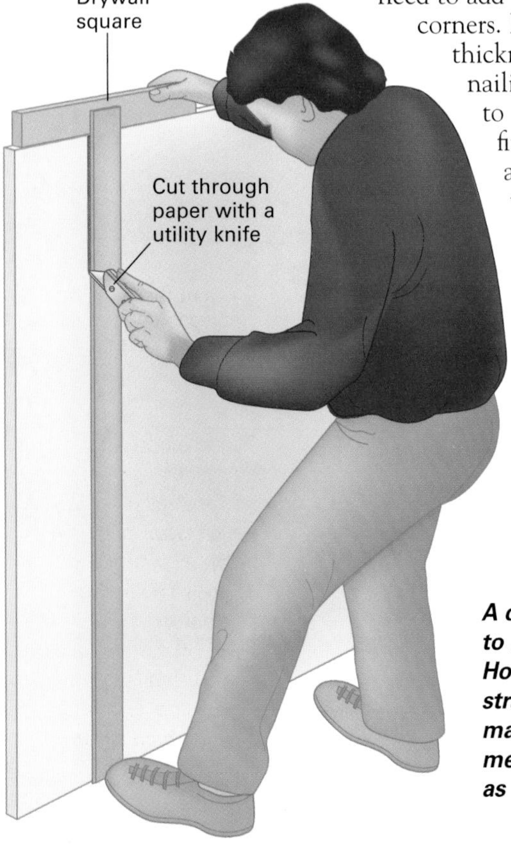
Drywall
square
Cut through
paper with a
utility knife

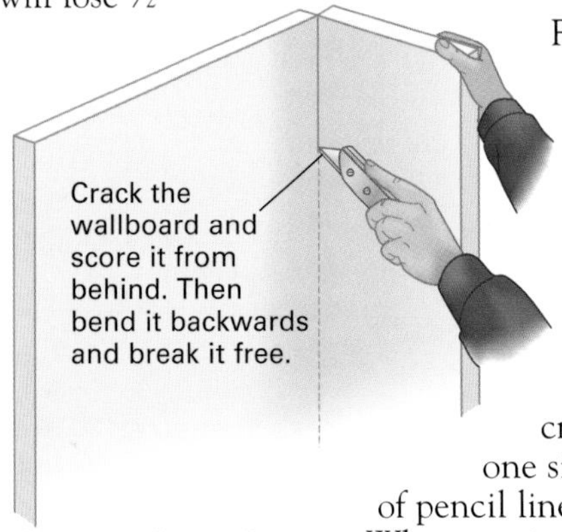
Crack the
wallboard and
score it from
behind. Then
bend it backwards
and break it free.

A drywall square is used to mark and cut wallboard. Hold it in place to guide straight cuts. Use it to mark stud locations, to measure for cutouts, and as a guide for rip cutting.

MEASURING AND CUTTING

Few things are more frustrating than missing a stud or joist while struggling to hold a heavy piece of wallboard. Take a minute or two to mark locations on the sheets. If your framing members are 16 inches apart, use a wallboard square (which has crosspieces 16 inches long on one side) to quickly make a series of pencil lines.

When cutting wallboard to length, cut the wallboard ¼ inch shorter than the measurement calls for; this compensates for the somewhat ragged edge of the cut. To make a square crosscut, make only one measurement mark. Hold the drywall square in place with your foot against the bottom,

VERTICAL OR HORIZONTAL?

Installing sheets with the tapered joints running up and down will mean that you avoid butt joints, which are very bothersome. However, it can be difficult to line up the edges so that they meet at the center of a stud (or "splitting the stud") all along their length.

Running the sheets horizontally may require butt joints, but it will be easier to split on studs. And, the horizontal tapered joints will be easier to tape than vertical joints running from floor to ceiling.

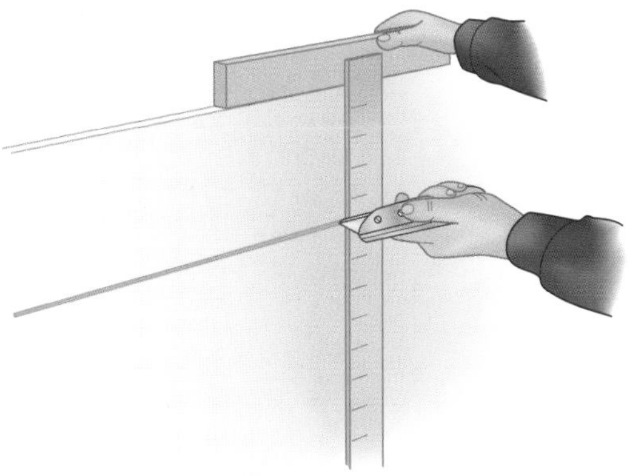

For long cuts, clasp the top of the drywall square, and press the knife blade against the correct measurement. Move square and knife together for a smooth rip cut.

and score through the paper. Bend the cut piece back, and cut through the paper on the other side. For a rip cut parallel to the edge of a sheet, use the drywall square to measure and as a guide *(above right)*. For rip cuts not parallel to edge, measure each end and chalk a line between; cut freehand.

Make cutouts for electrical boxes ¼ inch larger than the boxes. With a tape measure or drywall square, mark the two dimensions in one direction and then in the other direction, and draw a rectangle. Cut out the opening with a drywall saw or a knife *(right)*. To cut circles for pipes, measure to the center of the hole only, and use a circle cutter. Cut on both sides, and bang the hole out.

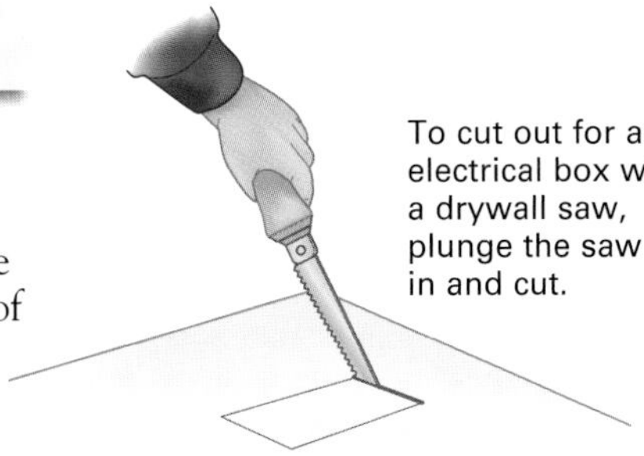

To cut out for an electrical box with a drywall saw, plunge the saw in and cut.

To cut out with a utility knife, score the outline and cut an X...

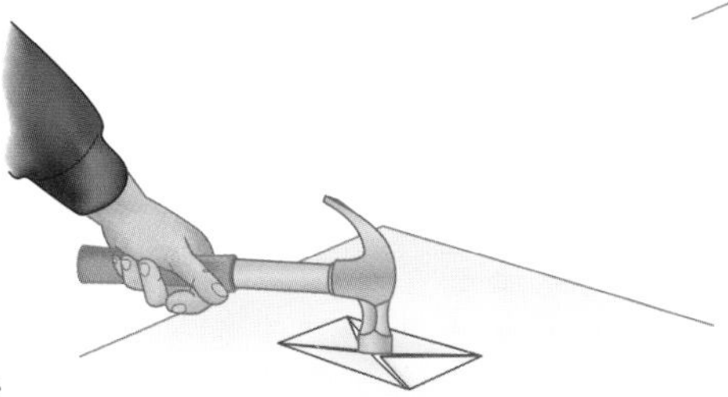

...smack the area with a hammer...

...cut the pieces out from behind.

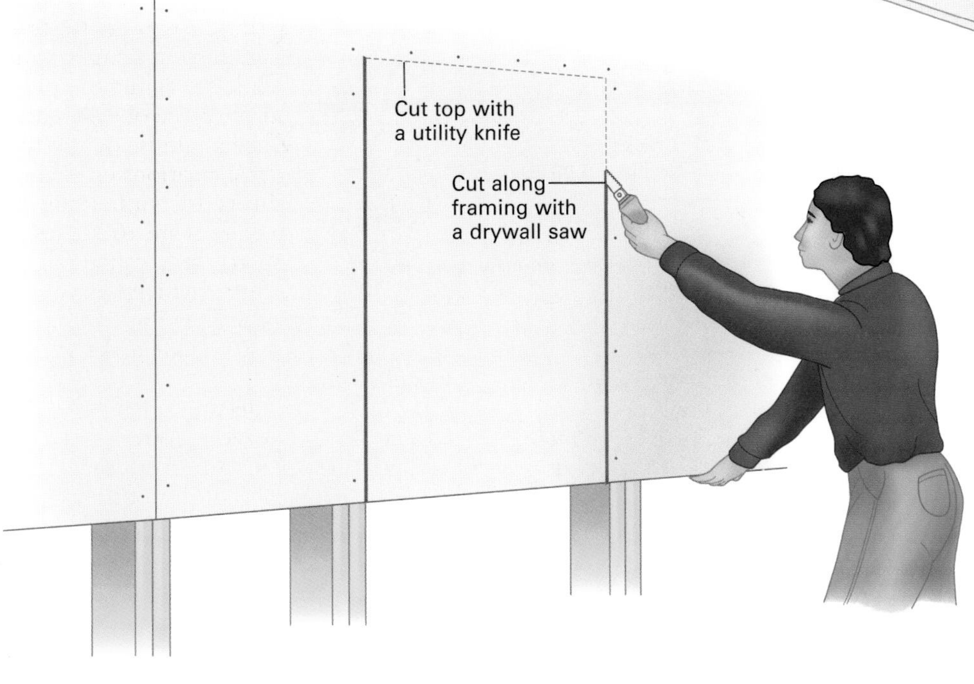
Cut top with
a utility knife
Cut along
framing with
a drywall saw

The easiest way to cut around an unfinished opening is to fasten the piece in place and cut out the scrap as shown. This method also eliminates joints at the top of the door, which often crack when the house settles.

INSTALLING WALLBOARD

continued

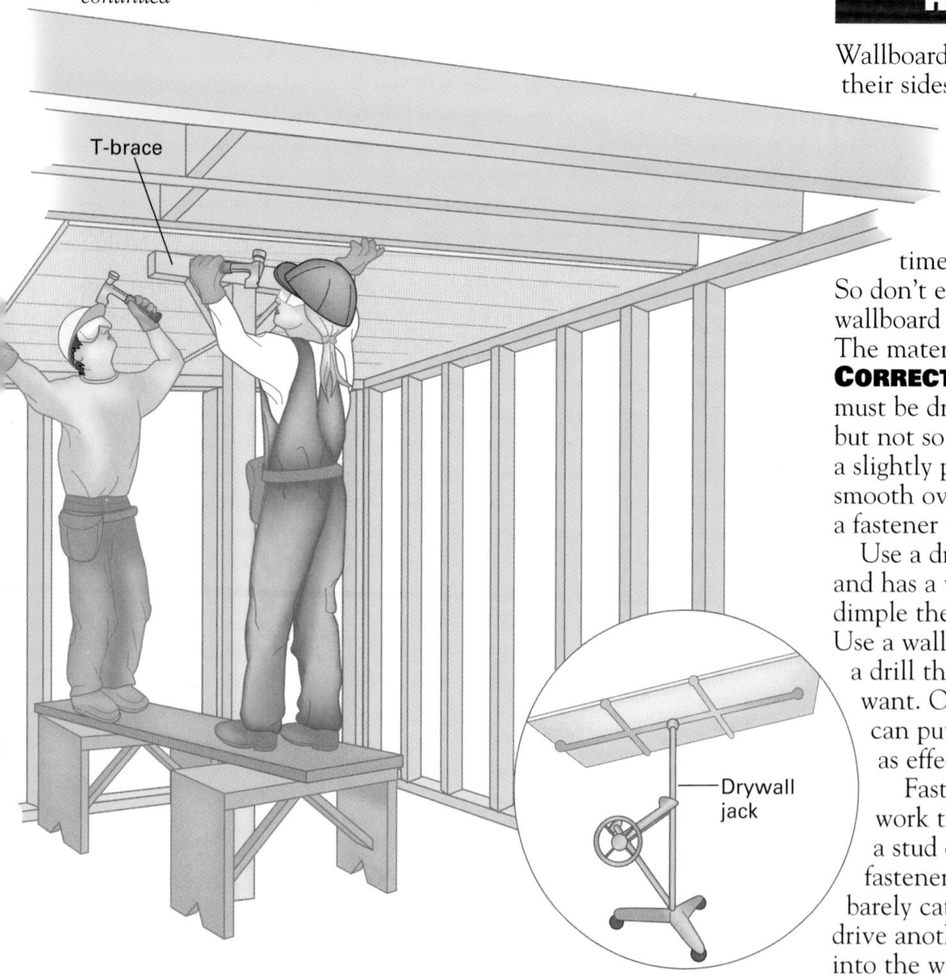

Mark the wallboard with nailing guidelines. When covering old wallboard or plaster, mark the walls and ceiling as well, to make it easy to hit the ceiling joists. When skinning over an old plaster wall, it is preferable—though not necessary—to split on the joists; gluing and driving 2-inch screws into the lath will hold well.

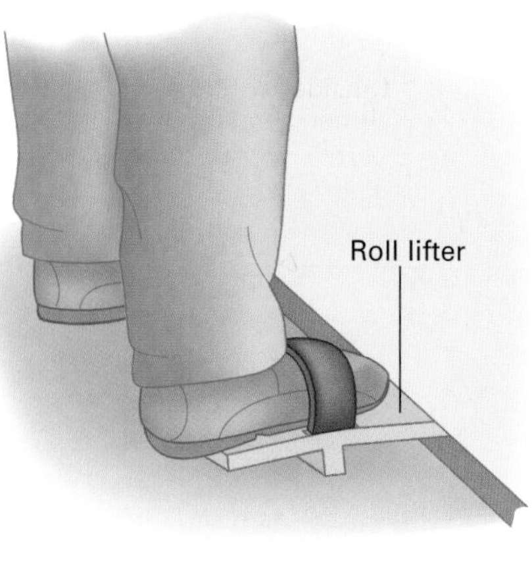

FINISHING DRYWALL CORNERS

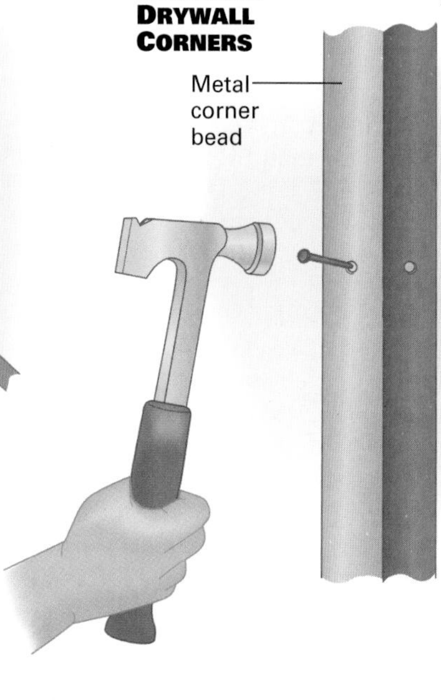

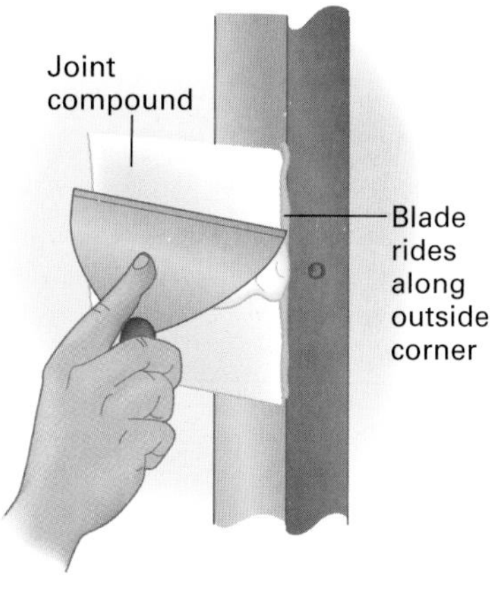

HANGING THE SHEETS

Wallboard sheets have tapered edges along their sides. When a tapered edge is butted against a tapered edge, the resulting joint is easy to tape and will not bulge out (*see page 87*). When sheets are butted end to end, however, that joint will take time and will never be truly straight. So don't economize by using cut pieces of wallboard if it results in more butt joints. The material is cheap, after all.

CORRECT FASTENING: A fastener's head must be driven below the face of the sheet, but not so far that it breaks the paper. Even a slightly protruding head is impossible to smooth over. And, if the paper is broken, a fastener is nearly useless.

Use a drywall hammer for nails. It is light and has a wider head that makes it easy to dimple the nails without harming the paper. Use a wallboard shooter to fasten screws. It's a drill that you can adjust to the depth you want. Or, buy a dimpling bit, which you can put on a regular drill and is nearly as effective.

Fasteners that do not grab wood will work themselves out in time. If you miss a stud or joist completely, remove the fastener and try again. If the fastener barely catches the side of the stud, angle-drive another fastener next to it and directly into the wood, to hold the first one in place.

Building codes have varying regulations concerning how many fasteners to use. To be safe, space nails or screws 7 inches apart on the ceiling and 8 inches apart on the wall. If you use wallboard adhesive, you'll need fewer fasteners.

ATTACHING TO THE CEILING: If you're not using a wallboard jack, at least have a helper, some solid scaffolding, and a T-brace made of 2×4s that can hold up part of a sheet temporarily. Wear a hat with a sponge in it to lessen the head and neck strain caused by holding up sheets with your head while you nail.

Start in a corner with a full sheet, if possible. With a helper, raise the sheet and place it fairly tight to the walls. Drive 10 or 12 fasteners, and move on to the next sheet; go back and install the rest of the fasteners after all the sheets are up.

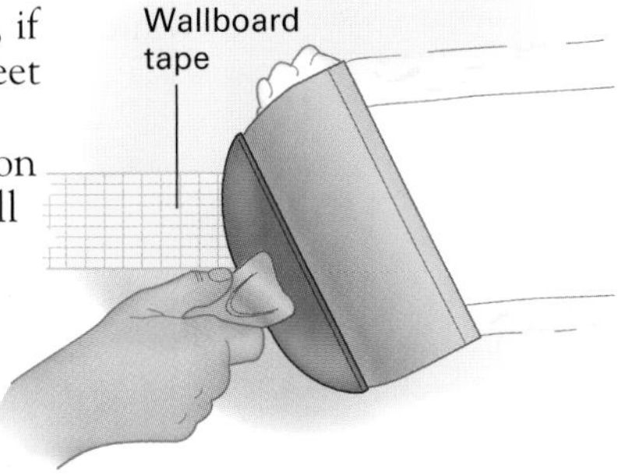

ATTACHING TO WALLS: To run the pieces horizontally, hang the top pieces first. Butt them tightly against the ceiling sheets. Avoid butt joints at doors and windows; cut the sheet out instead. For the bottom horizontal sheet, or if you are installing vertically, use a roll lifter (or fulcrum) to raise it so it butts tightly to the top piece.

TAPING

For this job, use 6-inch, 8-inch, and 12-inch taping blades, and a corner blade. Maximize strength by using dry-mixed joint compound for the first coat and ready-mixed compound for the following coats. You may want to scoop compound into a special tray, or simply hold a dollop of compound on the 12-inch blade and scrape it off with the 8-incher.

Clean your tools often and keep the lid on the joint compound because small pieces of dried compound will make it difficult to get a smooth surface. For all joints, you will need at least three coats of compound. Allow each coat to dry, and sand away any protrusions before applying the next coat.

NAIL HOLES AND TAPERED JOINTS: These are the easiest sections to tape. Press mesh tape into all tapered joints, using continuous pieces wherever possible. Spread a smooth coat of compound over the tape with the 8-inch blade. Fill in only the valley made by the tapers, so a flat surface stretches across the joint. Fill each nail hole with two strokes of a 6- or 8-inch trowel. The first stroke pushes the compound into the joint, and the second scrapes it away.

BUTT JOINTS: These are more difficult because the edge of the wallboard is not indented. Apply mesh to the joint, and feather the compound out 6 inches or more on either side, taking care not to scratch the tape. Feather out farther with each successive coat.

OUTSIDE CORNERS: Cut a piece of metal corner bead with tin snips. Hold the bead gently against the corner—don't press—and drive nails or screws on both sides. Check that the bead's flange and the fastener heads don't protrude; run a taping blade along each side. Apply the first coat with a 6-inch blade, then an 8-inch blade, then use a 12-incher.

INSIDE CORNERS: This is the most difficult. Apply a bed of compound with no gaps, using a corner trowel. Immediately embed paper tape in the compound. If you get wrinkles or bubbles, lift, insert more compound, and reapply. Use a corner trowel and a 6-inch blade to apply coats of compound over the tape.

NAILS OR SCREWS?

When wallboard comes loose, it is usually because the paper is damaged, and rarely because the fastener has come loose. So nails are just as effective as screws. But many prefer the clean holes left by driving a screw with a dimpling bit.

PAPER OR MESH?

Mesh tape is easy to install, but it isn't as rigid as paper. Apply mesh tape to tapered and butt joints; because you don't have to lay down compound first, the taping will not be as thick. Use paper tape at inside corners. The tape will help define the corner, and it will not fray if you scrape the trowel against it, as mesh tape is likely to do.

Hold the blade nearly flat as you first apply the compound. Tilt it up to scrape the surface smooth. Feather the compound out to the edges, and plan to sand down the middle.

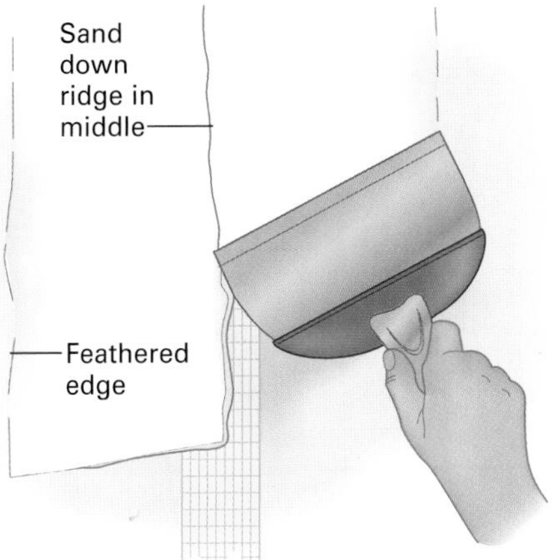

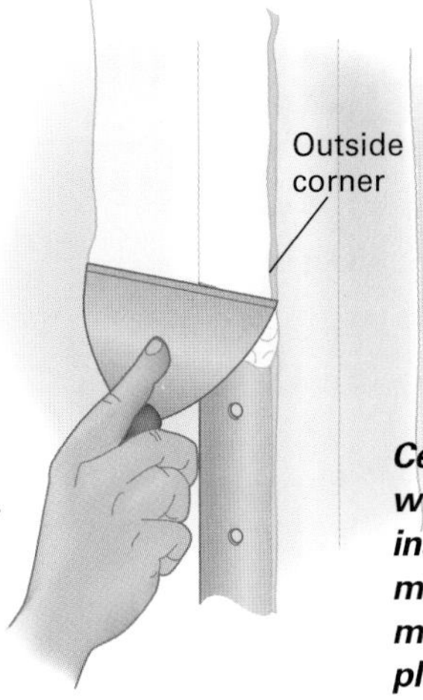

Ceiling corners, where three inside corners meet, are the most difficult places of all to tape. Consider installing crown molding, which eliminates the need for ceiling corner joints.

TONGUE-AND-GROOVE PANELING

Few projects change the look of a room more dramatically than installing wood paneling. Sheet paneling, which uses a thin veneer or even a paper coating over particleboard or plywood, is inexpensive and looks it. Solid pine tongue-and-groove planks, on the other hand, lend a warm, cabinlike feel. Installing them is relatively easy.

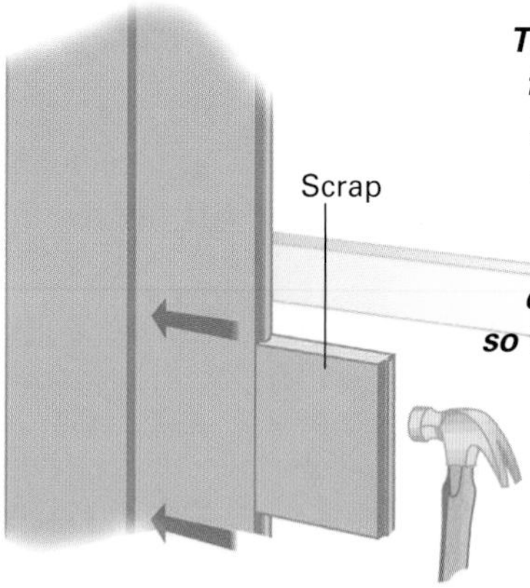

Tap the tongue firmly into the groove with a scrap piece of the same material. Set each nail flush so the next piece will easily fit tightly.

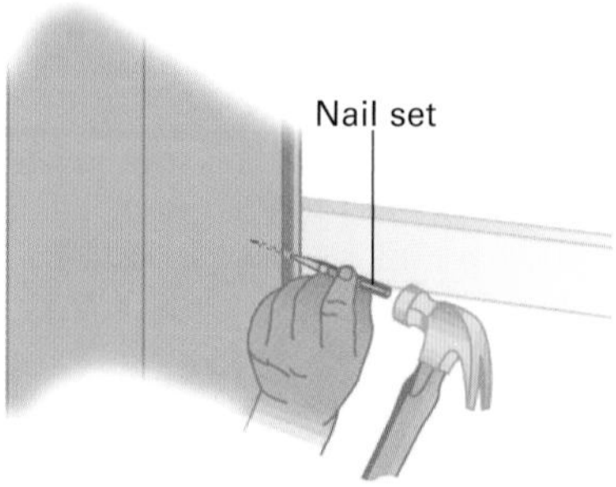

PREPARING THE WALL

Because studs run vertically, vertical planks will have little to nail to if installed directly on the wall. Installing with construction adhesive is risky because adhesive may fail; also, you will not be able to straighten out planks that are twisted or curved. You could run paneling at a 45-degree angle, driving long nails through tongues and wallboard and into studs. However, most people prefer the appearance of vertical planks. Do it correctly by first installing horizontal furring strips. It will save you trouble later.

IN A FINISHED ROOM: Remove casings, baseboard, and any other molding. It is usually not a good idea to butt up against existing molding.

You will need to move electrical receptacles and switches out from the wall. Shut off power and move them yourself if you're sure you can do it safely, or call an electrician. You can either move the boxes or install box extenders.

Mark the wall for stud locations. Install horizontal 1×2 furring strips every 2 feet or so by driving screws through them and at least 1 inch into the stud. Position the bottom strip all the way down and the top strip up against the ceiling to provide a nailing surface for moldings.

ON A BASEMENT WALL: If water leaks into your basement, fix the leak first. You also need to protect against moisture from condensation, however. Chip away any protrusions in the masonry surface where the furring strips will go. With a notched trowel, apply a coat of resin-based concrete adhesive, and lay a sheet of plastic over it; work carefully to avoid creases and bubbles.

Install 1×2 furring strips in the same configuration as in a finished room. To attach the furring strips, rent a nail gun that uses explosive charges to drive nails into masonry surfaces. You will need to experiment with different charges to find the one that sets the nail heads just below the surface of the furring strip.

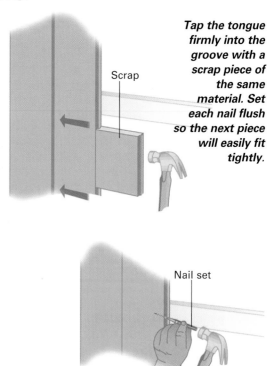

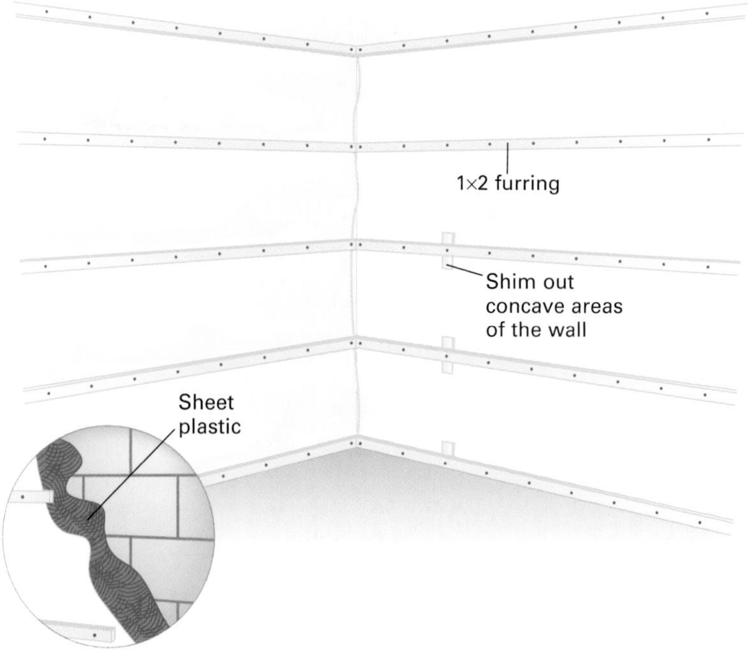

Furring strips set every 2 feet are sufficient because plank paneling is rigid. To install sheet paneling, place the strips every 16 inches. Install wallboard before attaching the paneling.

INSTALLING PLANKS

Figure your square footage and consult at a lumberyard to decide how many pieces you need. If you cannot buy pieces that all reach from floor to ceiling, plan a semi-regular pattern for staggering the joints so one area

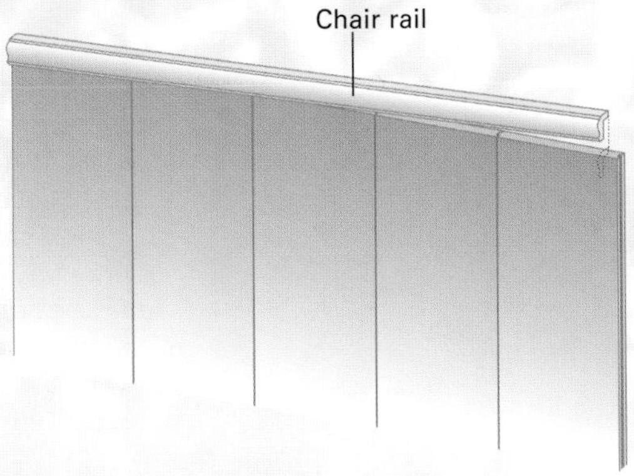

WAINSCOTING

For an old-fashioned look, cover the bottom half or so of a room's walls with wainscoting. For the easiest installation, use a thin material such as 5⁄16-inch beadboard. Remove the baseboard and install box extenders on the electrical receptacle boxes. Fill in any waves in the wall with joint compound. Cut all the pieces to the same length, apply paneling adhesive with a caulking gun, and press the pieces into place. Run the wainscoting all the way to the floor and you'll need no molding there. Cap the top off with a piece of chair rail.

of the room doesn't look different from the rest. Plan to put molding at the ceiling and floor; cutting paneling to match an uneven ceiling will only draw attention to the waves. Stack the planks in the room for a week or two so they can adjust to the humidity.

JAMB EXTENSIONS: Make jamb extensions as wide as the combined thicknesses of the furring strips and the planks, and attach them wherever the paneling meets a jamb.

NAIL THE PLANKS: Start at an inside corner with straight plank. Install the first piece perfectly plumb; the piece on the other wall that will butt against it will cover any gaps if the wall is not plumb. Put the groove edge out. Angle-drive a finishing nail through the tongue and into each furring strip. To avoid denting the plank, use a nail set for the last blow that drives the head flush.

Install subsequent pieces the same way, driving nails into each furring strip as you check for plumb every few boards. To straighten out a curved plank, set a scrap of plank against it, with the scrap's groove fitting over the plank's tongue. Then, tap the scrap with a hammer. If a plank is too bent or twisted to be tamed, return it.

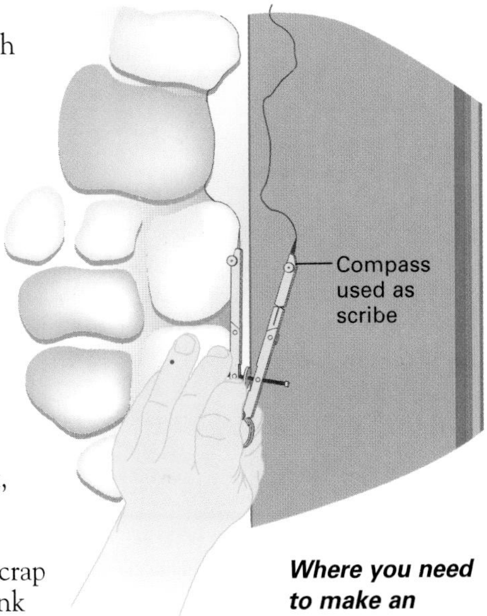

Where you need to make an uneven cut, use a compass to mark. Hold the two arms of the compass as level as possible when you mark.

OUTSIDE CORNER: Bevel cutting both pieces to form a mitered corner will be difficult, and even a perfect joint will be easily damaged. Set both pieces in place; use one to mark for rip cutting the other. Cover this butt joint with corner molding.

INSIDE CORNER: When turning an inside corner, make sure the first piece on the new wall is plumb. Install the final piece of the first wall so it fits fairly tightly; minor imperfections will be covered up. Tack in place the first piece of the adjacent wall, not quite a full plank's width away from the first wall. Check that it is plumb. Use another plank to mark a rip-cut line and cut the piece.

TRIM OUT: Casings and moldings at the bottom and top of paneling are traditionally large, for an informal look. Use ripped pieces of plank, or 3⁄4-inch pine quarter-round.

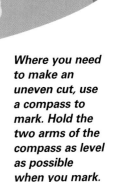

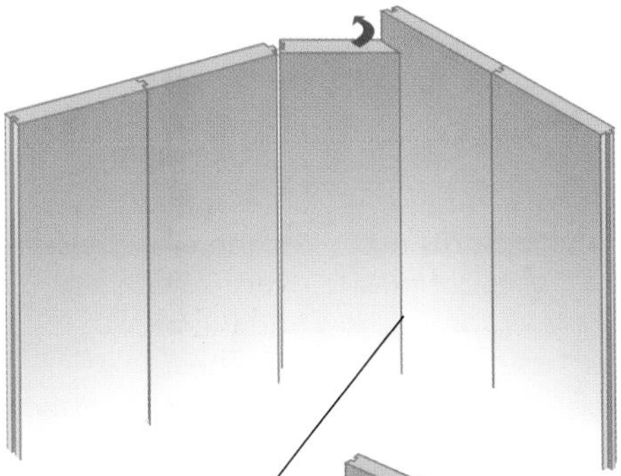

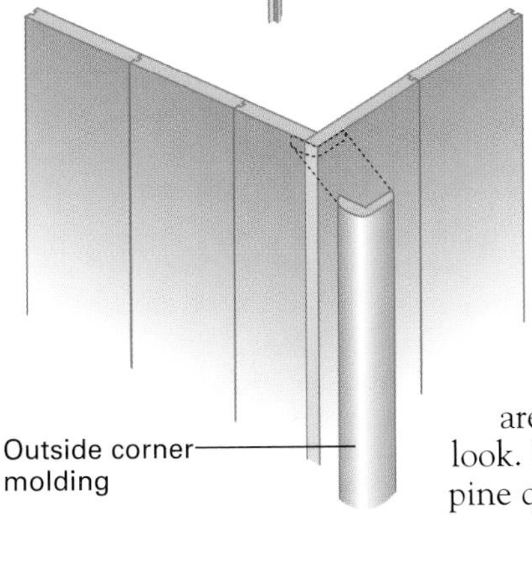

FLOORING PROJECTS

Even if you install vinyl or ceramic floor, most flooring projects begin with wood and carpentry. Here we show you how to deal with three flooring projects—underlayment, wood parquet, and laminate flooring.

UNDERLAYMENT

Lay scraps of underlayment in place and mark them to fill in after placing full sheets.

Underlayment can solve two floor problems. If a floor is uneven, installing ¼-inch plywood underlayment will provide a surface smooth enough for vinyl tile or sheet goods. If a floor is not strong enough to support ceramic tile (if it bounces when you jump on it, the tiles or grout will crack), a thicker underlayment will add strength.

WILL IT BE TOO HIGH?: If the combined thicknesses of the underlayment and the finished flooring will make the new floor more than ½ inch higher than an adjoining floor, the step up will be awkward-looking and a tripping hazard. You may be able to solve the problem with a wide, ramp-like wood threshold that you mill yourself. If the new surface will be too high, consider using a thinner finish material, or removing a layer of existing flooring.

LAY OUT: Buy ¼-inch underlayment in 4×4-foot sheets with a grid of "+" marks indicating a recommended nailing pattern. For thicker underlayment, use thicker sheets of plywood. For ceramic tile, cement board works best. Remove the base shoe and possibly the base molding as well. Keep and number the pieces if you plan to re-use them. Chip away any protrusions on the floor, and sweep thoroughly. Lay as many full sheets as possible. Don't butt the edges up to the wall or base molding; leave a ¼-inch gap to allow for expansion.

CUT, FASTEN, AND FILL: Fasten the full sheets with a grid of underlayment nails or all-purpose screws. Then cut the other pieces, maintaining a ¼-inch gap at the perimeter,

PARQUET WOOD FLOORING

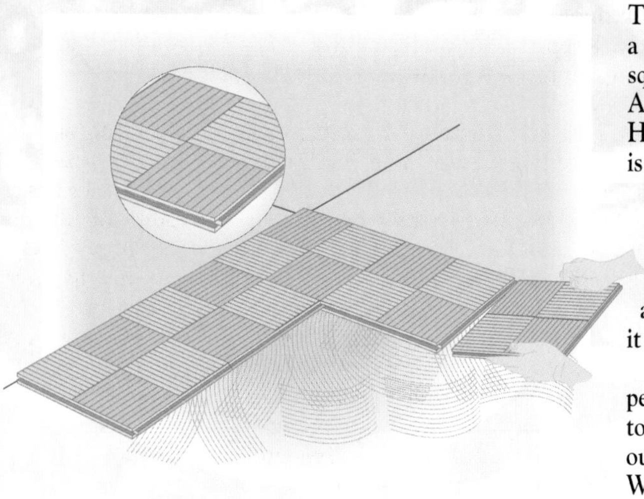

This is an inexpensive and relatively easy way to install a new hardwood floor. Parquet flooring comes in 12-inch-square pieces that interlock with tongues and grooves. A wide variety of patterns and wood tones is available. However, the special mastic required for gluing it down is surprisingly expensive.

Cut parquet with a chop saw, circular saw, or sabersaw. To install it, draw layout lines as you would for any tile floor; plan ahead to avoid placing small pieces in highly visible places. Cover only a small area with the thick mastic; it dries quickly, and once it "skins over" it will not bond with the parquet.

Use spacers to maintain a ¼-inch gap around the perimeter to allow for expansion. As you press the pieces together, watch to make sure tiles are not being pushed out of alignment. Install full tiles first, then cut tiles. Walk on the floor to make sure there is a good bond.

To add courses of laminate flooring, use a block to tap pieces in place. Stagger joints by at least 6 inches.

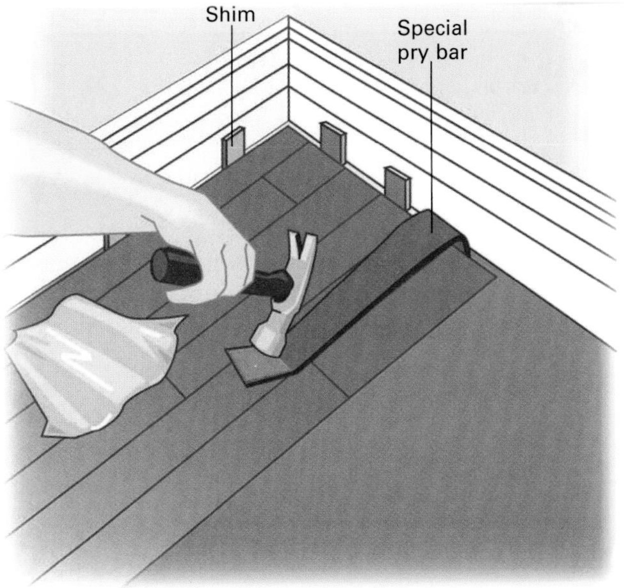

To snug in pieces at the end of a course, use the special tool designed for laminate flooring. Tap the tool to pull the pieces into place.

and install the same way. For a surface smooth enough for vinyl, fill all the gaps and fastener holes with flooring patch, then sand smooth.

LAMINATE FLOORING

This product has a finish similar to a plastic-laminated countertop, but it is durable enough to resist scratches.

The floor actually floats on top of the subsurface without being attached to it. One type is glued to the underlayment at the perimeter only. Another type rests on sheets of high-density polyethylene foam, making it slightly springy like a natural wood floor. No fasteners are used for either type; just glue the pieces to each other.

PREPARE THE FLOOR: Remove any protrusions, and sweep the floor thoroughly. If you are using underlayment sheeting, roll it out and tape the seams with duct tape. Cut the sheets with a knife. Use a scrap piece of plank as a guide, and cut the bottom of the casings *(see page 92)* so that you can slip planks under casings instead of making complicated cuts.

LAY OUT THE FIRST ROWS: Position ¼-inch spacers around the perimeter to hold the flooring away from the base mold. Without gluing, set two or three rows in place with the tongues facing outward. Cut them upside down to prevent splinters, and avoid using short pieces. Stagger the joints at least 6 inches for a better appearance. Use full pieces wherever possible.

GLUE THE PIECES TOGETHER: Pick up the second row, and apply glue to the grooves. Tap the pieces in place with a block of wood to prevent denting. Glue two or three rows, then wait an hour for the glue to set before installing the rest of the floor.

Continue cutting and gluing rows. To make sure the boards join tightly end-to-end, use a special pry bar that acts as a flooring snugger. You tap one end to pull the plank tightly into place. Keep a damp rag handy, and wipe away any excess glue immediately. Make sure each joint is tight before proceeding to the next row of flooring.

Once you've worked your way across the room, use the special pry bar to install the last few courses where you don't have enough room to swing a hammer.

THE LAST ROW: Rip cut the last row precisely so you will be able to install it tightly against the spacers. To mark for the rip cut, place the last-row pieces directly on top of the next-to-last row. Set a full-width plank on top, pressed against the spacers, and use it as a guide to scribe a cut line.

Test fit pieces for the last row, then apply glue to their grooves and install. If they are not pressed tightly to make a tight joint, tap shims in behind the spacers.

TONGUE-AND-GROOVE FLOORING

It's tedious to sand and finish, but nothing has quite the feel of real hardwood flooring. Choose "select" grade if you want uniform color. Or, spend less for "No. 1 common" and get a floor that is an interesting patchwork of colors and textures.

You can use these same techniques to install prefinished, wood laminated, tongue-and-groove flooring for a floor that you can walk on immediately.

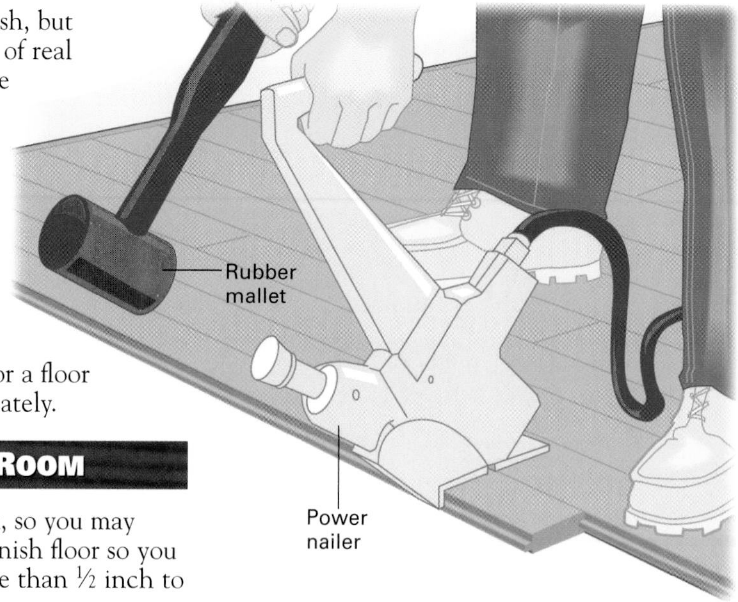

A rented power nailer reduces wear and tear on your arms and makes seams tighter. If one blow doesn't cinch a board up tight, strike it with the mallet a couple of times.

PREPARE THE ROOM

This material is ¾ inch thick, so you may need to remove an existing finish floor so you won't have to step down more than ½ inch to an adjoining floor.

PREPARE THE SUBSURFACE: If you reach an old plank subfloor, do not run the new flooring in the same direction as the subfloor planks or you will have waves. Install ¼-inch plywood underlayment first.

An older method called for "sleepers," strips of 1×3 laid perpendicular to the tongue-and-groove flooring. It's OK to install the new floor on sleepers, but it will not be as well supported, especially at the butt joints. A solid and even plywood surface is the best substrate.

Wherever possible, remove or cut back obstructions instead of cutting around them. Thorough preparation of the floor will minimize problems later.

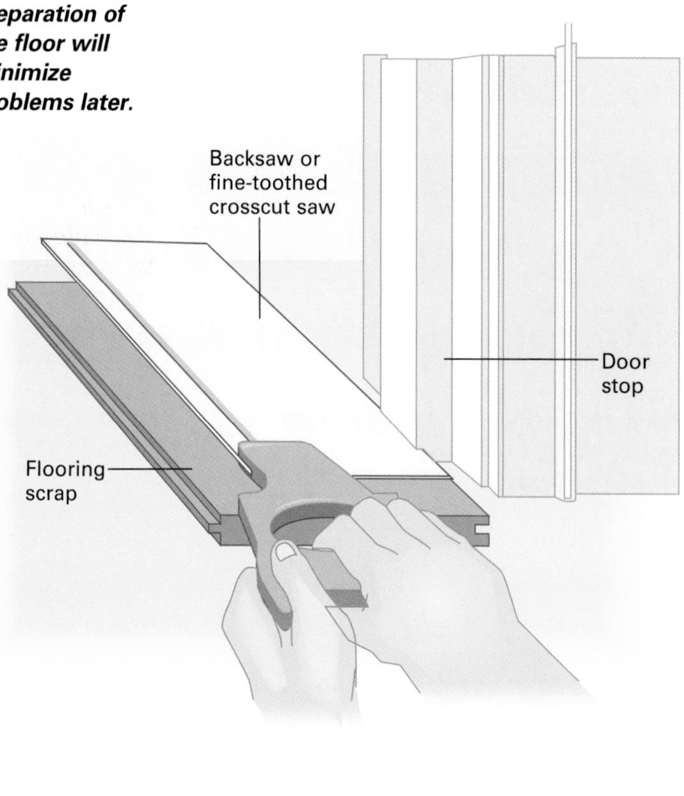

LAY PAPER: Remove the base shoe and any other obstructions. Remove or lift and support radiators. Sweep the floor completely clean, and tack down 15-pound roofing felt (tar paper), overlapping the pieces by several inches. The paper helps prevent squeaks.

CUT MOLDINGS: Cutting around casings, jambs, and stops is very difficult, and gaps will appear even on a perfect cut when the wood shrinks a bit as humidity changes. So, cut the bottoms of moldings and slip the boards under them. Use a scrap piece of flooring as a guide, and cut with a handsaw.

LAY OUT THE JOB

Your room is probably not perfectly square, so you may end up with flooring boards noticeably narrower at one end than the other. Don't let that happen on the most visible wall. Chalk an alignment line the entire length of the job, near an area you want to look best, such as a fireplace hearth. Dry-fit some pieces to get a sense of how the boards will look; you may want to make another line.

Measure over from the alignment line to a point one board's width from the wall where you want to start installing boards, and chalk a line parallel to it.

CUT AND NAIL

Leave the boards stacked in the room for a week or two to allow them to become acclimated to your room.

THE FIRST ROW: Start with very straight boards. Position them along the chalk line so that there is a ½-inch gap (but not more than ¾ inch) between the boards and the base molding. Drill pilot holes and face-nail the first few rows with 8d finishing nails. Start using the power nailer as soon as you have room.

TIGHT SEAMS, STAGGERED JOINTS: Use a scrap piece of flooring as a block, and tap subsequent pieces in place. Rent a power tongue-and-groove nailer. It will drive nails when you just tap it with a rubber mallet; if you need to move a bent board over for a tight seam, hit it hard. To prevent squeaks, drive plenty of nails—every 6 inches or so. Stagger the joints so that those next to each other and those separated by only one board are at least 2 inches apart. Keep a number of boards nearby so you can quickly shuffle through them to find one the right length.

THE LAST PIECES: Like the first pieces, the last ones will have to be face-nailed. Have a helper pull these boards tight with a flat pry bar and blocks of wood while you nail.

THRESHOLDS: Where the flooring ends, you can use a standard threshold, which sits on top of the flooring. But consider a classier look: Cut the flooring off straight. Score a line with a knife first to prevent splinters. Then cut the tongue off a piece of flooring the length of the threshold, and round off its edge. Install it against the flooring, rather than on top of it, using a biscuit joiner *(see page 39)* and face nails.

FINISHING: Though many do-it-yourselfers sand and finish floors themselves, we recommend that you hire a pro at least for the sanding. Sanding down a new floor requires a 220-volt sander, and an experienced hand; it's very easy to lose control for a second and leave an ugly dip in the floor.

Stain the floor lightly, and apply several coats of polyurethane finish. If you apply only oil-based polyurethane, the wood will eventually turn yellow.

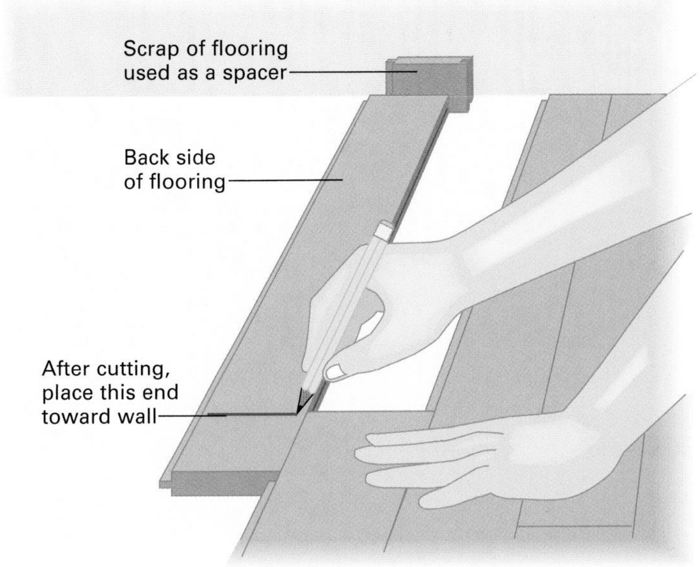

Fill out rows by flipping a piece over so it lays on its face side. Mark it as shown, cut it, and flip it over again so the cut side is against the wall.

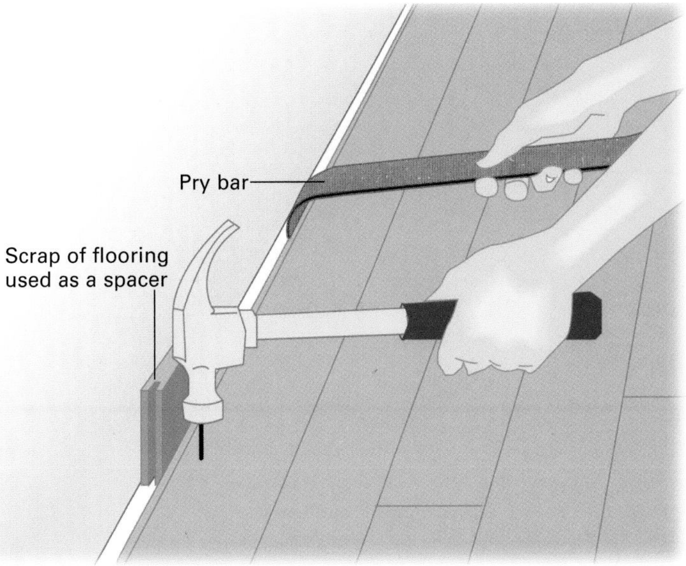

Use a pry bar to wedge pieces in the last row in place. Hold them with wood scraps and the pry bar until you can face them into place with a finishing nail.

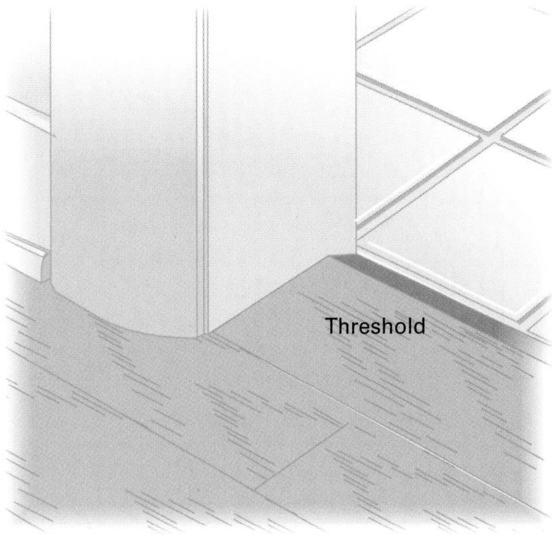

A flush threshold calls for extra work but looks much more professional. Use a piece like this to wrap around a threshold as well.

INDEX

Metric Conversions

U.S. Units to Metric Equivalents			Metric Units to U.S. Equivalents		
To Convert From	**Multiply By**	**To Get**	**To Convert From**	**Multiply By**	**To Get**
Inches	25.4	Millimeters	Millimeters	0.0394	Inches
Inches	2.54	Centimeters	Centimeters	0.3937	Inches
Feet	30.48	Centimeters	Centimeters	0.0328	Feet
Feet	0.3048	Meters	Meters	3.2808	Feet
Yards	0.9144	Meters	Meters	1.0936	Yards
Square inches	6.4516	Square centimeters	Square centimeters	0.1550	Square inches
Square feet	0.0929	Square meters	Square meters	10.764	Square feet
Square yards	0.8361	Square meters	Square meters	1.1960	Square yards
Acres	0.4047	Hectares	Hectares	2.4711	Acres
Cubic inches	16.387	Cubic centimeters	Cubic centimeters	0.0610	Cubic inches
Cubic feet	0.0283	Cubic meters	Cubic meters	35.315	Cubic feet
Cubic feet	28.316	Liters	Liters	0.0353	Cubic feet
Cubic yards	0.7646	Cubic meters	Cubic meters	1.308	Cubic yards
Cubic yards	764.55	Liters	Liters	0.0013	Cubic yards

To convert from degrees Fahrenheit (F) to degrees Celsius (C), first subtract 32, then multiply by $5/9$.

To convert from degrees Celsius to degrees Fahrenheit, multiply by $9/5$, then add 32.